Testimonials

"Everybody who worked on the picture was pleased as Andy is a wonderful pool player."
Woody Allen – Actor, Writer, Director – referring to his film "Sweet & Lowdown", starring himself, Sean Penn and Uma Thurman

"Very Nice… Like Magic."
Chris Cuomo – Host of Good Morning America

"I believe Andy is the best all-around competitor in artistic pool right now, and his record proves it. Andy is a fine example of what talent, passion, hard work, dedication and creative imagination in a sport can produce in a person. He's also a very good entertainer that can make people smile around a pool table and that's mainly what trick shots are about. Above all, he's a nice guy and a good friend."
Mike Massey – Former #1 world ranking and four-time WPA World Artistic Pool Champion

"Andy Segal is the premier trick shot player in the world today. His knowledge and dedication to the game is second to none. Andy does a great job telling his road stories as well as his behind the scene pranks. You will learn, laugh, and enjoy the great stories. This is a must read book!"
Bruce Barthelette – Owner of the Connecticut APA and author of Knack, Pool & Billiards

"Andy Segal is to trick shots today, what Mike Massey was 20 years ago. Andy has contributed more to the sport than anyone else through his promotion, innovation, creativity, and fierce competitiveness. Andy and I have met in the finals more times than I can count. Although I can say I've won a few, Andy has come out ahead more often than not. On or off the table, Andy always carries himself with professionalism and a deep set of values. It is my pleasure to call Andy a friend."
Jamey Gray – 2008 WPA World Artistic Pool Champion and member of Team USA for ESPN's World Cup of Trick Shots

"Andy is by far one of the most talented trick shot players in the world. In my eyes, he is destined for the Hall of Fame. He is my biggest adversary and great friend. I am looking forward to many more great matches!"
Nick Nikolaidis – 2013 World Cup of Trick Shots Champion & 2010 Masters Champion

"In 2003, when we produced Trick Shot Magic for ESPN, Andy Segal was a last-minute replacement for a champion player who had injured his shoulder. Year by year Andy became better and better, winning Trick Shot Magic, the World Cup of Trick Shots, and the World Championship several times. Today, Andy reigns over the sport, truly a Master of Trick Shots."
Bettiane and Matt Braun – Producers of the International Challenge of Champions, Trick Shot Magic, and the World Cup of Trick Shots

"Having been involved in the world of championship billiards for almost two decades, it's been my good fortune to watch and do commentary for the game's elite players, in almost every discipline. From the time he burst onto the world trick shot stage as an unheralded newcomer in ESPN's Trick Shot Magic, Andy has consistently proven to be one of the most talented, creative, and hard-working champions in the game. Add to that being a fantastic teammate and consummate professional, and you'll understand why it's been a privilege to cover Andy over his career."
Mitch Laurance - Play-by-Play Commentator, ESPN Championship Billiards

"Andy Segal is arguably the most creative and accomplished performer and competitor on the Trick Shot Circuit today. His knowledge of the game, coupled with his creativity and personality, has made him both one of the most feared yet likable players in the world."
Ewa Laurance – 2012 WPBA Masters Champion and 2-Time US Open Champion

"Andy is without a doubt, one of the best American trick shot artists to come from my time. He is entertaining, sharp on all of his shots, and he always makes time for his fans. Thank you Andy for the great years."
Johnny Archer – 2009 Hall of Fame Inductee

"Andy Segal is a good friend whose dedication to the sport I find remarkable. He has so much knowledge about billiards, in all disciplines, but more than that, he pays careful attention to small details that most people miss. He is hardworking and obsessive, two qualities that I just love! I have full confidence that anything he puts in a book will be a must read!"
Jeanette Lee - Former #1 ranking on WPBA & World Games Gold Medalist

"In my opinion, Andy is one of the top 3 greatest trick shot artists of all time! I am confident that this book will set you on the right path if you're serious about trick shots!"
Tony Robles – Pro Player & Owner of The Predator Tour and National Amateur Pool League in NYC

"Andy is a true artist in the world of pool. His ability to create and perform trick shots is unparalleled."

Jennifer Barretta - Star of "9 Ball The Movie" and 2006 Empress Cup Champion

"As a promoter and a player, I have been around Andy for many years. He is highly talented but humble, professional and extremely personable. Andy is an inspiration on and off the table."

Dawn Hopkins - Top 16 WPBA touring professional for 3 decades

"In my travels through the world of pool and billiards I have run across some entertaining people but none more accomplished and dedicated than Andy Segal. I produce billiards programs for television and I have seen the players who can produce under pressure, who can create interesting shots, and who conduct themselves with integrity while showcasing the sport. Andy Segal stands at the top. His talent and commitment to creating wonderful trick shots have captured our viewer's interest for several years. He is an artist and true professional who has a lot to share with the pool and billiard loving public."

Gregg Hovey – Billiards International – Producer of ESPN's Trick Shot Magic and World Cup of Trick Shots

"Since I first started Artistic Pool, Andy Segal has always been a 'reference' in our sport, and his remarkable skills made him systematically the favorite of any competition. But Andy isn't only the most efficient opponent I've seen on tour. He is also a great promoter with his 'Ultimate Trick Shots Tour', the only format that allows us to keep alive the creative part of trick shots. More than just a strong competitor, Andy is also one of the greatest ambassadors of our sport!"

Florian Kohler - 2012 World Cup of Trick Shots Winner

"Andy Segal is truly a magic man. In the game of pool, there is nothing that he can't do! When I think of hiring a pool shark for an event, I always call Andy, and you should too!"

Michael Chaut - President, Magical Nights Inc and Producer of Monday Night Magic in NYC, with appearances on FOX-TV, Good Morning New York, NBC's Today Show, CBS's Early Show, ABC's Good Morning America and The Wall Street Journal Report

"Andy Segal is a true master of the trick shot, not only a great player but a pleasure to film with."

Darlene Liebman - Vice President of Casting, Howcast Media Inc.

"I've known Andy for nearly 20 years and can confidently tell you that his passion and drive are second to none. He has always been on a clear-cut mission, giving each and every one 110% effort. I'm sure you'll see and benefit from this extra effort as you work your way through this book."
Joe Tucker - Professional Player & Instructor

"Andy Segal is clearly the best showman and most dominant player in Trick Shot Pool. Andy is the greatest artist that the billiard world has ever seen. No one else even comes close to being at the level of consistency that Andy has demonstrated year after year in Artistic Pool. Andy is at the top for one reason - he is the best!"
Eric Yow – Former WPA Massé World Champion

"When competing against the Magic Man, I know to always expect amazing creativity and close-to-perfect shot execution. Andy has been performing trick shots for a while now and always knows what to shoot and when to shoot it. He is professionalism at its best and definitely a great choice when it comes to entertainment!"
Steve Markle - 2013 Massé World Champion

"Andy is an amazing competitor, a true champion, and a good friend. I always enjoy competing against him."
Dave Nangle - 2008 WPA World Massé Champion

"Andy's imagination on the pool table (and dedication to the sport off of it) has helped catalyze the new trick shot movement, inspiring all of his competitors to improve their skills and create radical new inventions that push the envelope of trick shots. His metro-nomic consistency has made him the winningest player, certainly in the modern era, and perhaps ever. Yet, he is always willing to help even the most novice players perfect routine shots, sharing his experience and passion for the game."
Tim Chin - 2010 Ultimate Trick Shot Tour Champion

"Andy Segal is one of the most amazing trick shot artists who has ever walked the planet. Winning three world championships back-to-back-to-back is a feat that has never been done before and will probably never be done again."
Sal Conti - 2013 New England Pool & Billiard Hall of Fame inductee

"I used to be a firm believer that no player is unbeatable. Andy Segal just might be the only exception."
Abram Diaz - 2011 WPA World Stroke Champion

"I've never been able to figure out Trick Shots…but I want too! I can't wait to check out Andy's new book. Andy has mastered the Art of Trick Shots!"
Robin Dodson - Two Time World 9 Ball Champion and BCA Hall of Famer

"It has been my pleasure to know Andy and his wonderful family since 2004. During this time, I have found him to be a true gentleman who is as talented as he is honorable. Whether it be in competition or in life, he always finds a way to help others. His skills are unparalleled and the many titles he holds and standards he has set are a true testimony to his character. I am proud to know Andy, compete with Andy, and call Andy a friend."

Paul Danno - 2008 Masters Follow Shot Discipline Medal Winner

"Andy is one of the greatest champions ever! A true Aries!"

Jimmy Glanville - 2012 WPA World Trick & Fancy Shots Champion

"I have had the pleasure to know Andy for many years and I have found him to be a great competitor and friend. He has been one of the constants in our sport, inventing many new shots, and bringing new players into the sport. He is a fierce competitor with titles under his belt too numerous to count, and if history repeats itself, many more to come."

Jason Lynch - 2008 World Jump Champion

"Andy Segal comes up with very challenging, fun, and entertaining shots. I always look forward to new shots at our competitions."

Gordon Hedges - 2012 US Open Draw Shots Champion

"We have been friends for over 2 decades. Your dedication and professionalism has rewarded you with world titles and multiple championships. You have been an inspiration to our sport."

Tom Kinzel – Chairman of the Artistic Pool & Trick Shot Association

Andy Segal's Cue Magic
Inside the World of Modern Trick Shots

ANDY SEGAL

First Edition
Billiards Press, New York, NY

Andy Segal's Cue Magic
Inside the World of Modern Trick Shots

By Andy Segal

Copyright ©2013 By Andy Segal

Published by: Billiards Press
                 New York, NY

First Printing

Printed in the United States of America

10   9   8   7   6   5   4   3   2   1

Library of Congress Control Number 2013951700

ISBN 978-0-9898917-0-7

Cover design and diagrams by Janet Tedesco
Illustrations by Lorelei Arts, Nicholas Eriksen, Maritza Ortiz
Photos by Michael Pollan
Proofreading by Barbara Berkowitz, Kim Segal
Elevation Measurements by Jessica Segal

For my wife Kim, my daughter Jessica

and my parents Barbara and Billy Berkowitz.

Dedication

I first met my wife in Pittsburgh while attending college. At one of the billiard club meetings at Kim's school we made a small bet on a set of 9-ball – the loser has to buy the winner dinner. Long story short, I lost on purpose, took her out to dinner, and the rest is history. Once we both graduated, Kim quickly moved to New York, and we were married one year later in 1995. At our wedding, our best man, Jim Dale, had a great line during his toast. He said, "Andy thought that he was hustling Kim, but now that they are married, she, in fact, hustled him." As of the writing of this book, we have been happily married for 18 years, and each one has been better than the one before.

While in New York, we met multiple times per week after work at the Amsterdam Billiard Club, and we practiced together or separately for a few hours each night. In 1999, when Jessica was born, everything changed. Kim stopped playing pool on a regular basis, but she still supported me when I had to travel for a show or tournament. She later joined the Suffolk County APA and quickly became one of the better players in that league. When Jessica was able to reach the pool table, she loved going down into our basement and setting up trick shots for me. Every once in a while I would find her hitting a few balls around with a friend. Now that she is 14, Jessica is involved in dance, tennis and track – and she is an A student – who just started high school. Jessica is always there if I need help with something, whether filming a shot, taking pictures, or timing the speed of a shot for an ESPN event. While at a tournament, when things start to get intense, speaking with her on the phone is just the medicine I need to stay relaxed. When returning from a tournament win, I usually come home to find a new, hand-drawn poster, congratulating me on the victory – something which gets added to the trophy collection.

My parents, Barbara and Billy, were always full of encouragement. I used to be in the Information Technology field, and when I quit to purchase the Hudson County APA in New Jersey, they were an invaluable companion with their advice and support. The first tournament in which they had ever seen me play was a 9-ball event in Whitestone, NY – and I was overjoyed that they were there. Later, when I became involved with trick shots, they came up to see the U.S. Open in Southington, Connecticut. Today, whenever I have an extended trip for a tournament, they usually offer to come up from Florida and stay with our daughter, taking her to school, and to her after-school activities. I can't thank them enough for everything they have done for me over these many years.

Acknowledgments

I was very fortunate to have a team of people who shared my enthusiasm and dedication for this project. I would like to thank all of the people mentioned below, and any others who I may have missed for their help with this book.

Barbara Berkowitz did the preliminary editing of the text, giving each section a better flow, and making them easier to read. She spent long hours going through each individual word, and I would not have been able to produce this final product without her help. Phil Capelle performed the final edit, cleaning up the text to the point it is at now, along with putting his expertise in the billiard field to work in making the shots easier to understand. In the final weeks, I can't remember a day that passed where we didn't at least spend a few minutes on the phone. The final copy of this book would not have been possible without the assistance of Janet Tedesco, who spent countless hours working on the diagrams, the layout of each individual page, and the front cover design. It was a true pleasure to work with all three of them from start to finish.

Mike Pollan, the father of one of my daughter's friends, was responsible for the high quality photographs throughout this book. He went above and beyond what a standard photographer does by making this project his own, and by putting extra effort into making sure everything came out just right.

Laurie Edmonds (as Lorelei Arts), my cousin, did the illustrations for chapter 16, and the smaller icons that you will see describing the difficulty and power ratings throughout each shot. Nick Eriksen and Maritza Ortiz are two art students that I had the pleasure of meeting in New York City. They did a great job with the chapter introduction illustrations, and I would like to thank all three for their superb work.

In addition to the individuals who directly helped with the production of this book, there are a number of people throughout my life that have had a positive influence on my career. Starting with my high school years, I was introduced to the game of pool by my good friends Suji DeSilva, Eddie Tom, Pat Missud and Doug Roll. Once in college, Jim Dale, Alan Guilds, Steve Carpenter and Rich Kameda took over that role. Although I have lost touch with Alan and Rich, I still see Steve on occasion, and Jim and I remain best friends, living near each other, and getting together on a regular basis. Once we started playing at the University of Pittsburgh (my wife's school), I met some players who became good friends of mine and helped me to bump up my game to the next level: Anurag Mehta, Don Broggi, Chuck Farinella and JR Calvert.

After graduation, I moved back to New York and started the next step in my pool playing career. I met Ethan and Greg Hunt, the owners of the Amsterdam Billiard Club, who later sponsored me. The two brothers got me my first television commercial with AT&T, and they helped me acquire the role of Technical Advisor on a Woody Allen film (Sweet and Lowdown).

Among the top 9-ball professional players who I have met along the way have been Dawn Hopkins, Allison Fisher, Nick Varner, Tony Robles, George "Ginky" San Souci, Mike Dechaine, Steve Lipsky, Jonathan Smith, Jennifer Barretta, Jeanette Lee, and Rob Saez. All of these players were very influential with my 9-ball game and/or my trick shot career in one way or another.

Once I started getting involved in the trick shot world, there were quite a few players that I met, and I would like to thank all of them for their positive influence on me as a trick shot artist, and as a person. In no particular order, they are: Mike and Francine Massey, Bruce and Ann Barthelette, Sal Conti, Nick and Ewa Nikolaidis, Tom & Marty Rossman, Tim Chin, Paul & Elaine Danno, Steve Lillis, Mark Dimick, Abram Diaz, Steve Geller, Sebastian Giumelli, Jim Glanville, Brenda Lee, Javier Gomez, Jamey & Beverly Gray, Rick Hawkinson, Gordon Hedges, Jason Kane, Tom Kinzel, Florian Kohler, Jason Lynch, Matt MacPhail, Steve Markle, Jamie Moody, Dave Nangle, Jeremiah Owens, Curtis Robertson, Luke Szywala, Gabi Visoiu, Gerry Woodlief, Bogdan Wolkowski, Ralph Eckert, Chris Woodrum, Eric Yow, Iulian Cernatinschi, Jim Barnard, and Wayne Parker.

My career wouldn't have taken off the way it did if it were not for Matt and Bettiane Braun. They are the producers of the annual ESPN trick shot events, and their hard work and support have been invaluable. Mitch and Ewa Laurance were key people who encouraged and supported me during competitions, and who positively influenced me in other parts of my life as well. Allen Hopkins is another person that I would like to thank for his support during my career. Gregg Hovey, who is now working with Matt and Bettiane on the ESPN events, started off at Olhausen Billiards while helping me to become part of their organization as a player representative.

I would like to thank Bob Meucci for working with me and creating my first custom signature line of cues. We spent almost an entire week together designing and producing the cue line. Bob, and the entire staff at Meucci, have been a pleasure to work with.

Bruce Barthelette mentored me when I became a League Operator for the American Pool-players Association (APA) in 2007. Being involved with the APA has been so fantastic, from both a business and pool playing perspective, and it has enabled me to improve my relationship with my family as I was now home to spend more time with them instead of spending every waking hour either at work or on the train. The people at the APA (both the National Office and League Operators throughout the country) were very supportive with my franchise, and with my trick shot career. I would like to thank everyone at the APA, including (no particular order): Pam Aston, Terry Bell, Kevin Hinkebein, Jason Bowman, Greg Fletcher, Renee Lyle, Larry Hubbart, Bris Robinson, Traci Tufts, Gary Barsky, Bob Vandertoorn, Jerry Bayer, Melissa Cossidente, Brian Boyle, Mike Boyle, Terry and Valerie Justice, Lee and Jane Tiani, and, of course, all of the players in the Hudson County APA with whom I have had the pleasure of six wonderful years of friendship.

Finally, I would like to thank my daughter Jessica and my wife Kim. Jessica has spent a lot of time measuring the elevation angle on every shot, and she has also supported me in all my travels. Spending time away from Jessica and Kim is the hardest part of my job. Kim spent time proofreading the text, making sure it was understandable and, throughout my career, she helped me with the mental aspect of the game, teaching me to get over the fear and frustration of losing – and once I got over that hurdle, the only option left was to win. I have no one but her to thank for that.

Forward

Growing up in Chicopee, Massachusetts, I started playing pool when I was 4 years old. My dad purchased a used table from my uncle, and it didn't take long for me to fall in love with the game that would eventually reshape my life. In 1989, while I was playing in local pool leagues, I decided to take a chance and buy into a pool league franchise. Along with my wife Ann, we started the Connecticut APA Pool League, and have now become the second largest APA league in the world.

Running the pool league opened many doors for me. It gave me the chance to meet the legendary Mike Massey. Mike would come to our area and do trick shot exhibitions. It took a while, but Mike finally convinced me to play in the 2003 Artistic Pool US Open in New Bedford, Massachusetts. It was at that tournament that I first met Andy Segal. Andy, like me, was new to trick shots — starting about a year earlier. As I began to attend more events, Andy and I became good friends. We talked about how we could help get more tournaments and exposure for this great sport. We included Sal Conti, another great friend and fellow trick shot player, in our talks, and formed the strongest and most productive board that trick shots ever had. With Andy as president, and with Sal and I on the team, we took the sport of trick shots to the next level. In 2005, when the NHL went on strike, we were able to get the first non-ESPN televised trick shot tournament. It was at that tournament that Andy, Sal, and I came up with a new playoff format. There were a total of eight events, the most ever in any year, past or present.

Moving forward to 2013, Andy Segal has proven to be the top trick shot artist in the world. Having played and defeated everyone in the game, his record is nothing short of amazing. He has won every title that there is to win.

I would like to share two stories with you. First, when Andy was just starting out, he received a call from Matt Braun to fill in at Trick Shot Magic. Bogdan Wolkowski had thrown out his shoulder and was unable to play. Andy had about a week to practice for this event while the other competitors had months to prepare. In his first match, he defeated Stefano Pelinga, a veteran of the game. Andy won his next match, and ended up playing Mike Massey, the greatest trick shot artist ever, in the finals. Andy lost to Mike, but losing to a five time ESPN champ is nothing to feel bad about. From that time on, Andy just got stronger and stronger as a player.

In 2007, Andy and I traveled together to Russia for the World Championships. It was in mid-December and Andy was not feeling well, but he never said anything, and just played his matches. In the semi-final match, Andy played Luke Szywala from Poland. Andy was so dehydrated from being sick that he drank seven large bottles of water during the match. Andy went on to win the match, and had to face Sebastian Giumelli of Argentina in the finals. During this match, Andy was down early, but staged a great comeback. After consuming nine more large bottles of water, it came down to the very last shot. For Andy to win, he needed to make the Yo-Yo Masse, and he needed to make it on his first attempt! Andy went up and hit the shot perfectly to take home the trophy and the title.

In my opinion, Andy Segal is by far the best trick shot artist in the world. He has taken on all challengers and has won, and he has set the standard for all future trick shot artists. I could not ask for a better friend than Andy. It is always a great pleasure to work with him. We have both competed against each other and teamed up together. His wife Kim and daughter Jessica are always there to support him. In my opinion, Andy has it all.

Contents

Part I – Getting Started

Part II – Cue Magic

Part III – The Lighter Side

Andy Segal's Cue Magic

Inside the World of Modern Trick Shots

Part I

Getting Started

Some of these shots run the risk of one or more balls flying off the table. This is especially true when they are performed by someone just learning them. I urge you to use caution when performing these shots and to not shoot anything that you feel may result in a danger-ous situation. I will point out this risk on some, but not all of them. However, you must keep in mind that the shooter assumes any and all risks when trying the shots contained within this book.

Please be careful.

1: Introduction

Trick shots have been around for a long time. Originally they consisted of carefully aligning a few balls and making them all in one stroke. Some of these shots were given generic names like *3 in 3* (three balls made in three pockets) or *4 in 3* (four balls made in three pockets). Others were given memorable names such as the *Rosebud Cluster* or the *Just Showin' Off Shot*.

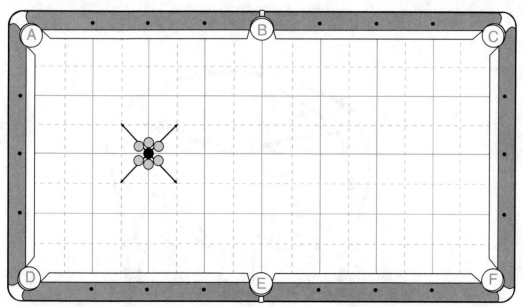

The *Rosebud Cluster* allows the center ball to be made in any of the four pockets shown. I set this shot up on Good Morning America for Chris Cuomo, the host, and he made it on his very first attempt.

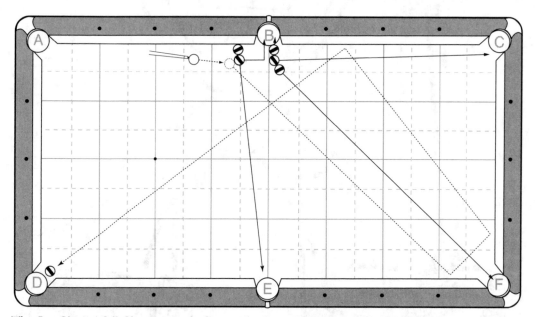

The *Just Showin' Off Shot* was made famous by Steve Mizerak in an old Miller Lite commercial.

With these older shots, the skill was mostly in the setup. Once the balls were aligned properly, any player could make it providing that they had a minimal amount of skill and could shoot straight. The problem was these shots took too long to set up. Still, these were all I had in my bag when I first started performing in trick shot shows, so I had to arrive an hour before show time, set up the shots, and tap the balls[1-1] so I could quickly reproduce the same configuration during the actual performance.

In 2000, Matt and Bettiane Braun[1-2] created ESPN's Trick Shot Magic, the first nationally aired and organized trick shot competition. If you were to look back at the first few episodes, a lot of the shots dealt with clusters of balls being set up and made in multiple pockets. Back then, one of the most innovative shots was a one-handed jump shot.

My first ESPN event was in 2003 at the ESPN Zone in Baltimore, MD. A last minute cancellation by one of the competitors and a phone call from the producer led to six days of preparation, resulting in a second place finish which is something I will never forget.

Not wanting to be a mere filler for the player who dropped out, I spent those six days working on new shots and modifying old ones, changing them in various ways so that I could hopefully catch the veterans off guard. With only two attempts per shot, I was counting on them not being able to perfect my new shots that quickly. My first match was against Italian trick shot artist Stefano Pelinga. Since each shot was worth one point, the match was essentially over when I assumed a three point lead with two shots to go.

I then waited for what seemed a very long time until my first televised match. Yes, it was only a day, but a case of the nerves prevented me from sleeping or having anything more than a few bites of food. In the semi-finals I was matched up against Charles Darling, a veteran player from prior ESPN tournaments. That match proved to be a lot closer and tougher than my first as shown by the final score of 11-11. We then moved into a sudden death tie-breaker, an eight rail bank onto the face of a $100 bill. I shot first and landed the cue ball a few inches from the bill. Despite all of the multi-rail kick shots he picked during our match, Charlie hit the cue ball four rails and scratched in the side. Now it was on to the finals against the two-time champion Mike Massey. Mike proved to be the great player he was by winning that match as he captured his third Trick Shot Magic title in four years.

I have since been invited to the ESPN events every year, and I have seen the shots evolve into what they are today. Very rarely do you see a setup shot, as they have been replaced by speed shots, multiple cue shots and a variety of skill shots. Almost none of these shots would ever come up in a standard game of pool, but they are very flashy and appeal to the television audience.

In this book, I have included a selection of the newer style of trick shots, leaving the older shots to the numerous books published in years past. Some of the shots in this book are difficult to learn, but they all rely on specific concepts which can be practiced and mastered. My goal in writing this book is to not only share with you this new collection of television shots, but to teach you the underlying concepts. I hope to encourage you to practice them and create the next generation of trick shots that will have me scratching my head in the future.

2: Terminology & Conventions

Whether you are a veteran or just starting out, please review this chapter. I have listed explanations for all of the notations used in the diagrams, plus a guide for the difficulty and power ratings. Advanced players can skip the sections which describe the pool table and some common terminology. However, there are some key tips listed in this chapter that even the more skilled players will find useful.

2.1: The Rails

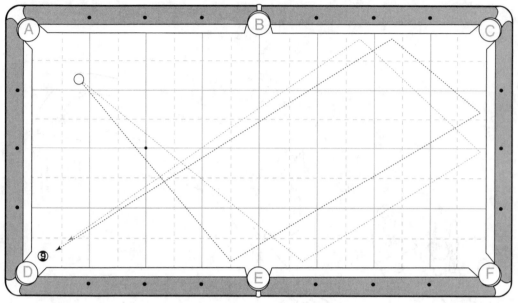

The term *rail* and *cushion* are used interchangeably throughout this book. The side pockets are located on the *long rail*, whereas the *short rail* is typically where you stand when racking or breaking the balls. When a trick shot is diagrammed showing a ball hitting a *rail*, it is always acceptable to make contact with that *rail* anywhere unless otherwise stated. For example, if you wanted to shoot the cue ball three *rails* to make the 9-ball, it would be okay to hit on either side of the pocket.

2.2: The Pocket

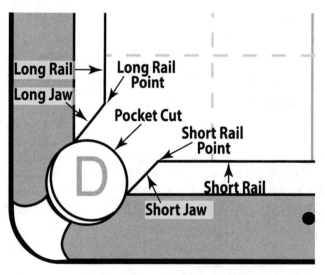

The *jaw* is the portion of the rail that is angled into the pocket. On some of the diagrams I may indicate that a ball should be frozen to the *long jaw*. This means you need to place the ball against the *jaw* that is part of the long rail.

The *pocket point* is where the standard rail and the *jaw* meet. The *corner pocket points* are shown in the diagram, however each side pocket also has two points. If I specify that a ball is centered at the *long rail pocket point* (or any of the other points), this means that the ball will be touching the corresponding *pocket point*, and if you were to draw a line perpendicular to the rail, the ball would be centered on that line.

The *pocket cut* is where the table ends and the ball drops into the pocket. Sometimes shots are described as having a ball hanging in the pocket with its back edge aligned with the *pocket cut*. When looking straight down from the top, the edge of the ball deepest in the pocket should be aligned with the *pocket cut*.

2.2.1: Hanging a Ball

When a ball is said to be *hanging*, you have the freedom to position the ball anywhere in the immediate vicinity of the pocket. Where a ball is placed can have a big impact on whether or not you make the shot. Besides hitting the ball directly in the center, there are two other ways to make that *hanger* [2-1]: hitting the rail first and clipping the edge of the object ball. The illustrations below show three common ways to miss the *hanger* if the object ball is not positioned properly.

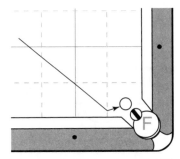 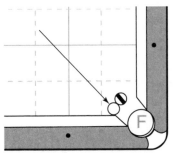 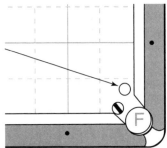

The cue ball hits the rail. If the ball is positioned too deep in the pocket, the cue ball may miss it.

The cue ball hits the ball and the rail at the same time. If the ball is too far out, it could be hit as shown and missed.

The cue ball is coming directly at the edge of the pocket, and the ball will be missed if it is too far to one side.

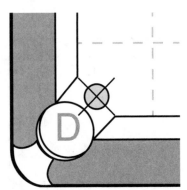

There is one place, however, that gives you the most room for error. Typically the best place to put the ball is directly in the center of the pocket, where the ball is also centered along the line connecting the pocket points.

2.3: Frozen Balls

Two balls are considered *frozen* when they are touching. A ball is *frozen* to a cushion when it is touching that cushion. It is not enough for the balls to be close, especially when the cue ball is involved, as even the slightest gap can mean the difference between making and missing a shot.

It looks as if both balls are *frozen*.

A closer look reveals a small gap.

2.4: Diagram Markings

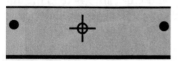

This indicates the point at which you should be aiming. It may also indicate an alignment point of two or more balls.

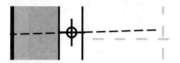

A dashed line may also be used to indicate the alignment point of two or more balls.

S - This indicates that you missed the shot 'short'.

L - This indicates that you missed the shot 'long'.

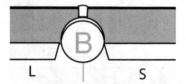

(S) - This shows you how to adjust to make the shot shorter (correcting a 'long' miss).

(L) - This shows you how to adjust to make the shot longer (correcting a 'short' miss).

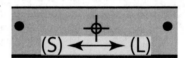

2.5: The Diamonds

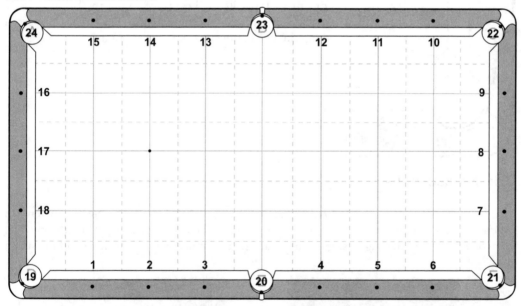

The *diamonds* are the markers on the rail which help guide you when shooting *bank* or *kick* shots. *Bank shots* usually refer to the object ball while *kick shots* refer to the cue ball. Shooting the cue ball into another ball, causing that ball to rebound off a cushion and into a pocket is a *bank shot*. Shooting the cue ball off one or more cushions in order to make another ball is called a *kick shot*.   The words are sometimes used interchangeably and either may be used throughout this book.

At first glance, it would appear there are only 18 *diamonds* on the table when actually there are 24. The center of each pocket is considered a *diamond* as indicated in the diagram above.

2.5.1: On the Line/Behind the Line

When playing 8-ball or 9-ball, you must break from *behind the line* or *behind the headstring*. This means the cue ball must be behind the second diamond [2-2]. Typically the position of the ball's base is the determining factor but in trick shots, we use the entire ball. In the diagram to the right, the difference should be obvious.

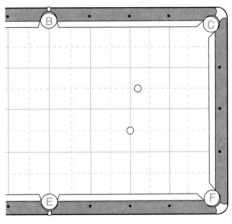

2.5.2: Measuring From a Diamond Line

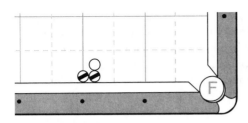

Sometimes balls must be positioned very precisely when setting up trick shots. This book may refer to the cue ball being one ball-width from the second diamond and one ball-width off the rail. Start by placing a ball frozen to the cushion, centered at the second diamond. We need to move one ball-width over and one ball-width off the rail. The final and correct position for the cue ball is shown in the diagram. Once in place, the two measuring balls can be removed.

2.5.3: Diamond Intersection Lines

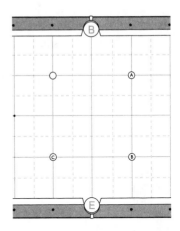

Normally the diamonds are counted only up to three. You wouldn't say a ball is on the *fifth diamond line*. Instead, you would say it is on the *third diamond line* and it would be obvious to which one you were referring. In the diagram, we would describe the cue ball as being on the 3,1 *diamond intersection point*. While it could be any of the other points marked 'A', 'B' or 'C', it should be easy to determine which one I am referring to.

2.5.4: Inside a Zone

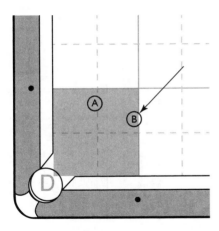

The 1x1 *diamond zone* near the corner pocket is shown in the diagram to the left.

The definition of '*inside a zone*' depends on whether you are referring to the ball's setup position or its final resting position.

When setting up a shot, if cue ball 'A' must start within this 1x1 *diamond zone*, the entire ball must be completely *inside the zone*, measured by the edge of the ball.

When executing a shot, if cue ball 'B' must come to rest inside this 1x1 *diamond zone*, any part of the ball can be inside it for the shot to be successfully made.

2.5.5: Spin

The term *spin* or *English* refers to hitting the cue ball off center. Hitting the ball above, below, left, or right of center will cause it to react differently during the course of a shot. The five basic types of *spin* are *top, bottom, left, right,* and *center. Top spin* results when you hit the cue ball above center, *bottom spin* (or *back spin*) comes from a below center hit, etc. *Center spin* (called *center ball*) occurs when you hit the direct center of the cue ball. Then there are combinations, like *top left spin, bottom right spin,* etc.

During a typical game of 8-ball or 9-ball, most average players and even most of the top players will limit themselves to the basic types of *spin* mentioned above, unless a rare situation comes up. When performing trick shots, the exact *spin* that's applied to the cue ball needs to be more precise. Sometimes *top left spin* needs to have more *top* than *left*, and sometimes it needs to have more *left* than *top*.

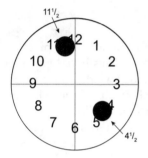

The *clock system* is the simplest way to explain the different points on the cue ball to hit. When describing a certain shot, I may instruct you to hit the cue ball at '12'. That means you should hit it with only *top spin* (above center, no *left* or *right*). If I say to hit it with '7', use *bottom left spin*, but more *bottom* than *left*. Basically, anywhere along the 7 o'clock line. Half and quarter hours may also be used in some situations. '4 1/2 ' means *standard bottom right spin*, and '11 1/2 ' means almost straight *top spin with a touch of left*.

The amount of *spin* is measured from the center spot on the cue ball, visualizing the width of a tip and moving away from the center along whatever *spin line* you are using ('2' English is shown in the diagram). Very few shots require *center ball spin*, even when playing 8-ball or 9-ball. Whether you are using top, left, bottom right, etc, the typical shot uses approximately two tips of English. Use this unless otherwise specified.

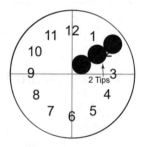

Running and *reverse English* may sound confusing to someone who doesn't play a lot of pool, but these concepts are really quite simple.

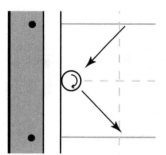

Running English helps the cue ball around the table, causing it to *run* (travel) further.

Reverse English hampers the movement of the cue ball, causing it to *reverse*, or travel less.

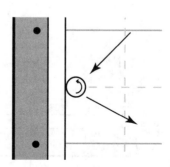

2.5.6: Deflection

Deflection occurs when you use either left or right English, which causes the cue ball to veer off your line of aim.

Line of Aim

Actual Travel Path

It is easy to understand *deflection* using this simple test: Place a piece of chalk on the table, put your finger perpendicular to the face of the chalk, and push. The chalk should move straight ahead, which is your line of aim. Turn the chalk slightly in either direction and give it another push. You will notice that the chalk does not travel along your line of aim, but is pushed at an angle.

Hitting a cue ball with left or right spin has the same effect. The point at which you are making contact with the cue ball has a tangent line similar to the twisted piece of chalk in the first example. Here you are hitting the cue ball with left spin, which will cause it to *deflect* slightly right of your line of aim.

Many things affect the amount of *deflection*. The more spin you use, the more *deflection*. The harder you hit the cue ball, the more it will *deflect*. A few cue makers have found ways to reduce *deflection* by crafting the shaft in their own proprietary manner. The shaft I have found that reduces *deflection* the most is the Ultimate Weapon shaft by Meucci[2-3].

Here is a word of caution for those of you that decide to go with a low *deflection* shaft. There are things that increase or decrease *deflection* other than the shaft. For example, a loose back wrist (which you should always have when shooting), will cause the cue ball to *deflect* more than will a stiff back wrist. I have tried some low *deflection* shafts and if I make my back wrist very loose (much looser than I would normally use), I can increase the *deflection* to where it is almost as much as with a standard shaft (with the Ultimate Weapon shaft by Meucci, I can only bring it up to about half of a normal shaft). If your game is at the point where your mechanics are pretty solid and you have a consistent stroke, a low *deflection* shaft may do the trick for you.

2.5.7: The Diamond System

I am going to now take you through a few of the many systems for using the diamonds. Since this is a book on trick shots, these explanations will be brief, but sufficient to give you a basic understanding.

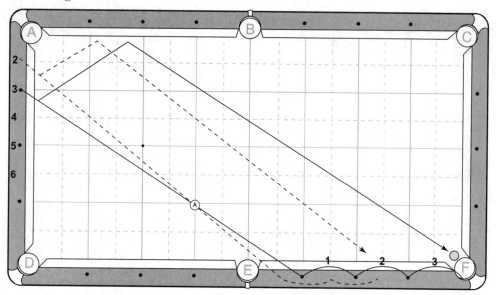

The diagram above shows a simple *two-rail system*. Cue ball 'A' is sitting on the line connecting the third diamond (on the long rail) and the first diamond (on the short rail). It may be a little confusing as to why that first diamond is labelled '3'. Start by drawing a line from that point, through the cue ball and into the long rail. As you can see from the cue ball's position, that line goes directly into the third diamond on the long rail. If you then count three diamonds over to the right, that is where the cue ball will return if you aim at the point marked '3'. In other words, aiming at the point marked '3' will cause the cue ball to return three diamonds down from where you started, as indicated by the solid lines in the diagram.

If you were to aim at the point marked '2' (with the same cue ball starting position), a different result will occur. Draw a line (dashed) from the point marked '2', through the cue ball and into the long rail. That is a point just to the left of the third diamond. Since you are aiming at the '2' point, the cue ball will return exactly two diamonds down from there.

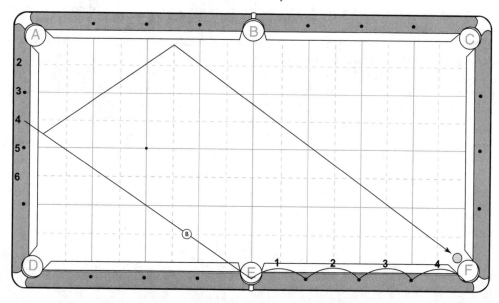

If you place the cue ball at point 'B' as shown in the diagram at the bottom of the previous page, it will be on the line connecting the side pocket (fourth diamond) and the short rail's 1 $^1/_2$ diamond mark (which is labeled '4'). Aim at that mark with running English and the cue ball will return exactly four diamonds down from where it started. Every table plays differently, so if you are playing on one where the cue ball doesn't follow the exact path described here, simply adjust where your '3' point is located. Instead of it being on the first diamond, you may need to shift it over an inch or two in either direction (and shift all other numbers as well). In all cases, use running English.

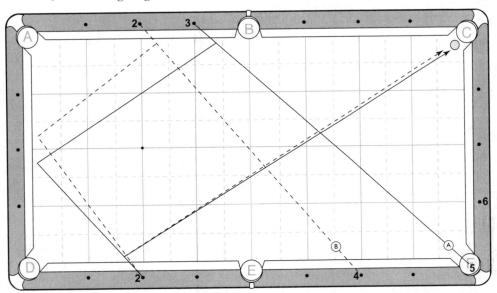

The *three-rail system* is a little more complicated. The most important thing to remember is that the corner pocket is numbered '5'. If you shoot cue ball 'A' along the path from the corner pocket (numbered '5') directly at the third diamond, it will hit the second diamond on the third cushion. This number is arrived at by simple subtraction; the cue ball starts at '5' and you are aiming at '3', resulting in a third rail hit at '2' (5-3=2). The complication comes when you move the cue ball away from the corner pocket.

When using the *three-rail system*, the starting position diamond numbers are adjusted by halves as you move up the long cushion, and by whole numbers moving along the short cushion. The diamond numbers for the first and third rails are standard. Cue ball 'B' is being shot along the line starting at the second diamond. Since we count by halves, this is actually point '4'. We are hitting the first rail at the second diamond so the third rail contact point will also be the second diamond (4-2=2). Since we are contacting the third rail at the same location, the cue ball should continue to make the hanger in the corner pocket. As with the two-rail system, you may need to adjust based on the table. The only thing you need to change is where the cue ball is hitting the third cushion, since the subtraction portion of this system should work on all tables. For example, while practicing, if you figure out that the cue ball must hit the third diamond on the third rail in order to make the hanger in the corner pocket, you would adjust cue ball 'A' to still start at '5', but aim at the second diamond (5-2=3), and adjust cue ball 'B' to start at '4' but aim at the first diamond (4-1=3).

2.5.8: Short & Long

Any shot that requires a ball to travel around the table (usually two or more cushions) will probably need some adjustments if the shot is missed. I will refer to the cue ball missing *long* or *short*. For example, if you see the letter 'S', showing you that the shot was missed *short*, you will need to find the corresponding '(L)', which shows you the adjustment for making the shot longer.

This three-rail shot shows the starting position and line of aim for the cue ball. The cue ball will miss *short* if it hits the long cushion, and it will miss *long* if it hits the short cushion first. I know this sounds backward, but it is based on the running English put on the cue ball. In the diagram, running English would be left spin. The cue ball misses *short* if it hits a cushion and the spin becomes reverse English. Missing *long* means the cue ball still has running English when it hits the rail. The original aim point is marked, and both misses are also marked near pocket 'D' using an 'S' to indicate the 'short' miss and an 'L' to indicate the 'long' miss.

There are multiple ways to adjust for missed shots. The most obvious is the line of aim. Shifting it left or right will cause the cue ball to travel *longer* or *shorter*. In the diagram, the arrow and mark '(L)' shows you the direction to change your line of aim in order to make the shot go *longer*. Similarly, the '(S)' shows you the adjustment that's needed to make the cue ball go *shorter*.

An alternative adjustment can be made to the speed at which you hit the cue ball. The harder it is struck, the *shorter* it will travel (shorter relating to the cushions, not distance). Finally, you can adjust the amount of spin used on the cue ball. As you increase the amount of spin, the *longer* the cue ball will go (assuming it is running English).

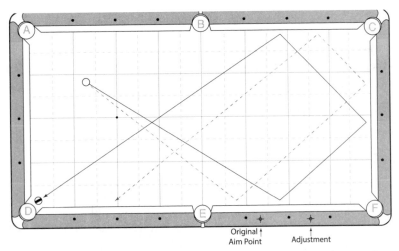

The original aim point brings the cue ball *short*. Adjusting your aim point in the direction shown in the diagram will cause the cue ball to go *longer*.

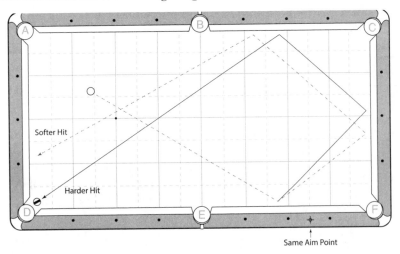

Use the same aim point and adjust the speed at which you hit the cue ball. Your original speed (softer hit) caused the cue ball to miss *long*, so hitting it harder will make it go *shorter*.

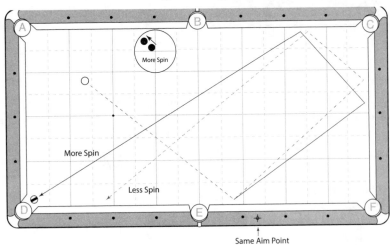

The same aim point is used here as well, while only adjusting the amount of spin. The original shot missed *short*, and more spin along the same line of aim will make the cue ball go *longer*.

2.6: Throw

Throw refers to the altered path an object ball takes when it starts out frozen to another ball. A common theme with older trick shots has the 1-ball starting on the spot (2,2 diamond intersection point), and the 2-ball is frozen to it.

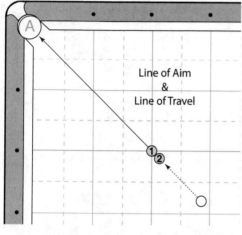

When two balls are lined up at the pocket's center, the second ball (the one closest to the pocket) will only go in if the cue ball hits it directly in line.

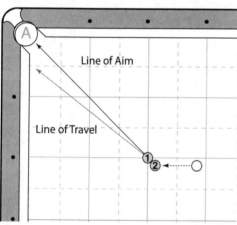

From this angle of approach, the momentum of the cue ball and the friction between the two setup balls cause the ball to be *thrown* off the line of aim, missing the pocket as shown.

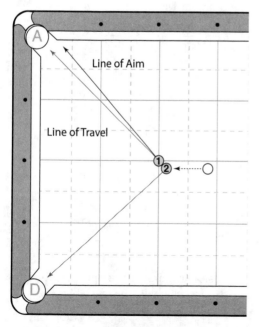

This setup works better. The balls are aligned for the long rail pocket point and the ball is *thrown* into the center of pocket 'A'. The nice thing about this setup is the other ball will also be made in pocket 'D'.

Throw also takes place when the cue ball is involved, but only when it is very close or frozen to the object ball. The image on the left shows a standard cut shot. The cue ball is hit to the right, which cuts the 1-ball to the left. The illustration on the right shows what happens when the cue ball is frozen to the 1-ball (or very close). The cue ball is hit to the right, which causes the 1-ball to *throw* to the right.

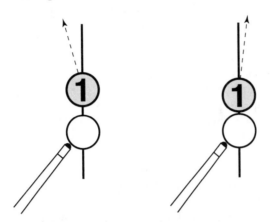

In the previous example, I showed *throw* when the 1-ball and 2-ball were frozen. In this example, the cue ball takes the place of the 2-ball and the cue stick takes the place of the cue ball. The friction between the cue ball and 1-ball, along with the momentum of the cue stick, causes the 1-ball to be *thrown* off the normal path.

Spin on the cue ball also affects *throw*, but only when dealing with a single ball. Shooting straight into the balls with right English will cause the cue ball to move left at the point of contact between the two balls. The friction between the two balls *throws* the 1-ball to the left, making it in the side pocket.

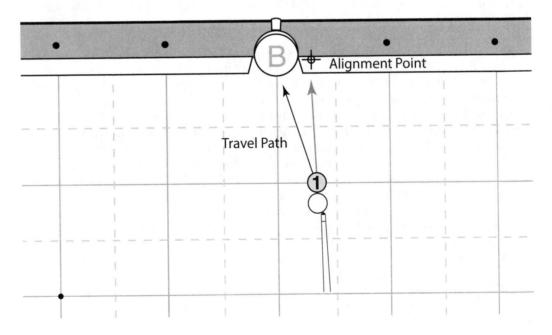

2.7: Shot Categories

The trick shots in this book are categorized by skill (jump, massé, etc). When a shot falls into multiple categories, the primary skill is used to classify that shot. For example, a shot where you need to jump a few balls into a pocket in less than ten seconds would be categorized as a speed shot (not a jump shot).

> *In competitions, every skill is considered. Jumping four balls in ten seconds would be a jump AND a speed shot, using up one in each category.*

In most trick shot competitions, players are only allowed to select two or three shots from any given category of skill. This rule forces each player to shoot a variety of shots for the audience, but it also prevents a player from taking advantage of an opponent's weakness in a specific skill. For example, a player cannot shoot ten speed shots.

The trick shots in this book are divided into the following chapters:

Bank/Kick Shots - Shots requiring the cue ball or object ball to bank or kick off one or more rails.

Speed Shots - Any shot that cannot be done at the player's leisure. A bunch of the newer trick shots require you to hit multiple balls, sometimes within some specified time frame or before another ball goes in. In other chapters there are shots that also use the element of *speed*, but since *speed* is not the primary skill, they have been included elsewhere.

Juggling Shots - These shots involve using your cue stick to hit a moving ball. The easiest example is to place the cue ball in the middle of the table and shoot it around three rails. After hitting the third rail and passing by the approximate starting position, re-hit the cue ball three rails again (along the same path). This can be done multiple times and is referred to as *juggling*.

Stroke Shots - Usually shot with a level cue, extreme spin is required for these shots. Occasionally you will need to elevate the cue stick, but usually by not more than 30 degrees. Sometimes it is a fine line between categorizing a shot as *stroke* or *massé*, but as you go through this book, the differences should become clear.

Massé Shots - The player typically shoots the cue ball with a vertical cue stick, hitting it straight down into the table. However, certain *massé shots* can be done with a partially elevated cue stick.

Jump Shots - The cue ball (or an object ball being hit with the cue stick) is *jumping* unaided over another ball or object. Oftentimes the cue ball is shot into a ball or cushion and that is what causes it to *jump* into the air and over something. In trick shot competitions, those are not considered *jump shots* because the cue ball really only needs to get about $1/8$ or $1/4$ inch airborne for the other object (ball or rail) to propel it high into the air, with no *jump* skill required for proper execution. In fact, sometimes amateur players do this without even trying!

Have you ever broken the balls in a game of 8-ball or 9-ball and the cue ball flew off the table? You may be surprised to learn that the cue ball is only about $1/8$ inch airborne when it hit the rack. That, in addition to the speed of the cue ball and the weight of the balls in the rack formation caused the cue ball to *jump* much higher. The shots categorized here as *jump shots* will require you to *jump* the ball without any help, usually over another ball, a cue stick butt or a block of wood.

Multi-Cue Jump Shots - *Jump shots* that require the use of *multiple cues* are placed in their own chapter in this book, but in televised competitions, they are all part of the *jump* category.

Wing Shots - These shots require the object ball to be in motion when it is hit by the cue ball. The most common version is when you roll an object ball down the table, then shoot the cue ball and cut it into the corner pocket (while it is moving).

Miscellaneous Shots – This diverse group of shots don't fit into any other category. In televised competitions, players are only allowed to select a certain number of shots from any skill category, but they may select an unlimited amount of shots from the *miscellaneous* category.

Partner Shots - These involve more than one player and in competition, the only place they have ever been used is in the World Cup of Trick Shots[2-4].

2.8: Difficulty Ratings

Each shot in this book is given a *difficulty rating*, which measures how difficult it is to execute for a non-professional trick shot artist. This applies to the average player and to the top 9-ball professionals, although the latter would find most of the shots a little easier to master. For example, a one-handed jump shot has become so simple over the past four or five years for a professional trick shot artist, that no player would even think of selecting that shot in an ESPN match since it could be easily matched by any opponent. On the contrary, there is no need for a one-handed jump in a 9-ball match, so most top 9-ball professionals may not have developed that skill to the level that trick shot artists have. For this reason alone, a one-handed jump shot may be given a *difficulty rating* of four (out of six), but for a professional trick shot artist, it would have a *difficulty rating* of one.

Easy Shots

1: This is for very easy shots. The player would be expected to have a modest amount of pool playing ability, like being able to shoot and aim straight, but mostly anyone would find this type of shot simple after a few tries.

2: Still relatively easy and no special skill is necessary, but some beginners may have problems with a shot like this. Better players should be able to make this regularly with a little bit of practice.

Average Shots

3: An average difficulty shot, where the good amateurs will need to dedicate some time to make this shot with any regularity. Most beginners would not be able to make this shot. Top 9-ball professionals should be able to handle shots at this level of difficulty with some practice.

4: Good amateurs will find that even with practice, these shots are quite difficult. Top 9-ball professionals should still be able to make these shots, but would probably require more than just a little practice.

Difficult Shots

5: Extreme spin, accuracy or an unusual skill is needed for these shots. Even very good players will have problems with them, and once learned, only the top 9-ball professionals will be able to make this shot with any consistency.

6: A very difficult shot, usually requiring some trick shot skill that no standard 9-ball player would ever need to learn. These shots are usually reserved for the professional trick shot artists.

2.9: Power

The *power* required for each shot is specified using a scale from one to nine, where one is the softest and nine is the hardest. Below are the nine different *power ratings*, along with an explanation of each. To learn the *power* needed for the various shots, start by placing the cue ball on the spot and aim straight down the table as if you were going to break an 8-ball or 9-ball rack. All of the power ratings specify how many table lengths (back and forth from short rail to short rail) the cue ball will travel.

I based the *power* scale around a standard stop shot. Place an object ball in the exact center of the table and the cue ball right behind the second diamond line. Give yourself a straight in shot to the corner pocket and shoot a stop shot. The *power* you've just used is what I call a '5'.

Soft Shots

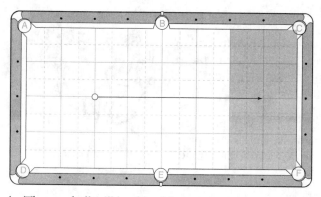

1: The cue ball will land in this zone.

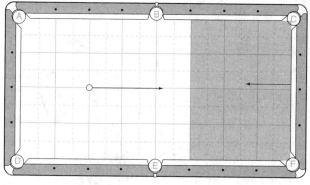

2: The cue ball will hit the cushion and rebound into this zone.

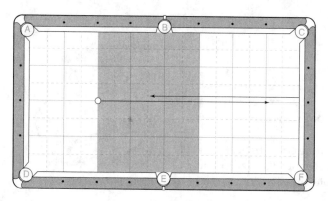

3: The cue ball will hit the cushion and rebound into this zone.

Medium Shots

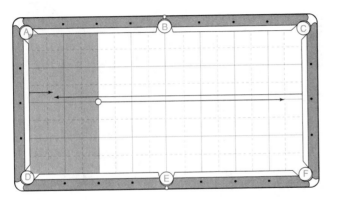

4: The cue ball will hit the cushion and either go directly into this zone, or hit a second cushion and bounce back into this zone.

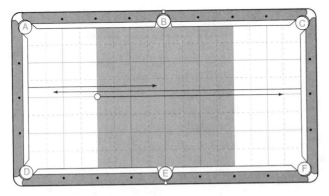

5: The cue ball will hit two cushions and rebound into this zone in the middle portion of the table. This is the speed at which you would hit most shots in a typical game of 8-ball or 9-ball.

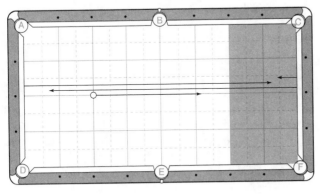

6: The cue ball will hit two cushions and either go directly into this zone, or hit a third cushion and bounce back into this zone. This is approximately the power you would use for a standard jump shot.

Hard Shots

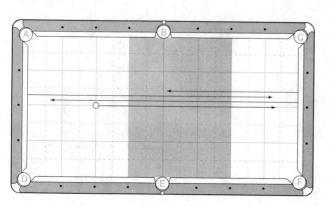

7: The cue ball will hit three cushions and rebound into this zone in the middle of the table.

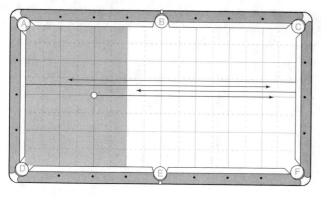

8: The cue ball will hit three cushions and rebound into this zone.

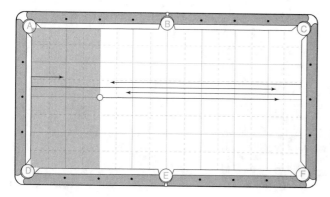

9: The cue ball will hit four cushions and rebound into this zone.

3: Trick Shot Concepts

Techniques in trick shots are sometimes similar to standard 9-ball concepts, but may also diverge into things that aren't obvious to most players. Please take a look at the material in this chapter before trying any of the trick shots included in this book. There are a few things you need to know, and some of the tips presented here may be the difference between making a shot, and missing it.

3.1: Tangent Lines

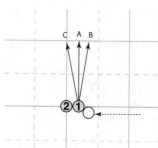

We all remember *tangent lines* from high school math class. The *tangent line* where two balls meet is the line drawn out from the contact point in both directions. If the cue ball were shot at the 1-ball, not directly but offset a little, the 1-ball should travel parallel to the *tangent line* and along path 'A'. Top spin will cause the 1-ball to have the small-

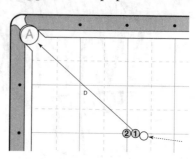

est amount of back spin, resulting in a slightly backward roll (path 'B'). Similarly, back spin on the cue ball puts top spin on the 1-ball, causing it to push forward and through the 2-ball (path 'C'). The effect of top spin on the 1-ball (even extreme top spin) is very slight, but with enough back spin (and a fuller hit) you can cause the 1-ball to force its way through and into the corner pocket (path 'D').

Adding an extra ball behind the 2-ball increases the push-back on the 1-ball (more weight = more push-back). Therefore, top spin will have an increased effect on the amount from which the 1-ball returns from the natural *tangent line* (path 'E'). In this diagram, you can compare the push-back with one ball (path 'B', taken from the prior diagram) and the push-back with two balls (path 'E').

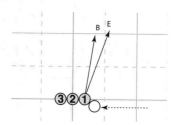

3.2: Aiming Systems

A commonly used *aiming system* in pool is to judge the direction of the cue ball based on the hit you are making (e.g. 1/2 ball hit, 1/4 ball hit, etc). While some trick shot artists use this technique, I prefer to use a *point aiming system*[3-1]. I select a point on a ball or a rail, and then aim my tip directly at that point. All I think about is hitting that point with my tip (not the cue ball). I may explain that you should aim at the center of a ball, or possibly two tips off the edge of the object ball. For shots like this, you need to visualize the width of a tip and mentally see a point exactly two tips off the edge. If this *aiming system* doesn't work for you, just try to understand the concept. Once you figure out where to aim on a particular shot, simply convert it into whatever works for you. For example, if I instruct you to aim one tip off the edge of a ball and you try it and realize that you are getting about a 1/4 ball hit, make a note in the margins of this book indicating that you should use a 1/4 ball hit for this shot.

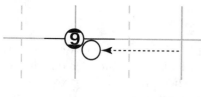

The cue ball is a 1/2 ball offset when hitting the 9-ball. This illustrates the commonly used *aiming system* mentioned above, where hits are measured as a 1/2 ball, a 1/4 ball, etc.

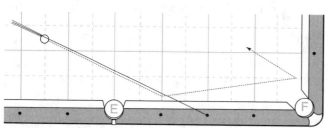

I am aiming my cue stick (not the cue ball) at the second diamond. When shooting trick shots, this is my preferred method of aiming.

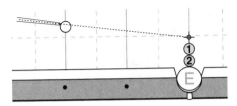

I am aiming at ¹/₂ ball-width off the 1-ball. In order to make this shot, you need to visualize another ball to the left of the 1-ball and aim at its center.

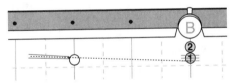

On this shot I aim at ¹/₄ inside the 1-ball (on the right side). You need to mentally divide the 1-ball into quarters.

3.3: Jump Shot Techniques

Many of the new and exciting shots involve jumping one or multiple balls, sometimes very quickly. Most 9-ball players use a standard grip when jumping a ball, but trick shot artists must vary their *jump technique* (grip, stance, elevation, etc.) based on the shot they are trying to perform.

The minimum cue length allowed is 40 inches, and a jump cue is just over that limit. They are also lighter than a standard cue. Additionally, most jump cues nowadays have a phenolic tip, which is a very hard material. Even hard, compact leather tips don't compare in firmness.

3.3.1: Standard Grip

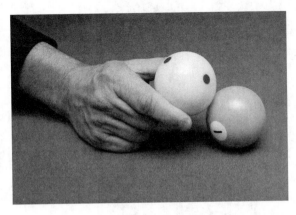

The *standard grip* technique is the most commonly seen when watching 9-ball players. Basically, you are holding the cue as if shooting a normal shot, only elevated (like you do when jacking up over a ball). Use a very loose back wrist and be sure to snap your wrist when making the final stroke. In order to understand how a jump shot works, place a ball on the table and hold another ball with your hand. At an angle of about 45 degrees, hit down on the ball's edge, being careful not to hit your finger. Observe that the object ball takes a short hop when struck. This is what you are trying to do with the cue stick. Hit the ball full, with some speed and a very loose wrist. If you have trouble clearing a ball, try jumping through a rack that is standing up on its edge (1/8 to 1/4 inch tall). Then progress to jumping over a piece of chalk, and finally over a full ball. This will take some practice. You must be able to jump over a full ball with ease before trying any of the jump shots in this book.

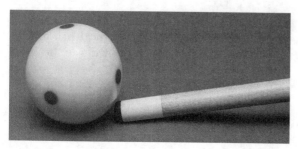

Many beginners start out playing jump shots by shooting with a level cue and scooping under the ball, shooting as low as possible. This is illegal since you are intentionally miscuing and hitting the cue ball with your ferrule. You also run the risk of ripping the cloth.

3.3.2: Dart Grip

While most trick shot artists will jump using a *standard grip*, there are some shots that call for what is known as the *dart grip*. Hold the cue between your thumb and first two fingers, similar to the way you would throw a dart. This technique makes it easier for higher elevations and you can also reach further across the table. Try using a *standard grip* and elevate to 80 degrees, or try jumping a ball in the center of the table, which requires that you stretch across its full length. It is much easier with the *dart grip*.

Dart Grip

The Popper

The higher you elevate, the quicker the cue ball will get up in the air. This enables you to jump over balls that are much closer to the cue ball. Of course the higher you go, the better the chances are that the cue stick will be in the way of the cue ball as it tries to jump. Fortunately, this problem can be easily solved by using a cue called *The Popper*[3-2], which is a very light cue with a large phenolic tip. When you jump with this cue, let go and *throw the cue* at the ball, just briefly.

The cue stick will bounce back and you will catch it, happening so quickly that it is almost impossible to see this in real-time. When you let go of the cue for that fraction of a second, the impact with the cue ball causes it to bounce back faster than the cue ball jumps, allowing the stick to get out of the way of the rising cue ball. This cue will allow you to jump over balls that are very close to each other. Jumping over a ball that is one inch away is no problem with this cue. In fact, I have jumped over a ball that is merely a credit card width away!

Close jumps can also be accomplished by only using the shaft of a jump cue, but since the regulation cue is 40 inches long, jumping that way is illegal. It is possible to make very close jumps with a standard jump cue, but this specialty cue makes it much easier and more consistent.

3.3.3: One-Handed Jumps

Jumping with one hand is very difficult. I have worked with a few of the top 9-ball players and they have all struggled with this, but all of them eventually succeeded after some coaching. The problem is that this kind of shot never comes up in a game, so why learn it? Of course, it is mandatory if you plan to compete in a trick shot tournament.

One Hand Jump (Front)

I haven't seen anyone jump one-handed consistently using a standard grip, so I will only show the dart grip here.

I like to hold the cue directly in front of my face and look straight down the line of aim. Keep your elbow in (i.e. don't hold it out to the side like you would if you were shooting with a bridge).

One Hand Jump (Side)

Some players like to hold the cue off to the side of their head. I can jump this way as well, but my aim is less precise. Try both to see which one works better for you.

3.4: Measuring Spin on a Jump Shot

When jumping, you can still put spin on the ball - and a few shots in this book will require just that. Since your stick is elevated, there are some differences because the cue ball's contact points shift.

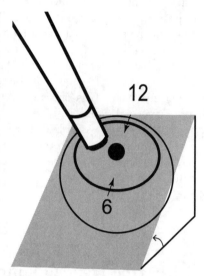

On a standard shot with no elevation, the cue stick goes directly into the ball, perpendicular to a vertical plane. When jacking up for a jump shot, the intersection plane must be at an *angle* to adjust for the cue's elevation. The same clock system I discussed in chapter 2 applies, but the points are placed on the *angled plane*. For example, when putting back spin on a jump shot, you are really hitting the cue ball near the center, not below center as you would when shooting with a level cue. The simplest way is to imagine a clock drawn on the cue ball, not straight up and down, but from the elevated *cue stick's perspective*.

3.5: Massé Techniques

Massé shots have always been a crowd favorite. The cue ball appears to defy the laws of physics, changing direction at unexpected times. Most trick shot artists employ at least one specially designed *massé cue*. These cues are shorter than a regular cue, but longer and heavier than a jump cue.

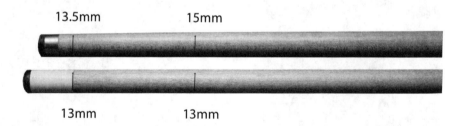

Standard pool cues have what is called a *pro-taper*. That is, if your shaft has a width of 13mm, it maintains that width most of the way down the shaft. In contrast, the *taper* of a massé cue's shaft is more like a typical house cue[3-3] – it is 13mm near the tip (mine starts at 13.5mm), but as you move down the shaft, the thickness increases and could be over 15mm just a few inches down from the tip. This gives the shaft more durability, which is a plus because on some massé shots the cue stick hits the table with a good deal of force.

Because of the cue's contact with the table, I always use a *break cloth* when doing massé shots. Most pool rooms will not allow you to massé even with a *break cloth*, but when practicing at home I still use a *break cloth* to protect my table. I am not worried about ripping the cloth since I have mastered massé shots and can avoid that disaster[3-4]. As a result, I am merely concerned with burning the cloth.

Massé shots require you to hit straight down on the cue ball, which causes an indentation in the cloth (resulting in a white mark). When you apply a lot of spin to the cue ball, you may notice that the white mark turns slightly brown. This is caused by the speed at which the cue ball spins, and the friction heats up and partially burns the cloth. I have slight yellow/brown discolorations on my cue ball from this as well, but there is nothing that can be done about that. The bottom line is this: *Always* use a *break cloth* when shooting massé shots, and be cautioned that performing them can result in ripped or damaged cloth, broken cues, or tips falling off. In short, they should be performed *at your own risk*.

3.5.1: Standard Grip

The *standard grip* has your thumb down, much like in a standard shot. This is the most common grip and is the one that I prefer.

Massé Standard Grip

3.5.2: Dart Grip

Massé Dart Grip

The *dart grip* is performed by simply turning your hand upside down. Some players, especially those from Europe, choose this style over the *standard grip*. Bruce Barthelette, one of my ESPN teammates, uses the *standard grip* for some shots, but finds that the *dart grip* gives him more success on others.

3.6: Measuring Spin on a Massé Shot

Measuring spin on a massé shot is the same as with a jump shot. That is, the direction of your cue should be perpendicular to the clock face at which you are aiming. The higher you are elevated, the more *angled* the plane needs to be for your clock. The center point (the exact top of the cue ball) is never used when shooting a massé shot - and you should take care not to hit any massé shot too close to the center of the cue ball (on the *angled plane* as already explained).

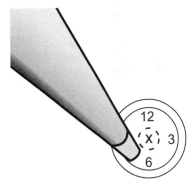

3.7: Aiming a Massé Shot

Aiming a standard shot is simple - just point the cue where you want the cue ball to go, and voila!!! If only it were that simple! But how do you aim a massé shot where the cue stick is *pointing down into the table?*

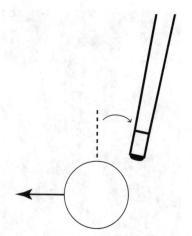

When shooting almost all massé shots, the cue stick is not perfectly vertical - it has a slight angle, maybe 75-85 degrees elevated. That slight angle is used to aim the shot. Take the angle of the cue and see in which direction you need to move the butt end to make it perfectly vertical (90 degrees elevated). That direction is the line along which you are aiming.

The cue stick is not perfectly vertical, but angled slightly. Since the shooter is using 6 o'clock English (straight backspin on the angled plane), the cue ball will travel in the opposite direction of the cue stick's angle.

This is the same shot, but from the shooter's perspective. Here you can see the 6 o'clock English and the expected travel path of the cue ball.

Line of Aim   Actual Travel Path

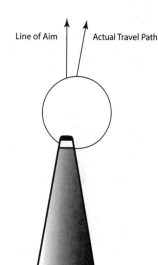

The direction that the cue stick is angled remains the same. The only change is that left English is now used. Instead of travelling directly opposite the cue stick's angle, we must account for some deflection.

If you shoot straight down (90 degrees), there is only one direction the cue ball can travel – opposite from where you are hitting (hitting at 6 o'clock causes the cue ball to travel toward 12 o'clock, and so on.

3.8: For the Southpaws

Some shots on a pool table are easier to reach for a right-handed person, where a lefty would need to use a bridge, or stretch to reach the shot. In trick shot competitions, players are not allowed to take advantage of this fact by setting up a shot that only a right-handed player can reach. The solution is called the *Mirror Image* rule – that is, a player is always allowed to flip any shot around so it is a *mirror image* of the original. Therefore, if you are having difficulty reaching any of the shots in this book, feel free to flip them around and shoot them from the other side of the table. As an example, take a look at the shot in the first diagram. The 1-ball is two ball-widths off the rail at the first diamond, and the cue ball is three ball-widths off the rail at the second diamond. Pocket the 1-ball with bottom right English (5 o'clock). The cue ball will draw back, hit the stick which makes the 2-ball, and roll down table to make the 3-ball. If you can put backspin on the cue ball, this should be a simple shot. However, if you are a left-handed player, this shot will be much harder. Right-handed players are able to stand near the cue ball, and lean over the table in order to have a comfortable body position. Left-handed players don't have that luxury – they need to either use the bridge, shoot behind the back, or just shoot with their opposite hand. Therefore, a left-handed player is allowed to *mirror image* the shot, which is shown in the second diagram. Except for the spin, everything else will remain the same. In this example, the spin used is bottom right. When performing the left-handed version, you must change right into left, so you hit this with bottom left (7 o'clock).

When practicing, I sometimes flip shots around if I am having trouble making them. I find that a different perspective (and English) gives me the very change that I need to get out of 'miss mode' and move into 'make mode'.

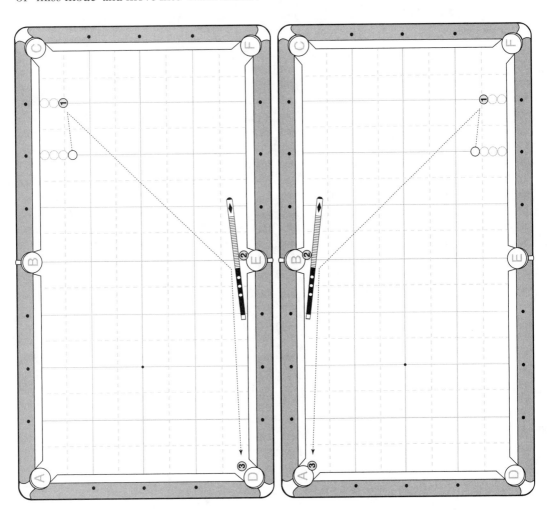

4: Equipment

People always ask me why I carry around so many pool cues, and my answer is always the same: When it comes to trick shots, you never know what you will need at any given time. Sometimes a shot can be made much easier with a specific type of cue. I like to use a golf analogy - golfers carry around different clubs for different shots, so I tell them that I have all different kinds of pool cues, like a nine iron, an eight iron, a seven iron, etc.

Below is a list of the cues I carry for a typical competition:

Standard Shooting Cue:
I only have one, but I carry 5 or 6 shafts. When I was in Kiev for the 2003 WPA World Artistic Pool Championship, I only had two shafts and the tip on the spare wasn't very good. I opened a bottle of sparkling water and it exploded all over my pool cue, shirt, and worst of all, my tip. Now I had to use the spare which I wasn't too happy about. Ever since then I have always made sure to carry at least 4 spare shafts.

Jump Cues:
I carry four standard jump cues; not as spares, but because I perform shots that require all four.

I carry a break/jump cue for certain shots. Here are a few examples from this book: 'Rainbow Shot', 'Cue Ball Toast' and 'Jump Fouette # 1'. As these shots come up frequently in competition, I always make sure I am prepared.

I'm not sure of their names, but I call them 'Mega-Jump Cues', and I carry around two (one primary and one back-up). They look like standard jump cues, but the tip is as long as a ferrule, and they are much heavier than normal (over 21 ounces). I typically use these cues for long jumps, but there are other types of shots where I feel more comfortable with a heavier cue, including 'Split Jump'. Depending on the type of tournament, I may carry up to five of my 'Mega-Jump Cues'. There is a shot performed by Jamey Gray using all five, so I have to be ready for anything.

I always carry two Popper jump cues, one as a spare. All of the close jumps and high jumps are done with these, such as the 'High Bar'.

All of the jump cues I've just talked about have phenolic tips, but I also like to have one with a leather tip. The 'Slalom' is a shot where I like to use a shorter and lighter cue (jump cue), but I need a leather tip to minimize the chances that I will miscue. I carry a Scorpion jump cue for this purpose.

Massé Cues:
I usually have three massé cues. Two are Eric Yow original custom cues, which are much heavier (about 24.5 ounces), and have a 13.5mm tip. I carry both so I have a spare, and because recently there have been shots that use two massé cues. With these types of shots, I prefer two massé cues that are exactly the same. My third massé cue is a Schuler – but I don't use it for massé shots! The cue weighs about 19 ounces and it has a smaller tip (about 12mm). There is one shot where I have to pocket a ball and draw the cue ball back using one hand, jacked up. I like to use a shorter cue, and this massé cue is perfect.

Prop Cues:
I usually carry two extra full length cues as props because I do a lot of shots where I need a cue butt or a full length cue on the table, and I don't want to use my expensive cues, especially when the balls are hitting into them with some speed

Add everything up and what do you get? TOO MANY POOL CUES!!!

4.1: Standard Cues

Every pool player should have his own cue stick, usually between 57 and 60 inches in length. The one shown above is a Meucci from the Andy Segal Signature Series, AS-4 Model. Most of the shots in this book can be performed with your *standard cue*, and the weight, shaft thickness and wrap style are all up to you. Whether you want to go with a heavier or lighter cue, or even a low deflection shaft, my advice is to use whatever you are comfortable with. Bottom line, don't feel like you need a special cue just for trick shots.

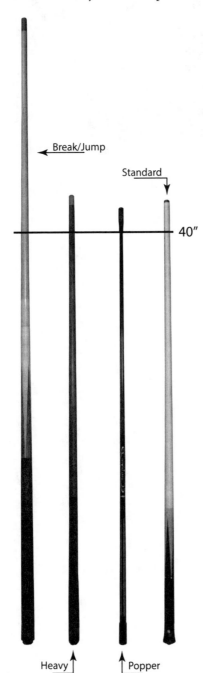

4.2: Jump Cues

Some players may already have a *jump cue*, which is shorter and lighter than a standard cue. Mostly any of the *jump cues* on the market will work as long as you feel good with it. Sometimes we use a *heavy jump cue* in competition for the longer jumps, but occasionally players will use it for short jumps. Jamey Gray, my ESPN teammate, likes a heavy cue for triple one-handed jumps (holding three cues in one hand and jumping three balls simultaneously — seen later in this book). Then there is *The Popper*, which is great for close jumps and very high jumps.

Almost all *jump cues* today are sold with a phenolic tip, which is much harder than a standard leather tip, and that makes it a lot easier to jump. In fact, many players have a *jump/break cue*. The hard phenolic tip allows for a more powerful break, and that cue's butt can be unscrewed to become a shorter *jump cue* when necessary.

4.3: Massé Cues

Massé cues are usually around 46-49 inches, which is longer than jump cues, but shorter than standard cues. As mentioned earlier, the shaft is tapered on an angle and the tip is any size you like, but these cues get wider very quickly as you move down the shaft. The one shown here weighs about 24 ounces.

4.4: Silicone

Some shots require the use of *silicone*. I use a standard spray that's commonly used on a shuffle board table. I spray a little of the quick dry *silicone* on the cue ball and wipe it down with a static free cloth. This removes a majority of the cue ball's friction which enables it to travel further before the spin kicks in. A lot of the shots I do with *silicone* can be done without it if I am performing on a brand new table with a brand new cue ball. Unfortunately, this perfect scenario isn't always available when doing a show – however a little *silicone* will cause the table to play like new for a few shots.

The only trouble is it may be difficult to bring *silicone* spray on a plane (with the security regulations nowadays), so here is what I do: I put a cloth in a zip-lock bag, spray like crazy, and close the bag. As long as I am careful, I can usually make this last for a few days, which is the typical duration of a tournament.

WARNING: Be careful with *silicone* and if you choose to use it, pay close attention to the warning labels on the side of the can. I wouldn't rub my eyes or put my hands near my mouth without washing them first.

5: Props

Several different *props* are used during a trick shot competition. The regular items include racks, bridges, prop cues, chalk, stacking balls and so on. In the televised competitions, the producer always asks that we use very non-standard stuff, so we have created shots with tripods, pillows, a four-foot self-standing frame made out of PVC tubing, heavy plastic boxes measuring two feet on all sides, and so on.

In addition to carrying around all of the pool cues we talked about in the previous chapter, I also carry a full bag of *props* – and every year that bag gets heavier and heavier. I do a shot where I need five racks, and another where I need a full box of pool balls. The list goes on, but lately I have been trying to limit the number of *props* I bring because, with all of the *props* and all of the pool cues necessary, I could wind up with a sore shoulder before I even hit one ball.

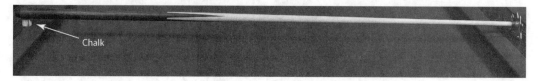

Cue stick butts are commonly used to enlarge a pocket and sometimes a shorter *butt* will be used (jump cue/massé cue) for the same purpose.

Chalk

Bridges are typically stretched across the table on the rail tops. On most shots, players have the option of raising the *bridge* slightly with a piece of chalk since the balls don't always fit under the entire *bridge*.

This specially made ball called a *stacking ball*, has a flat spot on the bottom, which keeps the ball from rolling, and a small hole (about $1/8$ inch) on the top, which holds the upper ball in place. Hitting the bottom ball with the cue ball causes it to move away (usually going into a pocket), and it results in the upper ball falling straight down in place[5-1].

Players like to use *bottles* or *cups* as obstacles to curve around, or to support other objects to jump over. Be careful if you are using glass which, incidentally, is no longer allowed on television, or in any other trick shot competition[5-2]. Plastic can be too light, therefore if necessary, marbles or anything else may be placed inside to weigh it down.

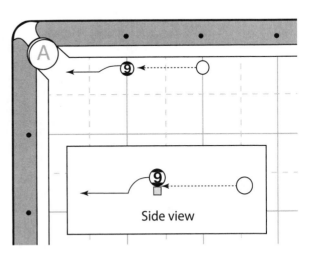

Chalk makes its way into some trick shots. In one common example, a ball is balanced on top and the cue ball hits it, causing it to fall off and roll into the pocket.

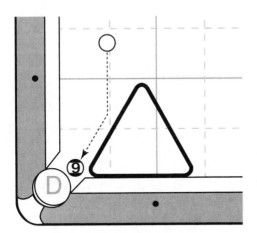

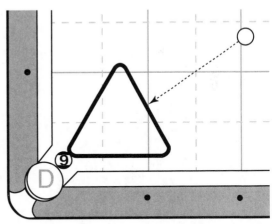

Racks can also enlarge a pocket, increasing the make percentage on certain shots. One way to use the *rack* is to place it against the rail, creating an area where the cue ball can enter and make a ball. Another method is to place the *rack's* point against a hanger and have the cue ball hit any part of the back edge of the *rack*.

The *props* in this chapter cover only a select few that have been used in recent trick shot competitions. I have used many other items from swinging racks suspended by a rope, to bouncing rubber balls, mini pool tables, basketballs, footballs, shipping tubes, and the list goes on. The point is to let your creativity run and you just might come up with something brand new. Take a new *prop* to the pool table and spend about 30 minutes messing around with different ideas. Maybe you will come up with something and maybe you won't. This is how I have developed many of my own trick shots.

Part II

Cue Magic

6: Bank/Kick Shots

All of the shots in this chapter require either the cue ball *banking* (or *kicking*) off one or more cushions, or the object ball doing the same. In the televised competitions, there is no *bank/kick* category, so these shots are usually assigned to the miscellaneous group.

Something strange happened at the 2013 WPA World Artistic Pool Championship, which was held at the Rio Hotel & Casino in Las Vegas during the BCAPL National Championships. We were in the convention area with over one hundred pool tables for the amateurs, about 20 for the one-pocket, 10-ball and straight pool tournaments, and three for our event. There had to be at least one thousand people in the place; players, vendors, spectators, you name it.

It was 7:30pm and we were getting ready to start the third round, which included five shots in the bank & kick discipline. We had just started with our designated practice time of four minutes per player when, about halfway through the practice, BAM!!! The lights went out and the room turned pitch black. It took about 30 seconds for the emergency lights to kick on, but all play had stopped. Fast forward about an hour and we were still waiting to find out what was happening. The tournament directors had to make a tough decision. It was still dark, but they couldn't delay the tournament because we all had plane tickets to leave on Monday morning.

Well, it was not completely dark. The table lights were out, and the convention hall lights were out. The only thing we had were the emergency lights, which were about 20-30 feet up on the ceiling. Add to that the large shadow stretched across half the table, which was caused by the table lights blocking the few rays coming from the ceiling. The decision was — play on!!! No one was happy, but we could do nothing. We had to play and the directors didn't have any other choice, so we played the bank/kick and stroke disciplines (10 shots total) in the half light of the convention hall. Only about half the balls could be used as the darker colored ones couldn't be seen that well, and the cue ball and whatever object ball we were aiming at had to be set up on the 'lighter side' of the table. It was certainly an adventure but we all made it through okay.

6.1: Compression Kick Back #1

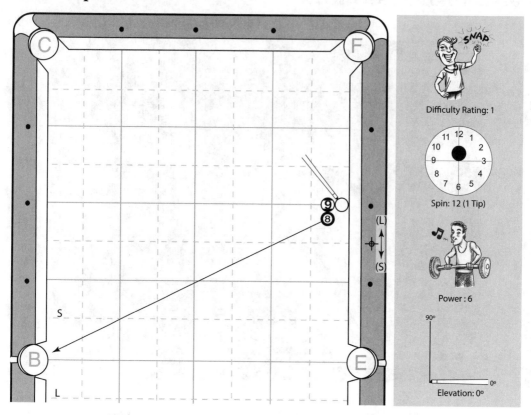

The *Compression Kick Back #1* is a great shot in a game of 8-ball (as if this position will ever come up), since you have to hit the 8-ball first or risk committing a foul and giving your opponent ball-in-hand. The objective is to pocket the 8-ball in the side pocket without moving the 9-ball. If you didn't know this shot, you could probably just give up ball-in-hand and let your opponent deal with the 9-ball - possibly trying to bank it. The shot is even more critical to know for a 9-ball game since giving up ball-in-hand will not work. If your opponent understands friction and throw, he will realize that hitting the 8-ball at an angle (toward the long cushion) will cause the 9-ball to throw in that direction and into corner pocket 'F'.

Setup: The cue ball and 9-ball are frozen in line along the second diamond. The 8-ball is frozen to the 9-ball, one ball-width from the cushion. The easiest way to set up this shot is to use a fourth ball, make a square with the four balls, then remove the extra ball.

Solution: Shoot into the cushion, aiming your cue stick at 2 1/2 diamonds as shown. Don't hit this one too softly, and be sure to follow through. The cue ball will compress the rail, giving it just enough space to escape without touching the 9-ball.

Adjustments: Three things can go wrong with this shot. If you are hitting the 9-ball, you are probably not hitting the cue ball hard enough, or you are aiming too far into the rail. Try adjusting your aim further up the long rail '(S)'. If you are making a nice, clean hit on the 8-ball but you are not making it in the side pocket, you simply need to adjust your aim. If you miss short 'S', aim a little more into the cushion '(L)'. If you miss long 'L', aim further up the rail '(S)'.

6.2: Compression Kick Back #2

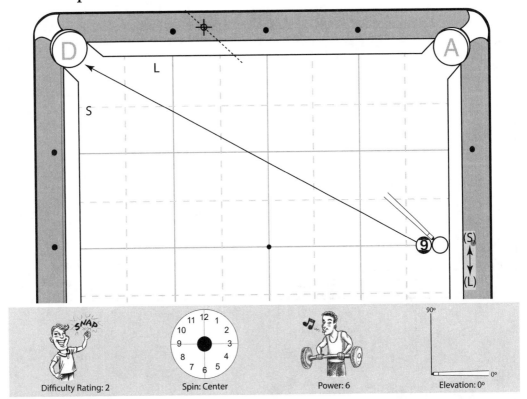

The crowd loves this shot, especially if it is made up of veteran pool players as most of them can't figure out what to do in this situation (unless they have seen the shot before). I always like to ask for ideas from the spectators before actually revealing the solution. *Compression Kick Back #2* is currently in the Artistic Pool Shot Program. You have to kick the 9-ball back into the corner pocket by shooting into the cushion and compressing the rail.

Setup: Place the cue ball frozen to the second diamond. The 9-ball should also be along the second diamond, and it is frozen to the cue ball.

Solution: I like to align my cue stick by using the butt end instead of simply aiming at a point on the rail. I look down and visualize a point about one-third of the way from the first diamond toward the middle diamond on the short rail. This usually falls right around the number counters if your table has them.

Adjustments: If you are missing short 'S', aim further up the long rail. This translates into shifting the butt of the cue to the left (to the left from your perspective – in the diagram, shift it to the right) Adjusting for missing long 'L' is the exact opposite. Take note how hard you hit the cue ball, and try to be consistent on your attempts. The harder the cue ball is hit, the longer the 9-ball will travel.

6.3: 5-Rail Chain Reaction

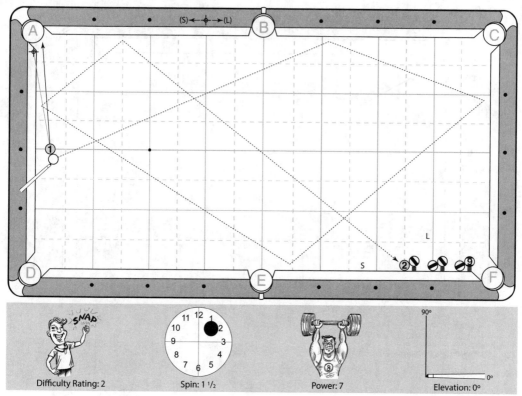

Difficulty Rating: 2   **Spin: 1 ½**   **Power: 7**   **Elevation: 0°**

The *5-Rail Chain Reaction* is also part of the Artistic Pool Shot Program, and it is always a crowd pleaser because most people who have never seen a trick shot show before enjoy watching the chain reaction at the end. They also like seeing the cue ball fly around the table, and with such accuracy. This shot begins with the 1-ball being cut into corner pocket 'A'. The cue ball then travels five rails, hits the 2-ball and starts a chain reaction, resulting in the 9-ball falling into corner pocket 'F'.

Setup: Place the 1-ball on the long center line of the table, exactly one ball-width from the cushion. The cue ball is frozen to the 1-ball, and it is lined up at the short rail pocket point. The six other balls on the opposite end of the table are about ¼ to ½ inch off the cushion, with every other ball propped up on a piece of chalk. Each pair should be frozen, and there should be about one ball-width between the groups.

Solution: Aim at the third diamond with 1 ½ English. Remember that the cue ball is frozen to the 1-ball, so instead of travelling along the line of aim, it will travel along the line as indicated in the illustration. The cue ball should kick five rails, hit the first ball in the chain of six, eventually causing the 9-ball to fall into the corner pocket.

Adjustments: The most common way to miss the shot is long 'L'. That is, the cue ball hits one of the other balls in the chain instead of the first one. If that happens, change your line of aim '(S)'. It is less common is to miss short 'S', and the adjustment is in the opposite direction '(L)'. If you miss the 1-ball, your initial setup was misaligned. If the 1-ball misses by hitting the short rail, change the setup so the balls line up a little closer to the pocket, and vice-versa.

6.4: The Slider

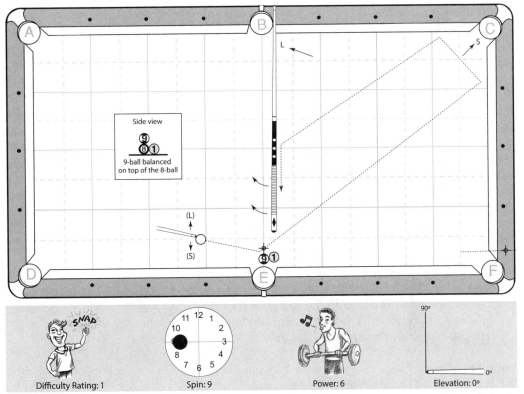

Difficulty Rating: 1   **Spin: 9**   **Power: 6**   **Elevation: 0°**

Your objective is to pocket the 8-ball (the lower ball in the setup) in the side pocket and the 1-ball in corner pocket 'F'. The 9-ball (the upper ball) will fall and sit in front of the side pocket. The cue ball will then travel two rails, hit the stick, slide it into alignment, and make the 9-ball. *The Slider* is one of my favorite shots to perform in competition. It is pretty easy to execute, but is still a little tricky. Estimating the throw on the 1-ball is not as simple as it may look, and judging how much the stick will slide has proven difficult, but this shot has provided me with many points during key matches, and at critical times in these contests.

Setup: Place a stacking ball directly in the center of the pocket and align the 1-ball at about the ⅓ diamond. The cue ball is positioned two ball-widths from the cushion, just behind the third diamond line. The shaft of the cue stick should be placed on the rail just to the side of side pocket 'B' and the stick is aligned for the 1-ball.

Solution: Visualize a point about ½ ball-width off the edge of the 8-ball/9-ball stack (slightly more than one inch). Use straight left (running) English, aim at that point and shoot.

Adjustments: Missing short 'S' can happen when the cue ball hits too close to the corner pocket. Adjust by moving the cue ball further from the cushion. If the cue ball hits the shaft end of the stick, you have missed long 'L', so move the cue ball closer to the cushion. Keep in mind that the harder you hit the cue ball, the more the stick will slide.

The stacked ball creates double the weight, increasing the throw on the 1-ball.

6.5: Pinball

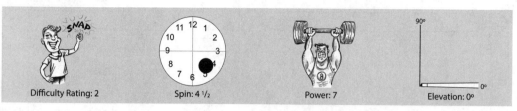

Difficulty Rating: 2   Spin: 4 ½   Power: 7   Elevation: 0°

It is always fun to watch the cue ball fly around the table, making balls in every pocket. On the *Pinball* shot you start out by making the 1-ball in the side and the 2-ball in the corner. The cue ball will then travel around the table, hit the stick (making both the 3-ball and 4-ball), then hit the rack (making the 5-ball), and roll off the rack into the 6-ball, knocking it off the chalk and into the corner pocket. This is a good shot for a show, so when I was first starting out, I used *Pinball* quite often as I only had a limited number of shots in my repertoire. As I developed more of my own collection of signature shots, I put this one aside because it takes a while to set up, and I prefer to keep the flow of an exhibition going with shots that can be set up in seconds. Still, it is one of my favorites.

Setup: The 1-ball is in front of the side pocket, and the 2-ball is frozen to it, aligned at the short rail point. The 3-ball is on the short rail near corner pocket 'F', the 4-ball is deep in the side pocket, the 5-ball is frozen to the rack, and the 6-ball is on a piece of chalk one or two inches outside the pocket. The rack is aligned about one inch from the edge of the 6-ball. The cue ball is placed even with the 1-ball, about one diamond away.

Solution: The cue ball is shot into the 1-ball, but the line of aim isn't as important as where the cue ball goes. Try to get the right hit to make the cue ball come off the long rail and hit the short rail close to the cue stick as shown. If the cue ball hits the short rail too soon, the impact with the cue may not have enough force to make the 3-ball. When the shot is hit with enough speed, the cue ball will bounce around the table, making all of the balls.

Adjustments: The stick should be angled so that the cue ball hits the rail before it hits the rack. If it hits the rack directly, it may not have enough speed to reach the 6-ball. If the cue ball is hitting the short rail too far from the stick, aim a little thinner on the 1-ball. Make the opposite adjustment if the cue ball hits the stick before the short rail.

Why use draw?
The answer lies with the first cushion. The cue ball needs to be hit with some speed, and the draw helps reduce the risk of the cue ball flying off the table.

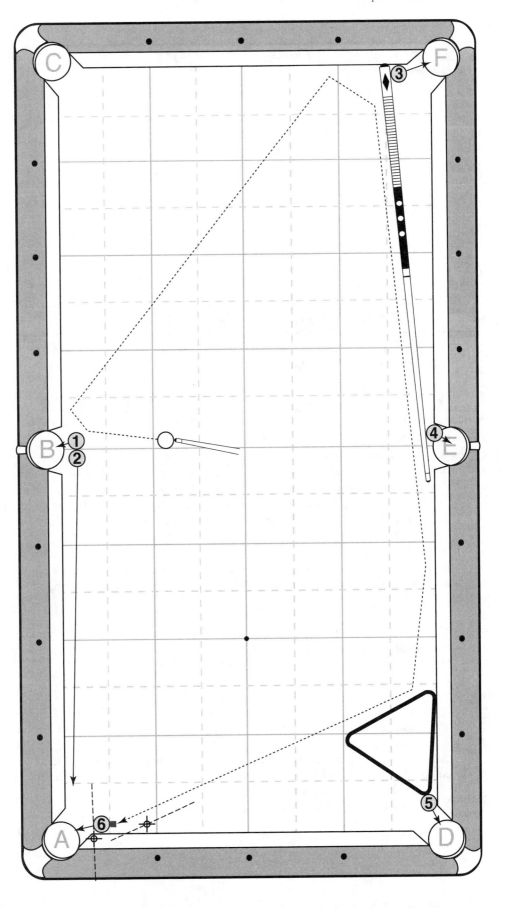

6.6: The Chaser

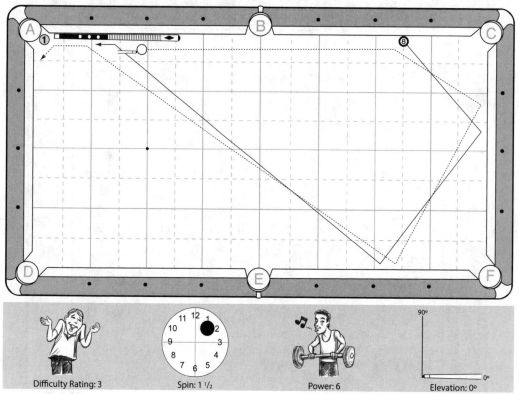

Difficulty Rating: 3   **Spin: 1 ½**   **Power: 6**   **Elevation: 0°**

The Chaser was introduced to me by Ralph Eckert (Germany) during the ESPN World Cup of Trick Shots. When doing a show, it is a good idea to come up with shots that can be applied to a real game, even if it never comes up. You are playing last-pocket 8-ball, and you have to make the 8 in the pocket where the 1-ball is now sitting. You need to hit into the 8-ball in such a way that both the 8-ball and cue ball follow the same path. The cue ball will arrive first, making the 1-ball and clearing the way for the 8-ball to go into the corner pocket.

Setup: The 8-ball is frozen to the cushion at the 1 ½ diamond line. A cue stick butt is frozen to the cushion, and the cue ball is one chalk-width from the butt, right behind the second diamond line. The 1-ball is hanging in corner pocket 'A', and it is currently blocking the 8-ball from going into that pocket.

Solution: Aim parallel to the cushion. If you hit the 8-ball correctly, the cue ball should travel two cushions with the 8-ball chasing right behind it. The cue ball will hit the butt, make the 1-ball and get out of the way, clearing the pocket for the 8-ball.

Adjustments: The most common error is to hit the 8-ball too thin. Though the cue ball will still travel two cushions as diagrammed, it will hit the short rail instead of the butt. In addition, the 8-ball will usually bank across the table instead of following the cue ball. You can fix this by aiming a little more toward the long rail. Similarly, if the 8-ball travels ahead of the cue ball, this usually is a result of hitting the 8-ball too full. Adjust with a thinner hit (aiming away from the rail). Another common mistake occurs when the cue ball blocks the pocket, not allowing the 8-ball a clean entry. It is important to place the 1-ball a little closer to the long jaw as this allows the cue ball to carom off the side, and to bank out of the way.

6.7: 6-Rail Kick

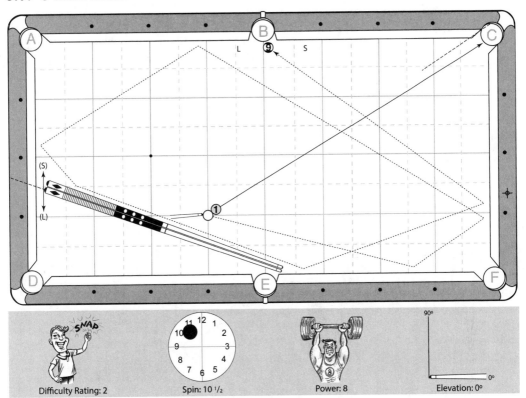

Difficulty Rating: 2   Spin: 10 1/2   Power: 8   Elevation: 0°

The *6-Rail Kick* begins by pocketing the 1-ball into corner pocket 'C'. The cue ball will travel four rails, hit and roll along the sticks, travel two more rails and make the 9-ball. This is a great shot for a crowd because the cue ball is flying almost twice around the table, and it isn't all that difficult since the cue sticks give you such a large margin for error (provided you have them aligned properly). Even if the cue ball misses the 9-ball, a simple adjustment on the cue sticks should get you pretty close on your second attempt.

Setup: Place the cue ball directly on the 3,1 diamond intersection line. The 1-ball is aligned for the long rail pocket point, and it is frozen to the cue ball. The 9-ball is hanging a little closer to the right edge of side pocket 'B'. Two cue sticks are placed as in the illustration, with the inside stick (the one closest to the long rail) lined at approximately the 1 1/2 diamond mark.

Solution: Aim at 1 1/4 diamonds on the short rail and hit it hard. Use running English, but avoid using too much - one-tip should be plenty. Hitting closer to the center will result in more power and speed for the cue ball.

Adjustments: The cue sticks make it unlikely that you will miss because of your aim. However, if you do hit the sticks before the short rail, aim a little longer (at 1 1/2 diamonds). The most common problem is misaligning the cue sticks. If the cue ball misses short 'S', shift the cue sticks so the butts move closer to the long rail. Should the cue ball miss long 'L', move the cues in the opposite direction.

6.8: Time in the Side

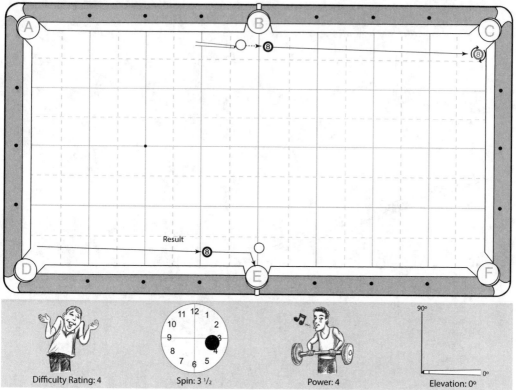

Difficulty Rating: 4   Spin: 3 ¹/₂   Power: 4   Elevation: 0°

Time in the Side is in the Artistic Pool Shot Program, and it is a favorite selection of Jamey Gray, the 2008 WPA World Artistic Pool Champion. Even though the shot is not that easy, Jamey makes it almost every time. His successes result in points on the board, and usually will extend his lead in a match. Bank the 8-ball one rail and have the cue ball stop in place. The 8-ball will come back and carom off the cue ball before going into the side pocket.

Setup: The 8-ball is placed about 1 ¹/₂ inches off the cushion, with its leading edge aligned with the pocket point. The cue ball's leading edge is aligned with the other pocket point, and it is positioned about ¹/₄ inch closer to the cushion.

Solution: Aim straight into the 8-ball with maximum right English and a little draw. The right English transfers a small amount of left English to the 8-ball, enabling it to spin back toward the long rail after banking off of the short rail (upper portion of diagram). The touch of draw helps the cue ball stop in front of the side pocket (as shown in the lower portion of the diagram).

Adjustments: The cue ball should stop after hitting the 8-ball. If it is sliding left or right, adjust your aim. If it is sliding forward, use a little more draw (and vice-versa). If the 8-ball is hitting the cushion, but it is not coming back into the long rail, use more spin or adjust the starting setup to create less of an angle for the two balls. Don't hit this one too hard because the increase in power will reduce the effect of the 8-ball's spin when it hits the far cushion.

6.9: Freeway

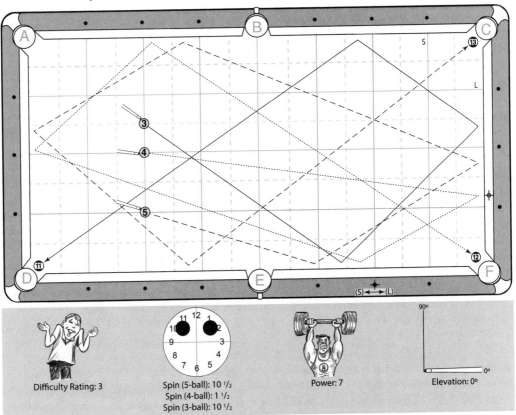

Difficulty Rating: 3

Spin (5-ball): 10 ½
Spin (4-ball): 1 ½
Spin (3-ball): 10 ½

Power: 7

Elevation: 0°

When playing the *Freeway*, shoot the 5-ball five cushions, making the 13-ball. Shoot the 4-ball four cushions, making the 12-ball. Lastly, shoot the 3-ball three cushions, making the 11-ball. All three balls (5-4-3) must be hit within four seconds. *Freeway* was the shot that enabled me to win the 2007 WPA World Artistic Pool Championship in St. Petersburg, Russia. I was up against Sebastian Giumelli from Argentina, in the finals. The score was tied, and *Freeway* was the deciding shot. Instead of having to make all three balls, players were given points based on how many and which ones of the three balls were made. Five points, four points, and three points were each awarded for the 5-rail, 4-rail and 3-rail shots respectively. With only one attempt per player, Giumelli missed all three balls. I was able to pocket the 13-ball (the 5-rail shot) and the 11-ball (the 3-rail shot) for the title!

Setup: The 5-ball is placed at the 2,1 diamond intersection line, the 4-ball goes on the head spot, and the 3-ball is positioned at the 2,1 ½ diamond intersection line. The 13, 12 & 11-balls should all be hanging in the pockets.

Solution: Aim the 5-ball at the second diamond, the 4-ball at the 1 ¼ diamond and the 3-ball at the second diamond.

Adjustments: I recommend shooting one ball at a time so that you can get the proper line of aim for each ball. Start with the 5-ball. If it misses short 'S', adjust by aiming further down the rail. If it misses long 'L', adjust the other way. Similar adjustments should be made for the other two balls.

6.10: Spinning Bank

Difficulty Rating: 5   Spin: 8 ½   Power (1st hit): 8   Elevation: 0°
                                                 Power (2nd hit): 4

I invented the *Spinning Bank* for the 2011 ESPN World Cup of Trick Shots, but I first saw the concept of banking a spinning ball during an exhibition by Jack White at the University of Pittsburgh in 1990. Getting back to 2011 and ESPN, this was originally designed as a two-player shot, where the first player would pocket the 2-ball and spin the 1-ball. The second player would then come to the table, position the cue ball, and shoot the spinning bank portion. I later adapted this to a one-player version and used it to win some competitions. To play the *Spinning Bank*, shoot the 1-ball into the 2-ball, making it in corner pocket 'F'. While the 1-ball is spinning in place, reposition the cue ball and shoot the 1-ball into the short cushion. The extreme spin on the 1-ball will cause it to bank around the 3-ball and make the 9.

Setup: The 1-ball and 2-ball are placed about one diamond apart, behind the second diamond line. The 3-ball is stationed at the 1,1 diamond intersection point as a blocker. Hang the 9-ball in the side pocket with a rack frozen to it. The cue ball should be within reach – at the ready.

Solution: The first part of the *Spinning Bank* requires that you pocket the 2-ball by using the 1-ball as the cue ball. Hitting the 1-ball with extreme left English will result in some deflection, so you will need to aim a little more to the left than usual. A little draw keeps the 1-ball from rolling too much. When hit just right, the 1-ball will spin rapidly in place after hitting the 2-ball. When repositioning the cue ball, most players will initially line it up parallel to the long rail – this results in the 1-ball spinning off the cue ball and into the long rail. The trick is to line up the cue ball and the 1-ball directly for the blocker ball. The extreme spin will push it off line just enough to miss that blocker.

Adjustments: It is easy to miss the 2-ball when you have to put so much spin on the ball. Due to the speed of the shot, it may be difficult to tell which side of the pocket you are missing on, so try to enlist the help of a friend. With a second pair of eyes, you will know if you are hitting the long or short rail first, and you can then adjust your aim accordingly. Keep in mind that the harder you hit the second part, the less effect the 1-ball's spin will have when banking off that far rail. Make sure you are getting the cue ball in position and are shooting the second part of the shot fast enough or else the extreme spin on the 1-ball may fade.

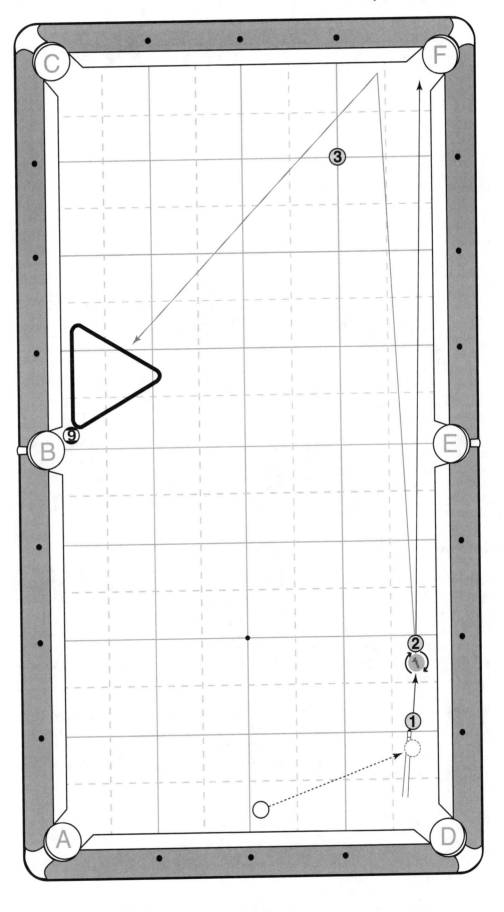

6.11: Ultra Thin Bank

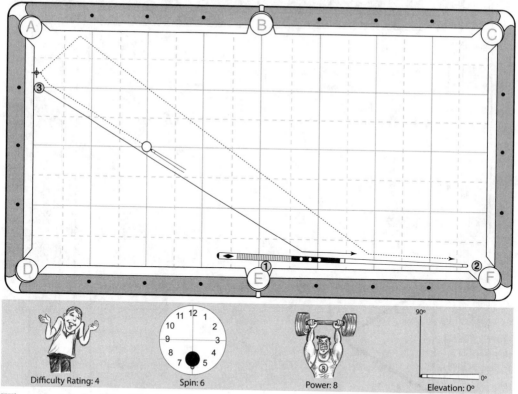

Difficulty Rating: 4   Spin: 6   Power: 8   Elevation: 0°

When playing the *Ultra Thin Bank*, back cut the 3-ball so that it banks toward corner pocket 'F' (where the 2-ball rests). The cue ball will hit the cue stick, make the 1-ball, and then roll down to pocket the 2-ball, clearing the way for the 3. When the *Ultra Thin Bank* was originally submitted by Mike Massey (2006 ESPN Trick Shot Magic), the idea was to bank the 3-ball with a double kiss. In other words, the cue ball would hit the 3-ball a lot fuller and not touch the short rail.

Setup: Place the cue ball on the 2,2 diamond intersection line. The 1-ball is hanging in the side pocket, the 2-ball hanging in the corner pocket (closer to the long jaw), and the 3-ball is frozen to the cushion at the first diamond. A cue is frozen to the 1-ball, and the tip is pointed straight at the center of the 2-ball, about 1/2 inch away.

Solution: Use straight draw, and visualize a point 3/4 of a ball-width off the edge of the 3-ball. That equates to a point between 1 1/2 and 1 3/4 inches off the edge of the 3-ball. You need to hit this one pretty hard, but don't blast it. The draw helps reduce the risk of the cue ball flying off the table.

Adjustments: Cutting the 3-ball too thin or too full are the two most common errors. If the 3-ball is not rolling fast enough to reach the pocket, aim for a slightly fuller hit. On the other hand, if the 3-ball is missing the cue and is hitting the short rail (on the right side of the diagram), aim a little thinner. If you would like to try the double-kiss method mentioned above, use 3 1/2 English and aim a little closer to the 3-ball.

6.12: Three Rails & Three Trays

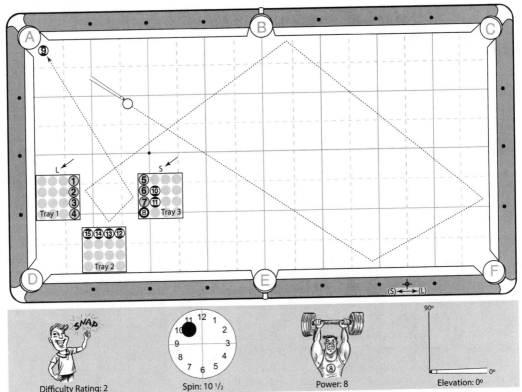

Difficulty Rating: 2   **Spin: 10 ½**   **Power: 8**   **Elevation: 0°**

I introduced *Three Rails & Three Trays*, which is one of my creations, at the 2013 Masters Trick Shot Championship during the Allen Hopkins Super Billiards Expo in Edison, NJ. It is always funny to watch a new shot get introduced. I was playing Karen Freire, who is a top APA player and was in her second professional trick shot tournament. As I was explaining the shot, I glanced around the room and saw multiple heads popping up, all top trick shot artists who were quickly taking notes and drawing this shot in their notebooks. Here is how it is played: Shoot the cue ball three rails – it will hit three trays, and then go on to pocket the 9-ball.

Setup: Hang the 9-ball in pocket 'A' and place the cue ball along the line between the corner pocket and the 1 ½ diamond marker. Three ball trays are used. The first is frozen to the short rail, with the first ball (4-ball) aligned with the first diamond. The second tray is frozen to the long cushion, with the first diamond line going right between the first two balls (14 & 15 balls). The third tray is even with the first tray, and the second diamond line goes right between the two rows of balls.

Solution: Aim the cue ball directly at the 1 ½ diamond mark (it is placed on the line between that mark and the 9-ball). The cue ball will lose a lot of speed as it rebounds off the trays, so make sure to hit this pretty hard.

Adjustments: If you miss short (hitting tray # 3), aim further down the rail (possibly at the first diamond). If you miss long (hitting the side of tray #1), aim closer to the side pocket (possibly at the second diamond).

6.13: Split Hit

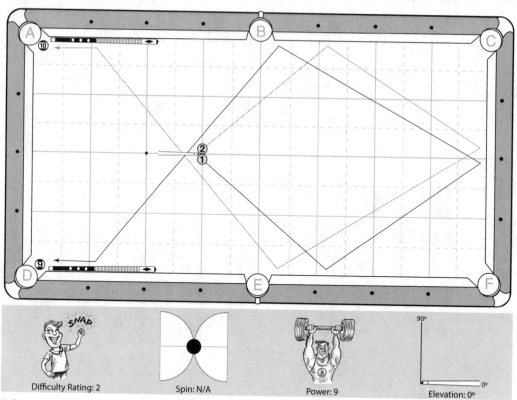

| Difficulty Rating: 2 | Spin: N/A | Power: 9 | Elevation: 0° |

I first saw the *Split Hit* played back in 2007. It was submitted by Sal Conti for the ESPN Trick Shot Magic competition. Although his was a slightly different version, it had the same concept of shooting between two frozen balls. In Sal's shot, the two balls were backed up a little and they were used to make hangers in the side pockets. In this version, you need to shoot between both balls, causing them to travel three cushions before they run into the two hangers.

Setup: The 1-ball and 2-ball are frozen along the third diamond line. The balls contact each other at the center line, but may be offset by up to 1/4 inch. The 9-ball & 10-ball are hanging. Two butts are placed along the cushions.

Solution: Shoot straight through and right between both balls. Based on their starting position, the two balls will travel three rails, hit the cue sticks, and make the hangers. You are hitting both balls very thin, so you will need to use extra power to get them around the table.

Adjustments: The most common error is a miscue, which is caused by not hitting directly between the balls. I advise against using a thin shaft. I recommend 13mm. Once you get a solid hit on both balls, you may find that they contact each other near the short rail. You can avoid such a collision by shifting the starting position to the left or right.

7: Speed Shots

Speed Shots, as the name strongly suggests, are focused on the element of *speed*. Some must be completed in a certain amount of time (using a stopwatch), while others use a *timer ball*. Shots of this nature usually involve hitting a ball, and then completing a certain task before that first ball is pocketed. Most players find these shots difficult because the element of *speed* is not used in a game of standard pool, but I urge you to not give up too quickly because these shots are fun to try, and they are very entertaining for a crowd.

In the televised competitions, there was a phase where some of the older style shots were being replaced with the new, flashy shots (e.g. speed). During that period, almost all of the new-comers created speed shots, and used them to gain points on the veterans. After all, new shots are sometimes hard to learn, especially when you are used to shooting only one kind of shot. However, after the older players practiced these newer style shots, they soon were able to hold their own against the new-comers. I remember one such match in which I selected a speed shot against Mike Massey and, after he made it, he loudly announced, "I may be old, but I'm not slow!"

7.1: 321-123

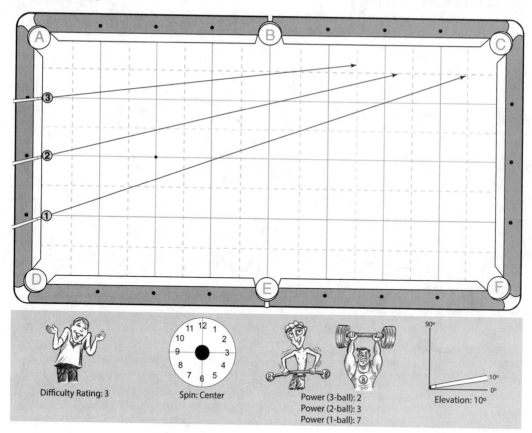

| Difficulty Rating: 3 | Spin: Center | Power (3-ball): 2
Power (2-ball): 3
Power (1-ball): 7 | Elevation: 10° |

The name *321-123* is derived from the order in which the balls are hit, and the order in which they go into the pocket. Shoot the balls toward corner pocket 'C' in 3-2-1 order. Vary the speed of each shot so the balls go into the pocket in 1-2-3 order – the reverse from which they were shot! I am not sure who invented this shot, but I seem to recall first seeing it during an ESPN Trick Shot Magic competition, and I believe it was Sebastian Giumelli who first performed it.

Setup: All three balls are frozen to the short rail at the diamond markers.

Solution: Shoot the 3-ball slowly so it barely reaches the pocket. The 2-ball is hit a little harder so it passes the 3-ball around the second diamond on the other end of the table. The 1-ball should be fired in as hard as you feel necessary to beat the 2-ball. The trick to this shot is in moving from ball to ball as quickly as possible.

Tips: The most common miss is on the 1-ball. To solve this problem, try removing the 3-ball and practice with only the 1-ball and 2-ball. Shoot the 2-ball first, and when moving over to shoot the 1-ball, don't take any practice strokes since you will not have time for them. Just move over and fire. Another common mistake is missing the 3-ball, either by hitting it too softly, or by hitting the long rail first. It seems like a very easy shot to shoot the ball straight in, but when you are thinking about what you have to do next, it is easy to get ahead of yourself and miss the ball. I hit the 3-ball a little harder than pocket speed[7-1] to guarantee that I don't hit it too softly. I can get away with this move because I have been shooting this shot for years and I can rapidly transition from one ball to the next.

7.2: Seven Ball Speed

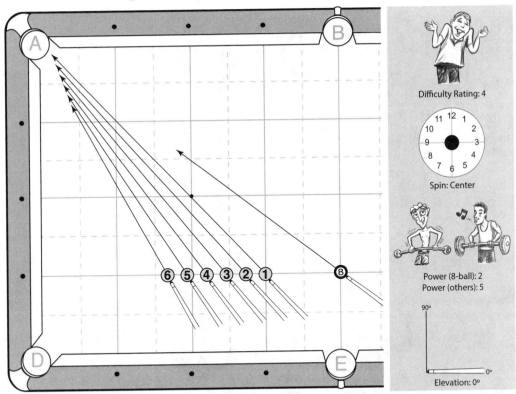

Difficulty Rating: 4

Spin: Center

Power (8-ball): 2
Power (others): 5

Elevation: 0°

I first came up with the *Seven Ball Speed* shot for the 2004 ESPN Trick Shot Magic, and then used it against Mike Massey in the semi-finals (I'm sure the underlying concept was around earlier than this, but I had never seen it). Shoot the 8-ball toward corner pocket 'A'. Before it goes in, you must quickly shoot the other six balls into the same pocket. The 8-ball goes in last.

Jessica, my daughter, was only five years old and she was just starting to experiment by setting up trick shots for me. She saw me practicing *Seven Ball Speed* and asked if she could set it up. It took her five full minutes, but she wanted to arrange the balls in 'rainbow color' order. I told her that I would shoot the shot on TV using her order, so instead of shooting the balls numerically, I shot them in this sequence: 3 (red), 5 (orange), 1 (yellow), 6 (green), 2 (blue), 4 (purple). That was the last time she was able to watch one of these events since she started school the following year, and the tournaments are on weekdays during the school year.

Setup: Place the 8-ball on the center line of the table and one diamond from side pocket 'E'. The 1-ball is placed at the 3,1 diamond intersection point. Each one of the other balls are positioned on the first diamond line, about 1 1/2 inches apart. There should be just enough space for the 1-ball to pass the 2-ball without hitting it. The closer the balls are to each other, the less distance you need to move, and the easier the shot becomes.

Solution: Start by positioning your body to shoot the 1-ball, keeping your feet together. Shift your right foot over and lean your body so you are in position to shoot the 8-ball. After shooting the 8, quickly move your right foot back to its original position and shoot the 1-ball. Don't be overly concerned about getting into proper body position and forming a stance for each ball as you move down the line; you will not have time, and that is a sure recipe for missing.

Tips: Try this shot with just two balls (and the 8-ball). When you can consistently make these balls, add a third ball, then a fourth and so on until you can make all six. Who knows? Maybe you will eventually be able to pocket more balls than described here. You will, of course, need a pocket capable of holding more balls, or optimally a table that has a ball return[7-2].

7.3: Pyramid

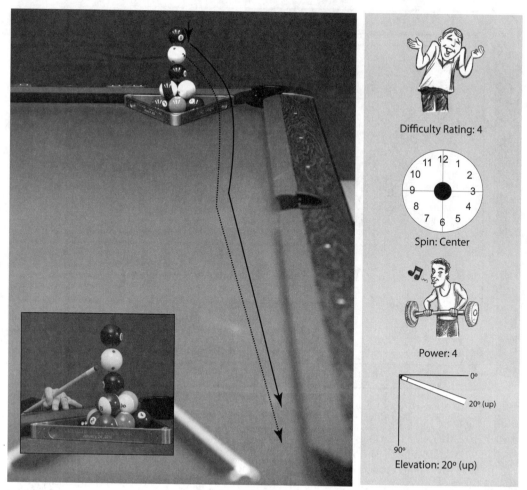

Difficulty Rating: 4

Spin: Center

Power: 4

Elevation: 20° (up)

The *Pyramid* is one of my own inventions. Build a pyramid of balls within a rack, with a stack of three at the top. Shoot the cue ball into the corner pocket. As the top ball falls (and before it hits and knocks down the pyramid), shoot it into the same corner.

Setup: From the bottom up, the tower consists of six balls, three balls, a stacker ball, the cue ball and another stacker on top. The lower stacker has the hole face up and the cue ball balanced within it. The hole on the top stacker is facing downward. The rack at the end of the table enlarges the pocket.

Solution: Kneel down behind the stack and aim at the cue ball. Aiming slightly upward will cause the top ball to move up before falling, giving you more time to strike it.

Adjustments: Take a series of quick practice strokes and keep that same rhythm when you shoot. Try to identify whether you missed the falling 8-ball by shooting too soon or too late – then adjust your rhythm.

If you are feeling adventurous, try stacking five balls. All three 8-balls are stackers. The bottom ball has the flat spot down, followed by a normal cue ball. The center stacker has the flat spot up, and the flat spot is down on the fourth ball. The top ball (9) is a normal ball [7-3]. I haven't yet figured out a shot for this mega-stack. Let me know if you come up with one.

7.4: How Many Can You Do?

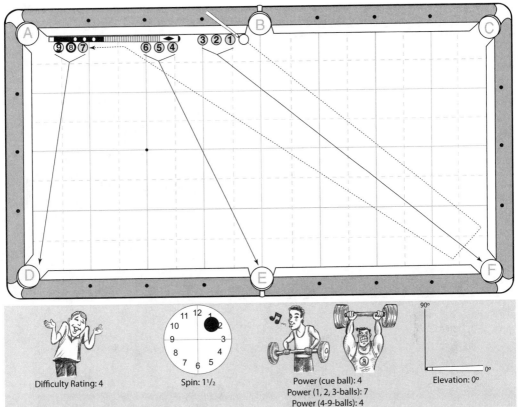

| Difficulty Rating: 4 | Spin: 1½ | Power (cue ball): 4
Power (1, 2, 3-balls): 7
Power (4-9-balls): 4 | Elevation: 0° |

This *How Many Can You Do?* shot came from a mix of three players: Dave Pearson, Sebastian Giumelli, and myself. In my first Trick Shot Magic competition, I saw Dave Pearson playing Mike Massey in the first round and he shot something similar to this, only the cue ball was shot three rails, and had to go directly into the corner pocket without a cue butt for help. A year or two later, Sebastian Giumelli executed this shot using seven object balls and the cue ball, but all of them went into the same pocket. I later combined the two and came up with my version. Shoot the cue ball two cushions and into the corner pocket (possibly with the help of the cue stick as shown in the diagram). While the cue ball is rolling, shoot the 1, 2, and 3 balls into the corner pocket, the 4, 5 and 6 balls into the side pocket, and the 7, 8, and 9 balls into the other corner pocket, clearing the path for the cue ball. As you improve on this shot, try adding more balls. I have used as many as 13 balls in competition!

Setup: Place a butt along the rail and balls 1-9 in line, either frozen to the rail, or to the butt. Leave a small gap between the balls.

Solution: Start your body in position to shoot the 3-ball and lean over to shoot the cue ball. This enables you to quickly shoot the cue ball and the first three balls without moving your feet, and this maneuver will hopefully leave you with enough time to shoot the rest of the balls.

Tips: Cue ball speed is the key, so practice by just shooting it a few times. The cue ball will barely drop when it is hit at the ideal speed, but in competition I recommend hitting it a little harder. If you hit the cue ball too hard, you can speed up on the object balls and still make the shot. If the cue ball is hit too softly, you will miss no matter how fast you shoot the others. This concept applies in golf — never leave a birdie putt short – give yourself a chance to make it. The secret is to ignore the cue ball when it creeps up on you while hitting the 7, 8, and 9 balls, It is so easy to get distracted and miss, so be sure to stay focused on the object balls.

7.5: The Twist

| Difficulty Rating: 5 | Spin: Center | Power (2, 4, 5-balls): 2
Power (1, 3-balls): 6 | Elevation: 0° |

The Twist was invented by Tim Chin for the 2011 ESPN World Cup of Trick Shots. He gave it that name because your body is twisting back and forth as the cue stick goes behind your back for every other shot. Tim danced "*The Twist*" after making the shot, so it is possible that that is where the name really comes from. The balls are hit in the following order: 2-1-4-3-5, but must be pocketed in numerical order. Also, there must always be a ball rolling on the table at all times. Finally, the 1-ball and 3-ball must be shot with your cue behind the back.

Setup: The balls are placed in the following order (L to R): 3-1-5-4-2. All five balls are on the first diamond line with a one ball-width spacing between them. The 5-ball is centered.

Solution: Shoot the 2-ball softly, then fire in the 1-ball (with your cue behind your back). Shoot the 4-ball softly (before the 2-ball falls), then fire in the 3-ball (with your cue behind your back). Finally, shoot the 5-ball before the 4-ball falls.

Tips: The key to this shot is to make a quick transition from ball to ball. When switching to a behind-the-back shot, I prefer to keep my back hand holding the cue and release my bridge hand. I swing the cue behind my back and re-grip the bridge. Be careful because it is very easy to slam your cue into the side of the table. Make sure you overdo it a little by bringing your cue stick up high. Another technique is to keep your bridge hand on the cue and release your back hand, stepping around the cue to get the behind-the-back shot, and vice versa. I use a jump cue because it is shorter, and it allows me more control.

7.6: Drop Kick

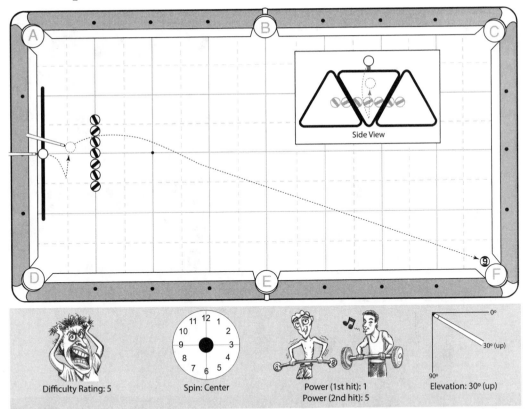

Side View

| Difficulty Rating: 5 | Spin: Center | Power (1st hit): 1
Power (2nd hit): 5 | Elevation: 30° (up) |

Drop Kick was created by Jamey Gray and it was introduced during the 2010 Ultimate Trick Shot Tour Finale in Las Vegas. It was just my luck that I was Jamey's first victim with this one. Shoot the cue ball off the rack, causing it to hit the table. As it bounces up, hit the cue ball again over the line of blocker balls and down the table to make the 9-ball.

Setup: Two racks are placed upright against the short cushion. A third rack is inverted and it is supported by the other two. The cue ball is placed on top of a chalk cube which is centered on the middle rack. The 9-ball is hanging in corner pocket 'F', and a line of seven blocker balls are frozen on the first diamond line.

Solution: Tap the cue ball lightly, using just enough force to knock it off the chalk. You must then quickly reposition the cue stick to shoot through the middle rack, so don't wait for the cue ball to fall before moving your cue. Get down there fast, and as soon as you hear the cue ball bounce, poke the stick forward and hit the cue ball.

Adjustments: Missing the cue ball while it's on the way back up is the most common way to miss this shot. Before knocking the cue ball off the chalk, pick a spot on the row of blocker balls. It could be the center of the third ball, the midpoint between the second and third ball, or any other spot with which you start off. After hitting the cue ball, reposition your stick, aim it directly at that spot, and poke forward. Try to determine if you missed the cue ball on the left, right, top, or bottom. If you missed it left or right, adjust your spot for the next attempt. If you missed it directly over or under the cue ball, you have the right spot, but you need to reposition your cue either higher or lower. Missing the 9-ball is a simple fix. Make sure during the entire shot that the cue stick is pointed directly at that ball. Don't try to hit the cue ball off the chalk straight up table and then change your angle for the re-hit. Aiming right at the 9-ball for both hits ensures the cue ball will make the 9-ball providing you get a solid re-hit after the bounce.

7.7: Jump and Reverse

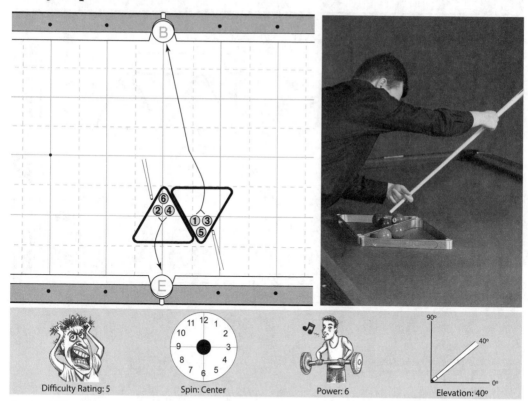

| Difficulty Rating: 5 | Spin: Center | Power: 6 | Elevation: 40° |

Jump and Reverse is one of my own inventions, but the concept of jumping backward was first introduced by Dave Nangle, one of the top trick shot artists in the world, and the 2008, 2009 & 2010 Masters Trick Shot Champion in the Draw Shots category. Stand behind the side pocket and jump the balls in numerical order. The 1, 3, and 5 balls are jumped forward into the opposite side pocket ('B'). The 2, 4, and 6 balls will be jumped backward, into the side pocket ('E') where you are standing. You will be alternating on each shot, jumping a ball forward, then backward, and so on. In competition, both feet need to remain on the floor and between both third diamond markers (within one diamond on either side of the side pocket). A timer, which is set at 12 seconds, is usually part of the requirements as well.

Setup: Center one rack between the side pockets, with the back edge exactly three ball-widths from the cushion. Take another rack and align the edge so they are touching. Three balls are placed within each rack, with the 1, 3, and 5 balls in the right-most rack and the 2, 4, and 6 balls in the centered rack. The balls should be in a triangular formation, close enough to the apex, and separated enough so you can comfortably jump each one of them.

Solution: The jump shots going forward (1, 3, 5) are standard jump shots. Jumping backward (2, 4, 6) takes a little more practice. To make a quick transition between the forward and backward jumps, it is important that you keep your right hand in one position on the butt of the cue. I recommend lining up a backward jump first, making sure you have a comfortable grip on the cue, then you are ready to jump the 1-ball and start the shot.

Adjustments: The most common error when jumping backward is to over elevate the cue. When players jump going forward, the cue is elevated 30-45 degrees. However, when they lean over for the backward jump, it is at 60-75 degrees, so try to consciously *under elevate*, as this should result in a perfect elevation for the backward jump. One last piece of advice to all of the men trying this shot: consider where you are standing and *do not* hit the backward jumps too hard!!!

7.8: The Original Speed Jump Shot

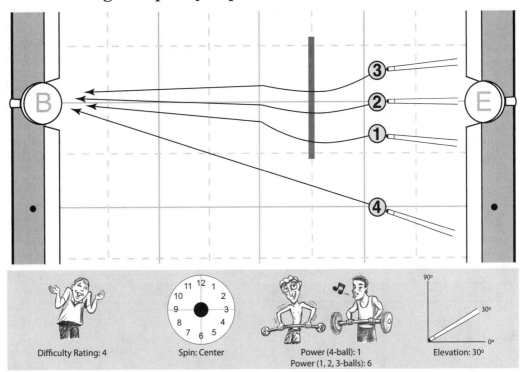

| Difficulty Rating: 4 | Spin: Center | Power (4-ball): 1
Power (1, 2, 3-balls): 6 | Elevation: 30° |

I invented *The Original Speed Jump Shot* back in 2004 for the ESPN Trick Shot Magic competition, and it ended up becoming the first of many speed jump shots to surface over the next nine years. Shoot the 4-ball slowly toward side pocket 'B'. Quickly jump the 1, 2, and 3 balls over the barrier and into the side pocket before the 4-ball falls.

Setup: The 4-ball is on the third diamond line, just behind the first diamond line from the long cushion. The 1, 2, and 3 balls are aligned with the 4-ball, with the 2-ball on the center line. Leave a small gap between each of the three balls. On television I used a row of dominos as the barrier, standing up in their shorter position. However, you can just as easily use a shaft, a butt, or a block of wood.

Solution: Getting the proper speed on the 4-ball is crucial. Also, you don't want to take practice strokes during the jump shots. While jumping, try to look at the object balls instead of the side pocket. Get a feel for the angle with which you need to aim the jump shots, and how much that angle needs to shift as you move from ball to ball.

Tips: A good way to practice this shot is to start by using only two balls - the 4-ball and the 1-ball. Lag the 4-ball and jump the 1-ball. Once you have that down, add the 2-ball, and finally add the 3-ball.

7.9: Speed Demon on Steroids

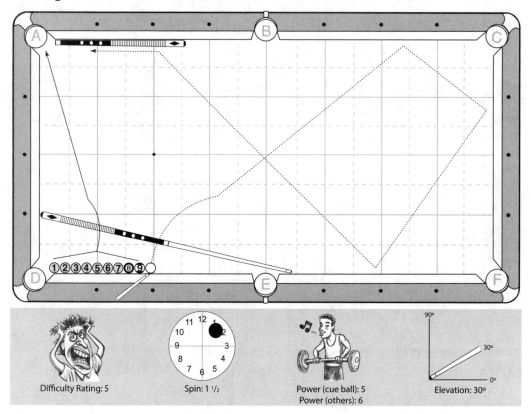

Difficulty Rating: 5	Spin: 1 1/2	Power (cue ball): 5 Power (others): 6	Elevation: 30°

Jamey Gray created this variation of a shot called the *Speed Demon*, by Nick Nikolaidis. I have always had trouble with this shot, and he was aware of my deficiency when he pulled this one out at the 2010 ESPN Trick Shot Magic competition at the Green Valley Ranch Casino in Henderson, NV. My first attempt during our match was the first time I had ever made this shot, both in competition and practice. The first step is to jump the cue ball over the cue, causing it to travel three-rails and into the corner pocket (probably with the help of the butt). Before the cue ball goes in, you must jump the 1 through 9 balls in order, into the same corner pocket.

Setup: Balls 1-9 are all frozen in a line and to the cushion, with the 1-ball starting at the pocket point. The cue ball is frozen to the 9-ball, and to the cushion. A cue butt is placed up against the opposite cushion to help the cue ball go in, but the object balls are not allowed to touch it. A standard cue stick is laying across the table, with the butt end frozen to the short cushion at the first diamond. The cue is placed at an angle so the tip is touching the long cushion.

Solution: I prefer to use a full length jump cue for this shot, even though any standard jump cue will do. It is important to hit the cue ball at the correct speed. Aim the cue ball short so that it will hit the butt, as this will give you more time to make the other balls than you would otherwise have if the cue ball went straight into the corner pocket.

Tips: The key to jumping the balls is to start slowly. Take your time (but not too much time) when jumping the 1-ball and 2-ball. As you progress down the line, increase your speed. If you try to go too fast on the first few balls, you will likely miss a shot or fail to jump one of them.

7.10: Lefty Righty Speed Jump

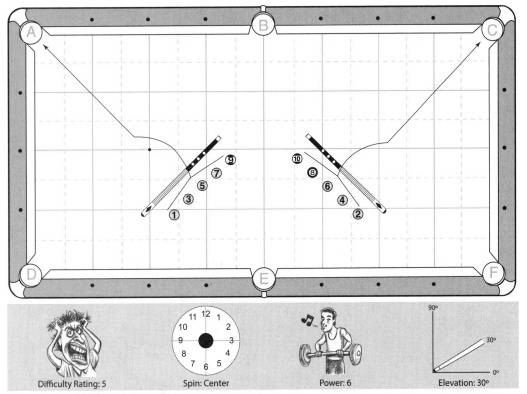

Difficulty Rating: 5	Spin: Center	Power: 6	Elevation: 30°

Nick Nikolaidis invented the *Lefty Righty Speed Jump*, and he can perform it in less than 20 seconds. However, on the ESPN competitions, if you use a stopwatch, you need to allow for a minimum of two seconds per ball hit. Since there are 10 balls in this shot, Nick wasn't allowed to specify anything less than 20 seconds. We had a $20,000 one-on-one challenge match in Montreal, Canada in 2011 where that two second rule wasn't in place, and the 20 second time limit was reduced. Here is how it is played: Jump the balls in numerical order into the two opposing corner pockets, alternating left side and right side. The balls jumping to the left (1, 3, 5, 7, 9) are jumped right-handed, and the balls jumping to the right (2, 4, 6, 8, 10) are jumped left-handed. Additionally, a 20 second shot clock puts a limit on the time you have to complete the shot.

Setup: Place a wood block or a butt diagonally across the table. Place the 1, 3, 5, 7, and 9 balls parallel to the butt, exactly two ball-widths from it. Create the mirror image of that setup on the other side of the table, this time using the even balls from 2-10.

Solution: As with most speed shots, start out slowly and then get faster as you go through the shot. The transition between your right-hand and left-hand is critical, so practice switching the cue a few times before trying to jump the balls. When ready, start with four balls (two on each side) until you get the feel for the motion.

Adjustments: The shots with your opposite hand (lefty in my case) are the easiest to miss. The key is to make sure you hit the balls in the center. It is very easy to hit these lefty jump shots with a little bit of English, which makes them curve out of the corner pocket. The harder you hit the ball, the smaller the curve, so you do have some room for error. However, you must be careful not to hit the balls too hard or else they will bounce off the table.

7.11: Blur Jump

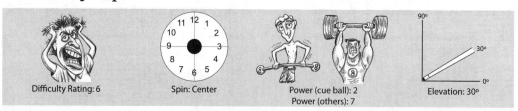

Difficulty Rating: 6   Spin: Center   Power (cue ball): 2   Elevation: 30°
                                                    Power (others): 7

Jamey Gray and I came up with the *Blur Jump* for the 2011 ESPN World Cup of Trick Shots. Though it was originally designed for two players, it is also possible to perform it by yourself if you reduce the number of balls. The cue ball is lagged across the table, causing it to bank back to where it started. While the cue ball is in motion, quickly jump the 1-7 balls into corner pocket 'F', then move to the 9-15 and jump them into pocket 'C'. Now, quickly move around the table and hit the cue ball to sink the 8-ball into the side. The cue ball must be re-hit before it stops moving, and before it hits the long rail where it started.

Jamey Gray and I love performing this shot together, but have never had much luck with it in competition. During practice, our make percentage is in the 70-80% range, but on TV, something always goes wrong that is not part of the actual shot.

The first year (2011), the shot was written up incorrectly in the book submitted for the World Cup of Trick Shots. We always practiced it like this: I lag the cue ball, Jamey jumps the 1-7, I jump the 9-15, and then move over to shoot and make the 8-ball. In the shot book, we didn't say 'Jamey' and 'Andy', but instead we used 'Player 1' and 'Player 2'. We didn't want the other team to know who would be selecting the shot! It read 'Player 1' (Andy) lags the cue ball, 'Player 2' (Jamey) jumps the 1-7, 'Player 1' (me) jumps the 9-15. However, there was a typo and it read 'Player 2' shoots the cue ball to make the 8. That meant Jamey was supposed to do it (according to the book), but I shot it during the competition. The referee called us on it and we didn't get credit for the make. The second year (2012) the cue ball was lagging across the table and it hit something, either a sliver of chalk or a splinter from the wood blocks over which we were jumping. In any case, the piece of debris bent the path of the cue ball into the wood, nullifying the shot.

Setup: Start with a block of wood ³/₄ inch tall (this is what we use on TV, but you can use two shafts). Stretch the wood (or shafts) across the entire width of the table. Place the cue ball frozen to the long cushion, and position the 1-7 balls and the 9-15 balls frozen to the short cushion. The 8-ball should be hanging in side pocket 'E'. Four racks are used to enlarge the corner pockets at the far end of the table, and a weight of some kind (a box of balls works well) holds everything in place.

Solution: Cue ball speed is the key - hit it just hard enough to make it back to the long cushion. When jumping the 1-7, start a little slower on the 1-ball and increase your speed as you progress down the line. When switching over to the 9-15 balls, the same thing applies (slowly on the 9, increasing to full speed when you hit the 15).

Tips: Let's assume that you are able to get the jumps off quickly. In that case, the most common error is to hit the cue ball with the object balls as it is rolling across the table. You have very large pockets, so you really don't need to aim when jumping. Just concentrate on jumping the balls over the *cue ball*, not the block of wood. Do that and you needn't worry about hitting the cue ball. Even if the cue ball is not in the way just yet, you should still think about jumping over it.

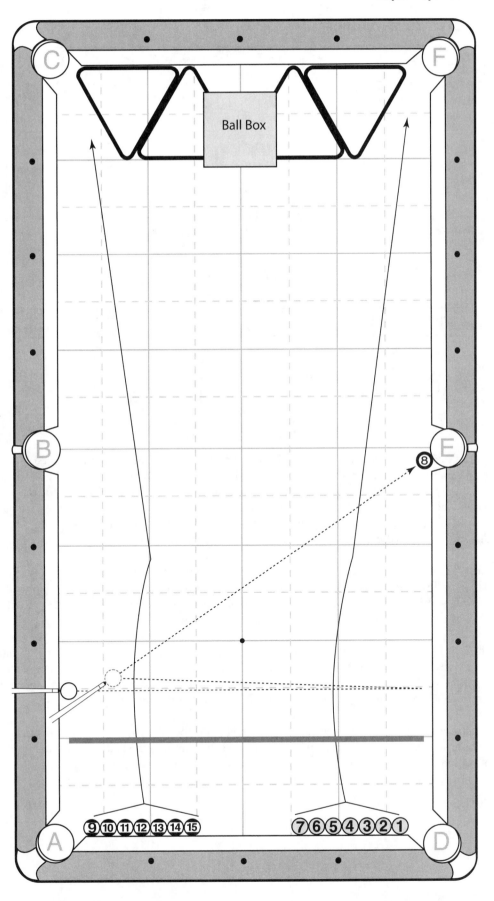

Ball Box

7.12: Markle's Madness

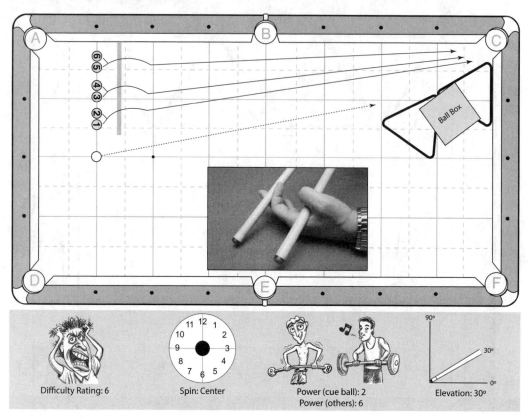

| Difficulty Rating: 6 | Spin: Center | Power (cue ball): 2
Power (others): 6 | Elevation: 30° |

I first saw *Markle's Madness* performed on YouTube by its creator, Steve Markle, the 2013 WPA World Champion in the Massé category. From the moment I saw Steve shoot it, I knew it was right up my alley, and I have been using it in competitions ever since. Hold on to two jump cues and lag the cue ball with one of them into corner pocket 'C'. Double jump the 1-ball and 2-ball (at the same time) over the barrier and into the corner pocket. Repeat for the 3 and 4 balls, and again for the 5 and 6 balls. The cue ball is pocketed last.

Setup: The cue ball is placed on the long center line of the table, one diamond from the short cushion. Three sets of two balls (1-2, 3-4, 5-6) are placed along the first diamond line and a block of wood is placed in front of them as shown. Two racks enlarge the pocket at the other end of the table, and there is a weight (perhaps a box of balls) to help keep them in place.

Solution: Hold both cues between your thumb and first finger (dart style). One of the shafts goes between your thumb and first finger, and the other goes between the first and second fingers. You should be able to separate the cues sufficiently to get a solid hit on both balls. Stand to line up for the first jump (the 1 and 2 balls), lean over, and hit the cue ball.

Adjustments: The gaps between each pair of balls must be the same, as this ensures that you do not have to waste time readjusting the jump cues. A common mistake occurs when the object balls collide with the cue ball. You can solve this by aiming the cue ball just to the left of the top apex of the rack, which will give you the most room for the object balls.

7.13: Catch & Release

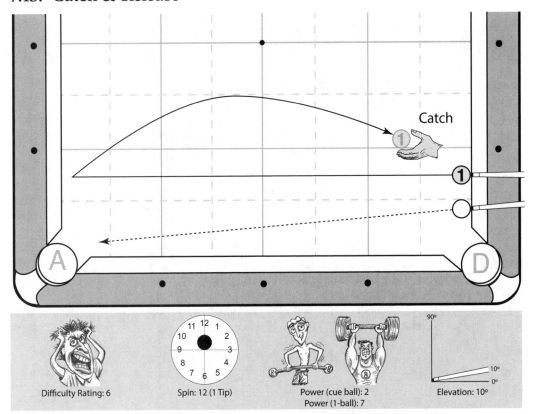

| Difficulty Rating: 6 | Spin: 12 (1 Tip) | Power (cue ball): 2
Power (1-ball): 7 | Elevation: 10° |

The *Catch & Release* is one of Bruce Barthelette's inventions. He has a version 2.0 which includes an extra ball, but I didn't want to go too crazy here. Sometimes Bruce can make it three or four times in a row, but it can also be missed. As captain of Team USA for the World Cup of Trick Shots, I am always a little hesitant to put in a shot like this where there is a chance of losing a point. However, Bruce always feels good about playing *Catch & Release*, and I have confidence in my teammates. Besides, he ALWAYS makes it in competition! The shot begins by shooting the 1-ball across the table with an elevated cue, causing it to jump back off the rail. Before catching the 1-ball, lag the cue ball toward the corner pocket. Then, catch the 1-ball and place it in the corner pocket before the cue ball gets there.

Setup: The cue ball and 1-ball are frozen to the cushion, with one or two inches between them.

Solution: The hardest part is in making the quick transition from a hard hit to a soft hit. When lagging the cue ball, speed is critical, so try to hit it so the ball will barely reach the pocket. I prefer to use a full length jump/break cue because it makes it easier for me to jump the 1-ball off the cushion; speaking of which, the 1-ball needs to be about 1/4 inch off the table when it hits the cushion so that it will jump back toward you. It helps to pretend you are jumping over a shaft. In one of the ESPN broadcasts, you can actually hear me whispering 'shaft' before I jump the ball!

Tips: After lining up the 1-ball, keep your cue in place, but look at the cue ball in preparation for the second shot. You don't need to look at the 1-ball when hitting it, and this trick gives you a quicker transition to the cue ball. If the 1-ball is not jumping, try only that part of the shot until you get used to executing it successfully.

7.14: Swing

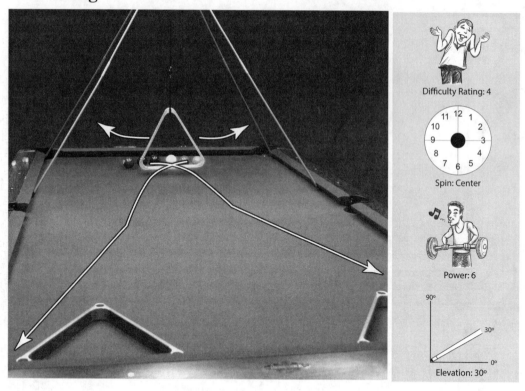

Difficulty Rating: 4

Spin: Center

Power: 6

Elevation: 30°

I was the first player to shoot the *Swing* in competition, but it was first diagrammed by Nick Nikolaidis a number of years earlier. He submitted it for the 2006 ESPN Trick Shot Magic competition, but he never selected it in an actual match. Hold the rack up and to the left, and then release it – this will create a swinging motion, back and forth. Every time the rack moves across, jump the next ball in sequence through the rack and into the far corner pocket (alternating pockets with each jump).

Setup: I use thin tent poles, but you can use an easel, or you can build something out of dowels or thin strips of wood. Hang a rack from the center so it is about 1 1/2 - 2 inches off the surface of the table. The 1, 3, and 5 balls are on the left, and the 2, 4, and 6 balls are on the right. Two racks are placed at the other end to enlarge the corner pockets.

Solution: As soon as you let go of the rack, immediately position yourself to jump the 1-ball diagonally across the table (I let the rack swing twice before jumping the first ball). Try to time it so you are jumping the ball as the front edge of the rack is directly in your path. Timing it in this manner should result in the rack's opening being in the proper position when the ball gets there.

Tips: Although this is a difficult shot, making the first ball is probably the easiest of the six. Most players miss when they move to the next ball. Try not to focus on whether that ball goes in. Just hit it at the appropriate time and move immediately to the next ball. Try to keep the rack in your peripheral vision, and do not take your eye off the next ball to be jumped.

7.15: Swipe

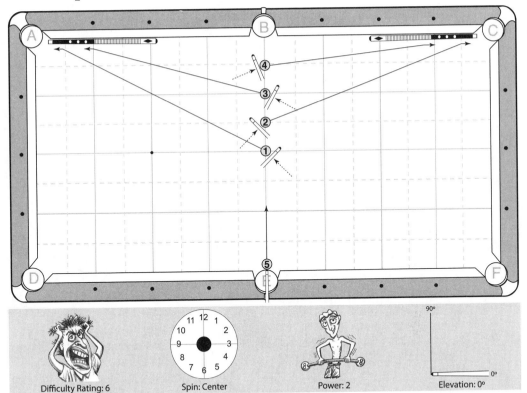

Difficulty Rating: 6 | **Spin: Center** | **Power: 2** | **Elevation: 0°**

The *Swipe* comes from an old concept, but I invented this newer version which requires making the 1-4 balls as you swipe them. This is one of the shots that I saved until the semi-final match against Jamey Gray (who else?) during the 2013 Masters Trick Shot Championship. He was familiar with the original version of the shot, but making the balls as you swipe them was just tricky enough to get me the point. I'm sure Jamey will have it figured out for the next competition, so I'll probably have to add a new wrinkle to it, keeping him off guard.

Shoot the 5-ball toward the side pocket. Using the side of your cue stick, swipe the balls in numerical order, alternating direction, so they go into the corner pockets. The 5-ball doesn't need to be made last, but swiping the balls must be done in order to clear a path for the 5-ball.

Setup: All of the balls are placed along the center line. The 1-ball is on the center spot. The 3-ball is positioned one diamond from the cushion. The 2-ball splits the 1 and 3. The 4-ball can be adjusted, and I like to place it a couple of inches past the 3-ball. The 5-ball should be hanging in the side pocket. Two butts are placed against the rails.

Solution: Lag the 5-ball softly so that it will barely reach side pocket 'B'. When swiping the balls left and right, hit them into the cues because this enlarges the pockets. An easier version (and the original version) is to just make the 5-ball and swipe the others out of the way without making them.

Tips: First try swiping the balls left and right without rolling the 5-ball. This will help you get used to that part of the shot, and it will give you a feel for how to properly swipe them so they all go in. It helps to use a jump cue because the shorter length prevents your body from getting in the way.

8: Juggling Shots

Juggling shots involve hitting a moving ball. The ball might be travelling around the table, coming toward you, moving away from you, or being tossed in the air. These are fun shots for an audience because they usually take a little time to fully develop. *Juggling* shots are not used in a standard game of pool, but invest some time practicing them. The first shot in this chapter is a great practice tool, so I recommend that you get the hang of this before moving on to the more difficult *juggling* shots.

Some players refer to *juggling* as 'circus' shots, and, in a way, they are. The producer of the ESPN events always asks us to come up with crazy shots that have lots of balls in motion, and that we use very unconventional props - the more motion, the better. I always go into a competition with the following thoughts in mind: entertain the crowd first, play the tournament second. Professional sports, whether trick shot competitions, 10-ball, bowling, or even baseball or football, would be nowhere without an entertained audience.

8.1: 15-Rail Kick

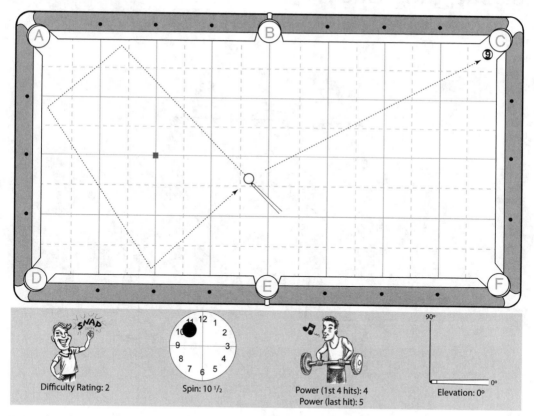

Difficulty Rating: 2	Spin: 10 ½	Power (1st 4 hits): 4	Elevation: 0°
		Power (last hit): 5	

When I shoot the *15-Rail Kick* in an exhibition, I start by asking the audience what is the most number of rails they think I can hit with the cue ball and still pocket the 9-ball. The typical responses are four, five, or six. When I announce 'fifteen', they look at me like I'm crazy. Once I re-hit the moving cue ball the first time, they all start laughing!

The shot begins by shooting the cue ball around the table three cushions. As the cue ball approaches the center of the table, re-hit it and repeat the process until you have hit the cue ball five times. The fifth hit will send it around the table to make the 9-ball.

Setup: Hang the 9-ball in the corner pocket and place the cue ball near the center of the table. A piece of chalk is placed on the spot.

Solution: Make sure not to hit the cue ball too hard, as it is easy to increase the speed on each re-hit. One helpful tip is to track the cue ball with your cue stick. In other words, don't stay in one spot and wait for the cue ball to arrive. Instead, move your bridge hand and cue stick as you track the movement of the cue ball. Then hit it when ready.

Adjustments: When hitting the cue ball for the last time, keep an eye on the diamond at which you are aiming. If the cue ball misses short, adjust your aim to a different spot; make the opposite adjustment if the cue ball misses long.

8.2: Three Ball Juggle

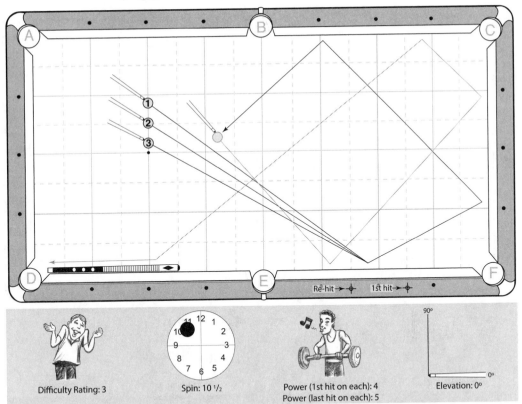

Difficulty Rating: 3

Spin: 10 ½

Power (1st hit on each): 4
Power (last hit on each): 5

Elevation: 0°

The *Three Ball Juggle* is one of my own creations. Shoot the 1, 2, and 3 balls in order, three cushions around the table. Re-hit the 1, 2, and 3 in order, only this time harder so that they will go into the corner pocket in order. The 3-ball must be re-hit before the 1-ball makes contact with the butt or goes into the pocket. I came up with this a long time ago, and have since seen other players improve on it, much to my delight. For example, I saw Steve Markle shoot this shot with seven balls, and I have seen a few others shoot it with three or four, but hitting them around the table more than two times.

Setup: Place the 1, 2, and 3 balls on the second diamond line. A cue butt is placed along the rail to enlarge the corner pocket.

Solution: The first hit on each one of the three balls should cause them to roll slowly. For example, if you didn't re-hit them, they would barely hit the butt and probably would not go into the pocket. The second hit on each ball can be made with a little more speed. Make sure that you track the balls with your cue stick rather than waiting in one spot. Try to hit all of the balls at the same speed to keep them from colliding with one another (which is not allowed in competitions). The ghost ball in the diagram shows the approximate place where you will re-hit each of the three balls.

Adjustments: A common mistake is for the 1-ball to interfere with re-hitting the 2-ball or 3-ball when it comes around the table for the second time. You can adjust for this by changing your angle. The first hit on the three balls should cause the balls to come around longer. When re-hitting the balls, aim shorter (closer to the side pocket) as this should prevent the balls from getting in the way.

8.3: The Phantom Shot

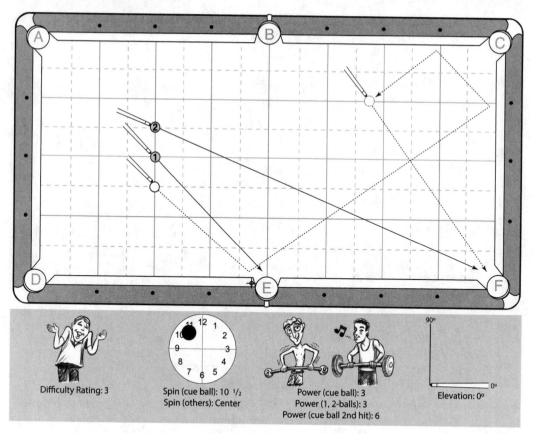

| Difficulty Rating: 3 | Spin (cue ball): 10 ½
Spin (others): Center | Power (cue ball): 3
Power (1, 2-balls): 3
Power (cue ball 2nd hit): 6 | Elevation: 0° |

Bruce Barthelette introduced *The Phantom Shot* back in 2005 when he was invited to the ESPN Trick Shot Magic competition for the first time. Bruce got the idea from a friend of his named Joe LeMaine. The cue ball is shot three rails around the table. While it is still rolling, shoot the 1-ball into side pocket 'E' and lag the 2-ball toward corner pocket 'F'. Re-hit the cue ball after it hits the third rail into the same pocket as the 2 before the 2-ball gets there. When Bruce shoots this in competition, he requires that you use a free-hand bridge. This means that your hand may not touch the table.

Setup: Place the 1-ball on the spot. The cue ball and the 2-ball are adjustable anywhere on the second diamond line, but I recommend that you place them as shown in the diagram.

Solution: Aim the cue ball at a point just before the side pocket and use running English. Quickly shoot the 1-ball, but not too hard because balls tend to bounce out of the side pocket when they approach it from that angle. Lagging the 2-ball at the correct speed is key. When re-hitting the cue ball, make sure that you move over to the side of the table. If you stay behind the short rail, the cue ball may travel too far and the rolling 2-ball will block its path to the corner pocket.

Adjustments: Don't be in a rush to hit the 2-ball immediately after hitting the 1-ball. Take a look first at where the cue ball is situated. If the cue ball has already hit the third rail, hit the 2-ball right away. However, if the cue ball is still rolling toward the third rail, wait a beat or two. If you hit the 2-ball too soon, that may not leave you with enough time to wait for the cue ball to hit the third rail. This common error happened to my opponent in the 2010 ESPN Trick Shot Magic semi-finals!

8.4: 1,2,3,4 Rails

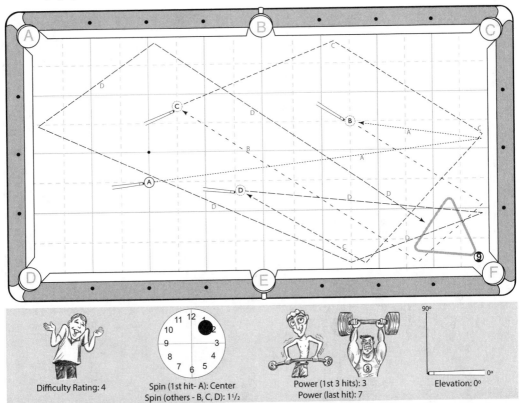

Difficulty Rating: 4

Spin (1st hit- A): Center
Spin (others - B, C, D): 1½

Power (1st 3 hits): 3
Power (last hit): 7

Elevation: 0°

I first came up with the *1,2,3,4 Rails* shot in 2008 for the ESPN Trick Shot Magic competition. Not only did I select this shot, but another competitor and friend of mine, Eric Yow, also selected it in his semi-final match against Tom Rossman. If you practice this shot, it isn't all that difficult. However, if you've never seen it played before, it can be tricky because you have to move quickly from shot to shot, and you don't want to get tripped up trying to remember where to go next. Shoot the cue ball one rail (from cue ball 'A'), then re-hit it two rails (from 'B'), then three rails (from 'C'), and finally four rails (from 'D'). Walk (or run) over to the rack and place it in front of the 9-ball. The cue ball will eventually make its way to the rack, hit it, and make the 9.

Setup: The cue ball starts on the second diamond line, and the 9-ball is hanging in the corner pocket. A rack is standing upright on the edge of the table.

Solution: The first hit on the cue ball (one rail) is angled slightly to the left. This will cause the cue ball to be closer to you, giving you a better angle for the second hit (two rails). The last hit on the cue ball should be aimed at approximately the first diamond on the short rail (near the 9-ball). This needs to be hit pretty hard, however, you should still have plenty of time to walk or run around the table to the rack. Place the point of the rack against the 9-ball and adjust the angle of the rack based on where the cue ball is travelling. Finally, make sure that your hand is out of the way before the cue ball arrives.

Tips: When I first invented this shot for competition, I put an eight second time limit on this shot, meaning the cue ball must be re-hit for the last time within eight seconds of the first hit. This is a big change because it requires that you hit the cue ball much faster than in the other juggling shots. I would recommend that you first try this shot without the timer.

8.5: Jamey's Juggle

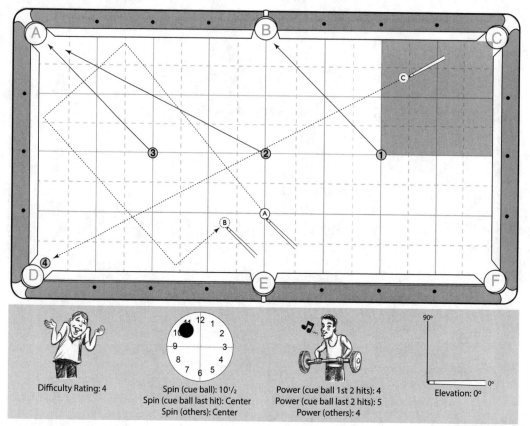

| Difficulty Rating: 4 | Spin (cue ball): 10½
Spin (cue ball last hit): Center
Spin (others): Center | Power (cue ball 1st 2 hits): 4
Power (cue ball last 2 hits): 5
Power (others): 4 | Elevation: 0° |

Jamey's Juggle was created by… wait for it… Jamey Gray. The cue ball is shot three cushions around the 3-ball from position 'A'. Move over and shoot the 1-ball into side pocket 'B'. Next, re-hit the cue ball, and then make the 2-ball in corner pocket 'A'. Re-hit the cue ball once more, and then shoot the 3-ball into corner pocket 'A'. Move down table and hit the cue ball (from 'C') one last time, making the 4-ball into pocket 'D'

Why, you may wonder, is the difficulty rating so high? Because there are two additional requirements: first, the cue ball must be within the 2x2 diamond zone as shown (without contacting an extra rail) before you can shoot it at the 4-ball. Second, the entire shot must be performed one-handed and jacked up, that is without touching the rail!

Setup: The cue ball is placed on the center line, one diamond from the side pocket. The 1-ball and 3-ball are on the spots, and the 2-ball is on the center spot. Hang the 4-ball in pocket 'D'.

Solution: Start out by hitting the cue ball softly. Remember that when you hit the cue ball for the third time (just before making the 3-ball), you need to hit it harder so it can make it to the 2x2 diamond zone.

Tips: This shot is difficult primarily because you must hit this one-handed and jacked up. First try *Jamey's Juggle* by using two hands with a standard bridge, just to get the feel for the shot. Use one hand, but only after you master the two-handed version.

8.6: Field Goal

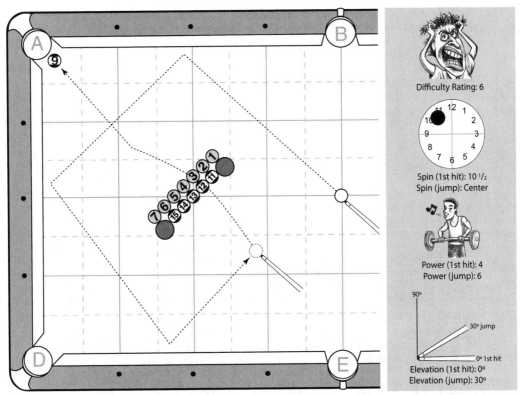

Difficulty Rating: 6

Spin (1st hit): 10 ½
Spin (jump): Center

Power (1st hit): 4
Power (jump): 6

90°

30° jump

0° 1st hit

Elevation (1st hit): 0°
Elevation (jump): 30°

In the 2009 ESPN World Cup of Trick Shots, Bruce Barthelette and I were finishing up our semi-final match. We were down by one point and Bruce was just about to go up to the table to answer one of Team Europe's challenges. We were discussing which shot he should pick next and he said to me, "I don't want to think about it. You find one and I'll shoot it." Out of approximately 300 possible shots, *Field Goal* is the one I selected. Before going up to shoot it, Bruce said, "I haven't shot this one in a few years!" The idea is to shoot the cue ball three cushions and re-hit it when it returns, causing it to jump over the balls, between the cups, and to pocket the 9-ball. The entire shot must be done with one-hand, and while jacked up. He ended up making it on his first attempt which, after one more shot, resulted in a tie. We went to the tie-breaker (an eight rail shot onto a $100 bill) and we emerged victorious.

Setup: The 12 object balls should be placed frozen in two lines (one line of five balls, and one line of seven). The center ball in the line of five balls is placed on the spot, and two plastic cups are placed at either end. The cue ball starts in the middle of the table, and the 9-ball is hanging in corner pocket 'A'.

Solution: You will need to practice jumping the cue ball while it is moving, but the key to this shot is making sure you get a good first hit on the cue ball as it is very easy to hit it too softly, or at the wrong angle. If the cue ball is too close to the line of balls when it returns, you will be unable to jump it without hitting the blockers. If the cue ball is too far from the row of balls, the jump will need to be hit too hard and the cue ball will fly off the table, which this shot prohibits.

Tips: As with all one-handed shots, I advise that you first try this with two hands until you get the feel for it. Hold the cue stick like you would for a jump shot for the first hit of the cue ball. This will keep you from having to fumble around with changing your grip for the actual jump shot.

8.7: Swipe Jump

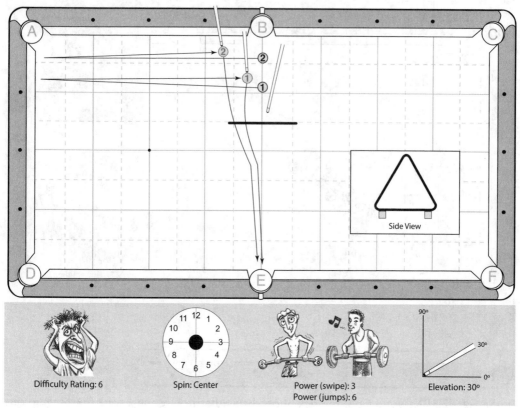

| Difficulty Rating: 6 | Spin: Center | Power (swipe): 3
Power (jumps): 6 | Elevation: 30° |

Using the side of your stick, swipe both balls so they bank off the short cushion and back to where they can be jumped through the rack, one at a time and into side pocket 'E'. The jump shots are done one-handed. Not only did I invent the *Swipe Jump*, but I also created a variation in which you swipe one ball to the right, and the other to the left. As the balls come back toward each other, jump each through the rack, one at a time, into the side pocket. Both versions have their difficult points. This one is tough because you have to swipe two balls at the same time, controlling their speed and direction, but the alternate version is even more difficult because you have to swipe twice, once in each direction, leaving you with less time to prepare for the jumps.

Setup: Stand a rack upright 1 1/2 diamonds from the long cushion. The rack is propped up on two pieces of chalk (one on each side). The 1-ball and 2-ball are placed along the center line with the 1-ball closer to the rack.

Solution: Be sure not to swipe straight across when swiping the balls. Instead, twist your stick so the tip end goes further. This will cause the balls to separate, and the 1-ball to reach the opening of the rack faster than the 2-ball.

Adjustments: The balls will be moving from your right to left, so you will need to aim the jump shots at the right most side pocket point (left point in the diagram). The momentum of the moving balls will bring them into the center of the pocket. You will need to judge how fast the balls are moving to determine how far to aim away from center pocket.

8.8: Lefty Righty Juggle

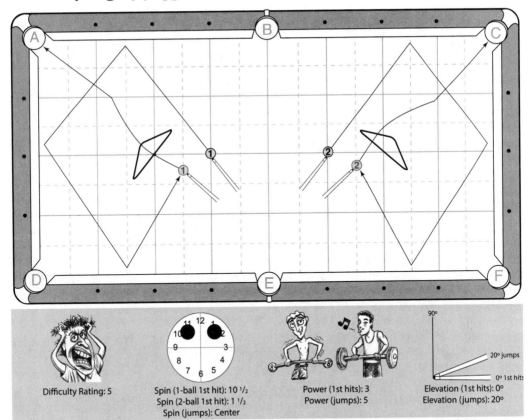

Difficulty Rating: 5	Spin (1-ball 1st hit): 10 ½ Spin (2-ball 1st hit): 1 ½ Spin (jumps): Center	Power (1st hits): 3 Power (jumps): 5	Elevation (1st hits): 0° Elevation (jumps): 20°

The *Lefty Righty Juggle* was created by Nick Nikolaidis, the 2010 Masters Trick Shot Champion and a four-time winner of the ESPN World Cup of Trick Shots as a member of Team Europe. Shoot the 1-ball three cushions around the rack, right-handed. Shoot the 2-ball three cushions around the other rack, left-handed. Next, jump the 1-ball through the opening into corner pocket 'A', right-handed, then jump the 2-ball into pocket 'C', left-handed.

Setup: Two racks are standing upright, at about 45 degrees to the table. Both are centered at the spots. The 1-ball and 2-ball are at the intersection of the center line and each third diamond line.

Solution: You can use a full length jump cue or standard cue since you are only jumping over the edge of the rack (approximately ¼ inch). However, I still prefer to use a standard jump cue because it is shorter, which makes it easier to switch hands. You need to get the approach angles off the third rail just right so that the balls are not too close or too far from the racks as they come around the table.

Adjustments: Missing the jump shots can be solved by aiming at the short rail corner pocket points when jumping, allowing the momentum of the balls to adjust the line into the center of the pocket. Another common error is having the 2-ball stop short of the opening of the rack. If you are a righty, this means that the 2-ball is being hit with your opposite hand, so you will need to hit it a little harder so that it will have enough speed to come around for a clean jump through the rack.

8.9: Easy Button

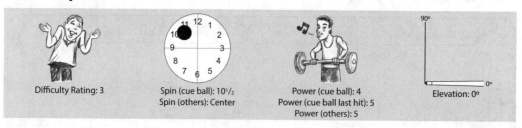

| Difficulty Rating: 3 | Spin (cue ball): 10½
Spin (others): Center | Power (cue ball): 4
Power (cue ball last hit): 5
Power (others): 5 | Elevation: 0° |

The *Easy Button* begins by shooting the cue ball around the table and then pocketing the 1-5 balls into corner pocket 'F'. Re-hit the cue ball around the table and pocket the 6-10 balls into side pocket 'E'. Re-hit the cue ball again, only this time a little harder so that it makes it all the way into the far corner pocket 'D' (probably with the help of the butt). Before it arrives, switch hands and shoot lefty to make the 11-15 balls into the same pocket.

I invented the *Easy Button* shot back in the mid-2000s, and it has since gone through several variations. The first called for juggling two cue balls. The next version required that I juggle one cue ball, but I had to alternate hands when shooting the object balls (1-ball righty, 2-ball lefty, 3-ball right, etc.) The last variation is similar to the one presented in this book, but everything must be shot one-handed and jacked up. I am working on a new variation, which will be in a future book, but only after I have used it in competition. After all, I don't want to give my opponents any hint of what might be coming down the road!

Setup: All of the balls are placed on the long center line of the table. The 5-ball on the spot and the 1-5 balls are frozen together. The 6-10 balls and 15-11 balls are frozen with the 10-ball and 15-ball sharing opposite sides of the spot. The cue ball is positioned at the center of the table, and there is a butt against the long rail to enlarge pocket 'D'. This shot got its name due to my using an 'Easy Button' as the obstacle, and it is placed one ball-width away from the 5-ball. Any obstacle will do (a piece of chalk, another ball, etc.)

Solution: The key is to hit the cue ball hard enough so that it just makes it past the center of the table after it has travelled three rails. If the cue ball is hit properly, you should have plenty of time to shoot the balls into the pockets. On the last shot, be sure to hit the cue ball short so that it hits the butt because this gives you the most time to pocket those last five balls.

Tips: There are no adjustments other than the speed of the cue ball. If the last hit is made at the proper speed, the cue ball should always go into the pocket because of the butt. You can try this shot without switching hands for the last five balls, but I actually find it easier to switch because then I don't have to stretch to make them.

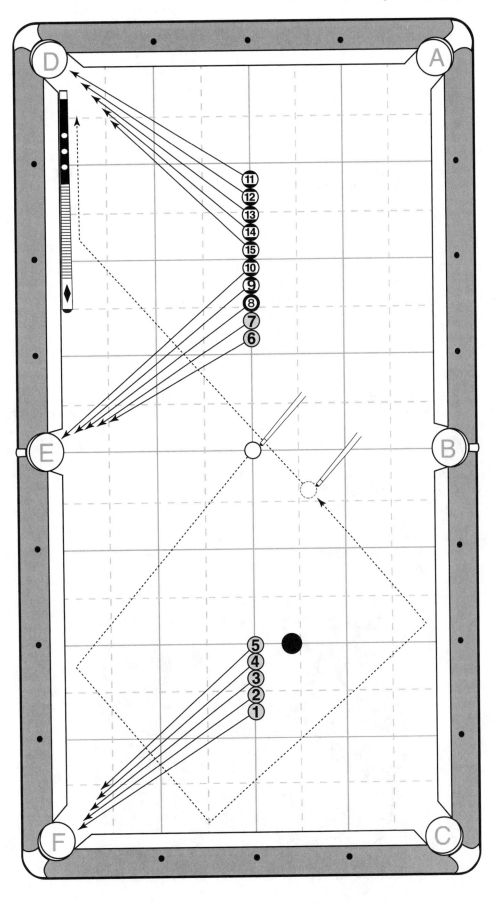

8.10: Down the Line

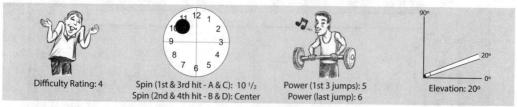

| Difficulty Rating: 4 | Spin (1st & 3rd hit - A & C): 10 1/2
Spin (2nd & 4th hit - B & D): Center | Power (1st 3 jumps): 5
Power (last jump): 6 | Elevation: 20° |

Down the Line is one of my own inventions, which I introduced at the 2013 Masters Trick Shot Championship during the Allen Hopkins Super Billiards Expo in Edison, NJ. The objective is to jump the cue ball through each rack in order, causing it to travel three cushions. The jump shot through the last rack takes the cue ball directly into the corner pocket. We had an award for 'Most Creative Shot', which is decided by a vote of the full field of players. Almost half the players voted for this one, winning me the medal.

Setup: Stand four racks in an upright position. Their centers are each aligned with the long center line of the table and the 1/2 diamond markers (2 1/2, 3 1/2, 3 1/2, 2 1/2). The racks are also aligned at approximately 45 degrees to the table, in alternating directions. The cue ball ('A') is positioned fairly close to the first rack.

Solution: Even though you are only jumping over the edge of the rack (probably 1/4 inch), I advise that you over-elevate for this first shot. You want the cue ball to lose speed as it goes around the table and as it is approaching the second rack. If it is rolling too fast you will have problems with the second jump. Apply this same principle to the second and third jump. For the fourth jump, just hit it hard and directly at corner pocket 'C'. I prefer to use a full length break/jump cue because it helps me to reach some of the jump shots. If you use a standard jump cue, you may find yourself stretching for shots, which increases the difficulty.

Adjustments: Try just the first jump and make sure that the cue ball comes directly toward the center of the second rack. If not, change your starting position and aim point. Now add the second jump and aim at a point on the long cushion. If the cue ball comes around perfectly for the third rack, go with it. Otherwise, reset the shot and try a different aiming point for the second jump shot. The third jump shot is tricky, and you may need to hit the cue ball with extra English and curve it a little for it to be in position to jump through the last rack and into the pocket. I try to aim long (near the first diamond) with extra left English.

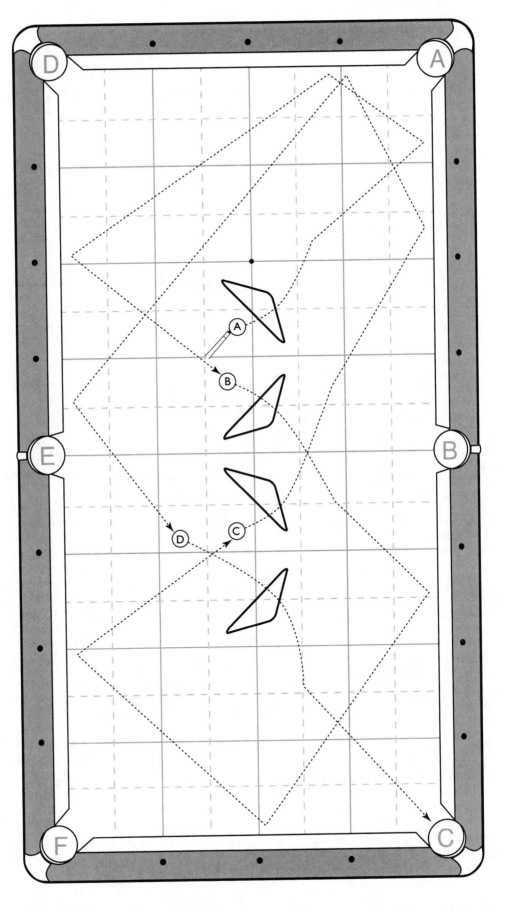

8.11: Slalom

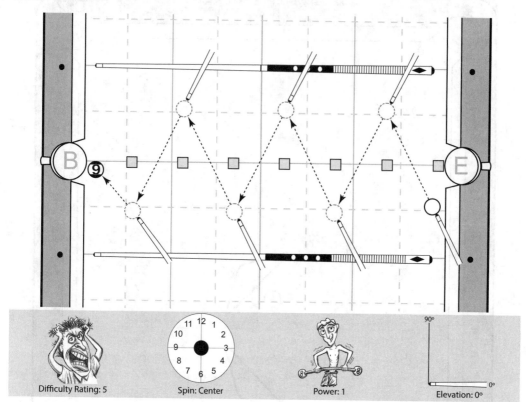

Difficulty Rating: 5   **Spin: Center**   **Power: 1**   **Elevation: 0°**

To play the *Slalom*, shoot the cue ball one-handed (lefty) through the opening created by the first two chalks. Re-hit the cue ball one-handed (righty) through the opening between the second and third pieces of chalk. Repeat this back-and-forth until you finally hit the cue ball for a seventh time and pocket the 9-ball.

The *Slalom* was actually invented by three people. In the first World Cup of Trick Shots in 2006, Bruce Barthelette and I created a similar shot, but it was done as partners (it is called "Bruce's Weave", and it appears later in the book). I would stand on one side while Bruce was on the other, but instead of switching hands, we would hit the cue ball back and forth to each other. The following year at Trick Shot Magic, I came up with a way to make this shot by myself for this individual competition. It was essentially the same shot included in this book, but I held two cue sticks, one in each hand, and volleyed the cue ball back and forth. The following year, Nick Nikolaidis came up with the shot you see here, using only one cue stick, which is transferred from hand to hand.

Setup: Start with a piece of chalk on the center line and whose edge is even with the pocket cut (where you are standing next to pocket 'E'). Six additional pieces of chalk are positioned along the center line, each at a three ball-width gap from the previous one. Hang the 9-ball at the far side pocket 'B' and place two jump cues along each third diamond line as shown.

Solution: I prefer to use a jump cue because that makes it easier to shift the cue back and forth between both hands. I also shift my body left and right so I can get a nice, solid hit on the cue ball. Speed is critical, and you can allow the cue ball to come close to the cue sticks before hitting it. This gives you the most time to set up for the next hit, and you will be able to hit the cue ball when it is travelling the slowest.

Tips: What makes this shot so hard is the unsteady grip you have on the cue stick. I like to hold the stick only 4 or 5 inches from the tip because this gives me a solid grip and a steady hand to make each shot.

9: Stroke Shots

The *Stroke Shots* chapter contains shots that require the use of extreme spin, so you must have a good stroke. These are great shots for the audience because the cue ball typically changes direction unexpectedly. When I'm performing for a crowd that doesn't play pool very well (i.e. a trade show or an expo hall), I usually pick the easier (high percentage) shots because they are only interested in seeing balls go in the pocket. However, these *stroke shots* are great when performing at a pool room for a more advanced audience, because even if I come close but miss, the crowd still appreciates the amount of skill involved in putting that amount of stroke on the ball.

During a free-style competition in Las Vegas, I was in the practice room working on a shot by Dave Nangle. It was a stroke shot where I had a line of five balls (four plus the cue ball), and I had to stroke through all of them and make the cue ball draw back and pocket something else. The trouble was that the cue ball kept flying off the table and, after it landed, it still had a ton of spin. That gave me an idea: I set up the shot toward the side pocket. I was now trying to make all of the object balls in the side, and then have the cue ball jump forward over the pocket and table, and onto the floor! The cue ball would then spin backward under the table, hit a combination I had set up on the floor (near my feet), and make a ball roll into a plastic cup. I must have worked on this shot for an hour when Dave came up and was wondering what I was doing. I was halfway through recapping the situation with his shot, and my idea for a new one, when he reminded me that in that tournament, no balls are allowed to fly off the table. Oops!!!

9.1: Rendezvous Fouette

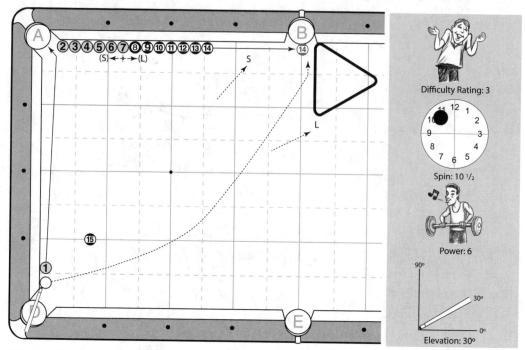

The *Rendezvous Fouette* is the brainchild of Sebastian Giumelli. He always seems to come up with the prettiest shots, and this one is no exception. The artistry begins when you shoot the 1-ball into corner pocket 'A'. The 1-ball will carom off the 2-ball, causing the 14-ball to travel up the rail, hit the rack, and sit in front of the side pocket. The cue ball will curve around the blocker ball and pocket the 14-ball, possibly using the rack as a guide.

When I shoot this shot, the cue ball usually swings way out, almost to the second diamond, before diving toward the rack. At the 2013 Masters Trick Shot Championship, I moved the blocker out near the second diamond to see if the other players could meet the challenge. The first match I tried the harder version was against Jim Glanville, a friend and competitor from Massachusetts. He made it on his first attempt, foiling my plot to win a point. In truth, I half expected him to make it since he is a very good player.

Setup: The cue ball and the 1-ball are frozen to the cushion, and the back edge of the cue ball is placed even with the pocket point. There is a 1/4 inch gap between the two balls. The 2-14 balls are frozen in line and to the cushion, and the 2-ball is overlapping the pocket slightly. The blocker ball is placed four ball-widths from the cushion along the first diamond line, and the rack is placed near the side pocket as shown.

Solution: Make sure the 2-ball is positioned so the 1-ball cannot go into the pocket without hitting it. Just don't move it too far into the pocket or else the 1-ball will double kiss it and bounce back out. Aim at the sixth ball in the line (the 7-ball), elevate your cue stick, and use top left English.

Adjustments: If the cue ball is hitting the blocker, you are probably double hitting it. Aim more to the right, or use more left English. Another common mistake is to have the cue ball miss short 'S' or long 'L'. Adjust by changing the elevation on your cue stick. If you miss long, the cue ball isn't curving enough, so elevate more. If the cue ball curves too much and the shot is missing short, decrease the elevation of your cue. Another solution is to change your line of aim. For example, if you are missing long, aiming more to the left (possibly at the fifth ball). This will keep the cue ball from swinging out as much before it begins curving to the left.

9.2: Zig Zag

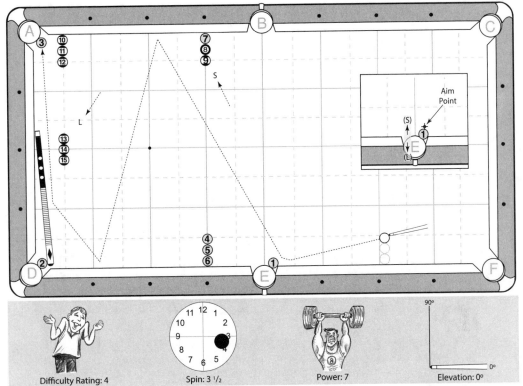

Difficulty Rating: 4   Spin: 3 ½   Power: 7   Elevation: 0°

The *Zig Zag*, which is one of Mike Massey's creations, made its first appearance at the 2007 ESPN Trick Shot Magic competition. It is a very pretty shot and it is still used today in the Artistic Pool Shot Program. Start by making the 1-ball in side pocket 'E'. The cue ball will zig zag across the table, hit the butt, make the 2-ball, and then travel across the table to sink the 3.

Setup: Hang the 1-ball in side pocket 'E' and freeze it to the point. Place the 2 and 3 balls in the jaws as shown, and position a butt against the 2-ball, angled slightly into the rail. Twelve blocker balls are frozen in four separate lines which run parallel to the short cushions. The 4, 5, and 6 balls and the 7, 8, and 9 balls are on the third diamond line on either side of the table. The 10, 11, and 12 balls are ½ diamond off the short rail, near the 3-ball, and the 13, 14, and 15 balls are centered, ½ diamond off the short rail. The cue ball is behind the second diamond line, and I like to place it two ball-widths from the cushion.

Solution: Use maximum right English and a touch of draw, and aim to hit the rail first. The hit on the 1-ball determines if you will make the shot. Keep in mind that the more you aim into the rail, the thinner you will hit the 1-ball. When you use the aim point marked in the diagram (see insert), it looks like the cue ball will not hit the rail first, but remember that you are hitting this with extreme right English. The deflection will cause the cue ball to veer toward the rail – enough so that it will strike the cushion ahead of the 1-ball.

Adjustments: If the cue ball is hitting the 7, 8, and 9 balls (missing short), you need to hit the 1-ball thinner. The solution is to aim your cue more into the rail. If the cue ball going too far down table and hitting the 13, 14, and 15 balls (missing long), hit the 1-ball fuller by aiming less into the rail. Another adjustment for missing long is to use a little more draw.

9.3: Reverse Four Rail Kick

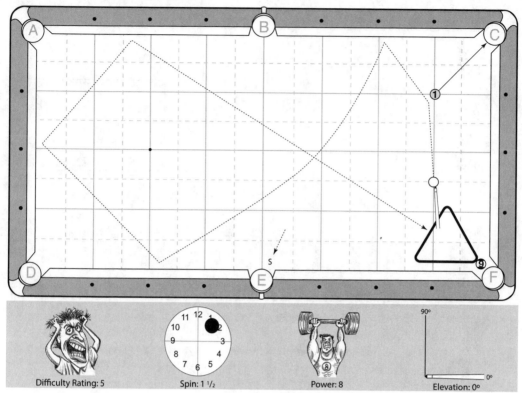

| Difficulty Rating: 5 | Spin: 1 ½ | Power: 8 | Elevation: 0° |

I am not sure who first came up with the *Reverse Four Rail Kick*, but I do know that it has been around for quite a while. Shoot the 1-ball into pocket 'C'. The cue ball will then hit the first cushion and travel three rails, hit the rack, and sink the 9-ball. You need to have a brand new table with brand new balls, or else the spin will die out too early. If your conditions do not meet these criteria, then do what we fellow trick shot artists usually do: spray the cue ball with silicone, which removes the friction and allows the spin to last much longer.

Setup: The 1-ball is placed on the 1,1 diamond intersection line. The cue ball is also on the first diamond, and it is 1 ½ diamonds from the long cushion. The 9-ball is hanging in front of pocket 'F' with a rack against it. Silicone spray is used on the cue ball.

Solution: After pocketing the 1-ball, the normal rebound angle will take the cue ball back toward side pocket 'E', but you can bend the path of the cue ball by hitting it with top spin. The right English doesn't have much effect on the first rail (where it is considered reverse English), but once the cue ball gets to the second rail, it turns into running English, and that helps to propel the cue ball around the table.

Adjustments: If the cue ball hits the side pocket after banking one rail (missing short), use more top spin. This extra top spin will cause the cue ball to curve more, so that it will now miss going in the side pocket. Since you need to make the 1-ball, you cannot adjust by aiming for a fuller hit. Missing long is very uncommon, but if that happens, hit the cue ball with less top spin. Most failures occur because the cue ball runs out of steam before it gets to the rack, and yet hitting it harder often doesn't work because the extra speed reduces the effect of the top spin, and you will likely scratch in the side pocket. My advice is to hit the cue ball at the same speed, but to use more right English. The running English should give the cue ball just enough kick off the rails to lengthen out the distance and to reach the rack.

9.4: Silicone Follow

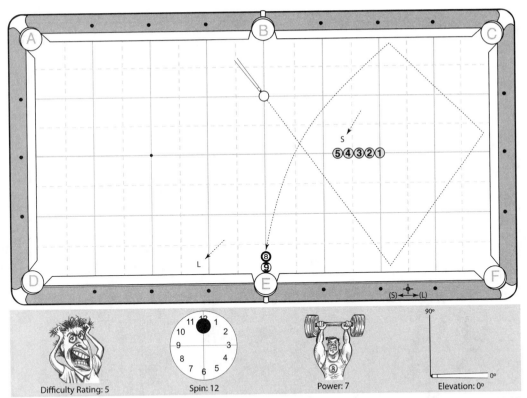

Difficulty Rating: 5   **Spin: 12**   **Power: 7**   **Elevation: 0°**

The *Silicone Follow* is one of my own inventions. The first time I performed it was in the 2010 Ultimate Trick Shot Tour Finale and it proved very successful. Here is how it goes: Shoot the cue ball three cushions, around the blocker balls, and into the combination. For a top trick shot professional, it isn't that difficult. The problem arises, however, when the shooter is playing it for the very first time because he must figure out the exact aim point, angle, and power – and that is tough to do in only three attempts.

Setup: The cue ball is located one diamond from the side pocket, on the center line. Five blocker balls are frozen to each other. The lineup starts on the spot and extends up the center line of the table. The 8-9 combination is hanging in the side pocket. Silicone is sprayed on the cue ball.

Solution: The 1-5 balls block the natural three cushion bank, so you need to make the cue ball bend sharply after it hits the third rail. Start by aiming at the 1 1/2 diamond marker, and use a lot of top spin. That angle would normally send the cue ball beyond the combination so that it would hit 1-1 1/2 diamonds past pocket 'E'. However, the top spin should alter the path of the cue ball enough so that it curves it into the combo.

Adjustments: If you miss long, use more top spin. You can also hit the shot a little softer so the spin kicks in sooner, or try aiming at the 1 3/4 diamond mark. If you miss short, you probably ran into the blocker balls. You can fix this by aiming further down the table (closer to pocket 'F').

9.5: Hood Variation

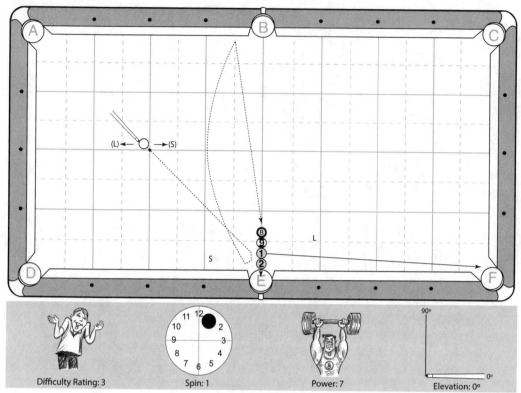

Difficulty Rating: 3	Spin: 1	Power: 7	Elevation: 0°

The *Hood Variation* calls for shooting to make the 1-ball in corner pocket 'F', and the 2-ball into side pocket 'E'. The cue ball will carom off the 1-ball, bank back and forth across the table, and into the 8-9 combination. I am not quite sure of the origin of this shot, but I do know that it is a variation of a famous shot from the early 1900's, and that it comes from the Joe Hood book. When I perform at a show, a member of the audience will usually tell me about a shot setup just like this, but where all four balls go into different pockets (1-ball in the same corner, 2-ball in the same side, 9-ball long banking one rail into corner pocket 'D', and the 8-ball going into the opposite side pocket). After performing the requested shot, I like to follow-up with this one, which looks exactly the same, but has a very different result.

Setup: Four balls are lined up along the center line, all frozen to each other. Start by placing the 2-ball with the edge even with the pocket cut. The cue ball is positioned behind the long center line, and I prefer for it to be located just behind the spot.

Solution: Aim to hit only the 1-ball, being sure to miss the 9-ball. Use top right English, with more top than right. The right English will pull the cue ball back after it hits the first rail, and the top will make the cue ball curve forward, adjusting its path so that it hits the combination. You will need to play around with your hit on the 1-ball and the English to achieve the desired effect.

Adjustments: If you miss short, the cue ball is not curving enough. The solution is to aim for a thinner hit on the 1-ball. Alternatively, try starting the cue ball further down table (closer to the short rail, further from the balls). This gives additional forward momentum to the cue ball, helping it to curve more. If the cue ball is curving too much and is missing long, shift its starting position in the opposite direction, hit the 1-ball fuller, or possibly use a little more right English.

9.6: Double Kiss Follow

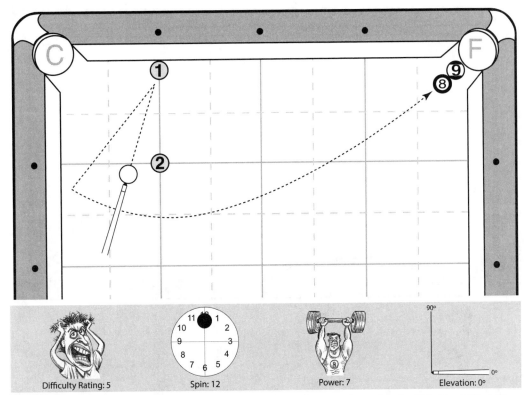

Difficulty Rating: 5   Spin: 12   Power: 7   Elevation: 0°

The *Double Kiss Follow* is a tough one, so when it was first put into the Artistic Pool Shot Program, nobody selected it. After a while, I decided to start practicing it, and once I found the proper alignment and stroke, I found that I was making it 40-50% of the time. At the 2011 World Artistic Pool Championships, I selected it for the first time in the playoffs, and this one neglected shot helped me to secure my second World Championship title! The cue ball will double kiss off the 1-ball, curve around the 2, and make the combination.

Setup: The 1-ball is frozen to the cushion at the first diamond. The 2-ball is at the 1,1 diamond intersection. The 8-9 combo is hanging in the pocket. Though you have cue ball in hand, it must be positioned at least one diamond from the short rail. I prefer to place it right behind the first diamond line, two to three ball-widths from the cushion.

Solution: Shoot the cue ball straight into the 1-ball with lots of top spin, and be sure to hit it hard enough so that it double kisses past the 2-ball. With enough top spin, the cue ball will curve forward and make the combination.

Adjustments: If the cue ball double kisses back too far and doesn't curve enough, aim for a slightly thinner hit on the 1-ball (to the left). Similarly, if the cue ball doesn't bounce back enough, hit the 1-ball fuller (to the right). Sometimes you must adjust the cue ball's starting point. Remember, the further from the rail that you place the cue ball, the more double kiss you will get.

9.7: Circular Follow Pinball

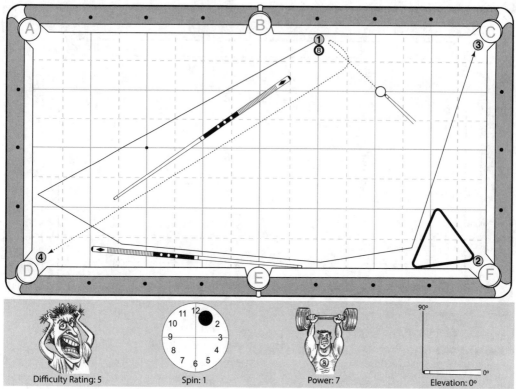

| Difficulty Rating: 5 | Spin: 1 | Power: 7 | Elevation: 0° |

The *Circular Follow Pinball* is another beautiful shot by Mike Massey. I avoid using it in my shows because it takes a while to set up, but it is a great selection when I'm in a competition. Actually, during some shows I will bring this shot out when things are winding down and a few players are still hanging around the pool table as I am packing up. I don't have to worry about the set up time since I am not in the middle of a routine. Here is how it is played: Shoot into the 1-ball, sending it two rails and into the stick. The 1-ball will ride down the stick, hit the rack (making the 2-ball), and carom off it to eventually make the 3-ball. In the meantime, the cue ball will curve around the 8-ball, hit the diagonal stick (optional), and pocket the 4-ball.

Setup: The 1-ball is frozen to the cushion at the third diamond, and the 8-ball is frozen to the 1 and is straight out from it. Hang the 3-ball in pocket 'C', and then hang the 2-ball in front of pocket 'F' with a rack against it. Make sure that the edge of the rack is pointing at the 3-ball. The 4-ball is also hanging in the jaws of pocket 'D'. Place one stick against the long rail, and the other cue should be aligned from the 8-ball to the 4-ball. It helps if this diagonal cue is shorter (such as a jump or massé cue). You have cue ball in hand, but it must be placed at least one diamond from the 1-ball. I like to place it along the first diamond from the long rail, and right behind the second diamond line.

Solution: Cue using top right English (more top than right). The right English will pull the cue ball back beyond the 8-ball, and the top spin will help it to curve into the cue stick.

Adjustments: If the 1-ball banks two rails and hits the diagonal stick, adjust the cue ball's starting position further away from the long rail. If the 1-ball banks two rails and misses the long rail stick, or hits the 4-ball, move the cue ball closer to the long rail.

9.8: Force It Back

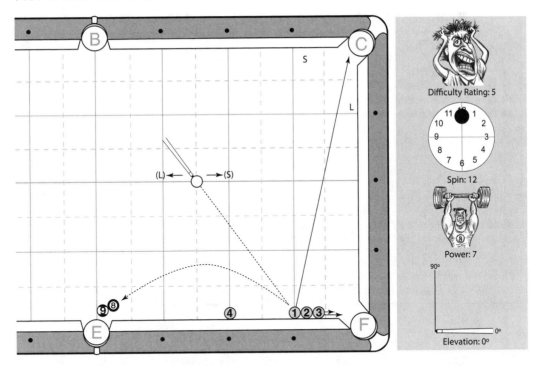

I don't know the origin of the *Force It Back* shot, but I do know that I have seen it before; never actually performed, but written up as a diagram. In trick shot competitions, I am the first person to ever attempt it (which I made, thank you very much). Shoot into the 1-ball and make balls 1, 2, and 3. The 1-ball banks into corner pocket 'C', and the 2 and 3 balls go directly pocket 'F'. The cue ball then double kisses back and around the 4-ball on its way to pocketing the 8-9 combo.

Setup: The 1, 2, and 3 balls are frozen in line and to the cushion, with the 1-ball positioned at the first diamond. The 4-ball is frozen to the cushion at the second diamond. The 8-9 combo is hanging in the jaws, and the cue ball is placed on the long center line of the table, 2 1/2 diamonds up from the short cushion.

Solution: Shoot the cue ball straight into the 1-ball. The momentum of the oncoming cue ball causes both the 2 and 3 balls to force their way into the pocket, and it also makes the 1-ball push through slightly and at an angle into the opposite corner. The double kiss on the cue ball must be hard enough to send it back past the 4-ball before the top spin kicks in and bends its path toward the 8-ball, making the combo.

Adjustments: Controlling the cue ball is accomplished by adjusting the top spin. The more top spin you use, the further and quicker the cue ball will curve into the rail. The most common miss is on the 1-ball. If it is missing long 'L', move the cue ball closer to the short rail to reduce the force. And, if the 1-ball is missing short 'S', move the cue ball further from the short cushion.

9.9: Resistance Jump

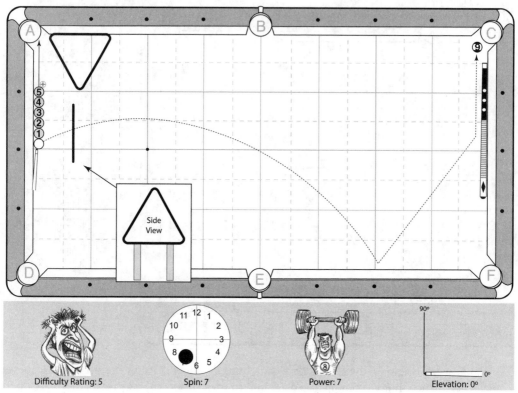

| Difficulty Rating: 5 | Spin: 7 | Power: 7 | Elevation: 0° |

The *Resistance Jump* requires that you shoot and make all five balls into the corner pocket, jump the cue ball through the rack, make it spin back, and then bank one rail into the butt, pocketing the 9-ball. Luke Szywala (Poland) and I combined to create this monster. Luke invented a similar shot where everything is the same, only you jump the cue ball over a row of balls, not a rack elevated by plastic cups. He demonstrated his version at a competition in Kiev, Ukraine back in 2003 and I modified it after being invited to Trick Shot Magic.

I first used the *Resistance Jump* (Luke's version) on television against Mike Massey, and he went up to Luke afterwards and laughed about how he should have paid more attention to the shot while we were all in Kiev. I later found when practicing it that my cue ball would jump very high into the air, so I naturally wanted to find a way to force everyone else to do that. So, I added the rack for the 2008 Ultimate Trick Shot Tour Finale in Las Vegas. The other players were making the first version, but they had a difficult time with the higher barrier – except for Bruce Barthelette, who was the only player in that competition to make the shot.

Setup: The 1-5 balls and the cue ball are frozen in line, and to the cushion. The end ball is at the first diamond. The 9-ball is in the jaws of pocket 'C'. A butt is placed against the short rail near the 9-ball. A rack increases the effective size of corner pocket 'A', and another rack is propped up on two plastic cups. The center of the rack is even with the ball next to the cue ball, and the cups are between two and three ball-widths from the setup.

Solution: Place your bridge on the rail, aim away from the cushion, and use 7 English. Stroke right through the cue ball, and be sure not to poke at it or else it will not jump. Force through the ball so it has nowhere to go but up.

Tips: The most common miss happens when the cue ball does not jump high enough to go through the rack. You just have to get a feel for it. Try replacing the upright rack with a line of balls about two ball-widths from the setup (this is Luke's version). You will not need to jump nearly as high, so you should have more success.

9.10: 2mm Gate Draw

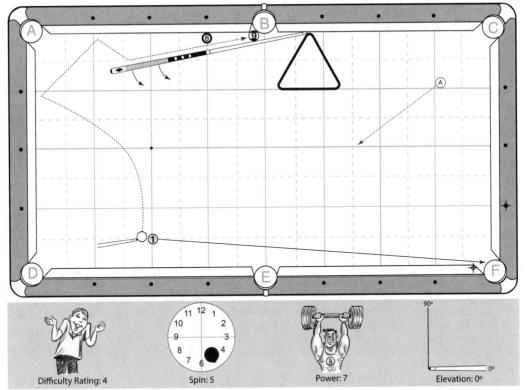

Difficulty Rating: 4	Spin: 5	Power: 7	Elevation: 0°

The *2mm Gate Draw* begins by pocketing the 1-ball into corner pocket 'F'. Draw the cue ball two rails, and hit the stick so that it swings it out, allowing the cue ball to go around the 8-ball, and then sink 9 in the side. I am not 100% sure, but I think that this is one of Mike Massey's shots. An easier version, called 'The Gate' shot starts with the cue ball at the diagonally opposite corner pocket (position 'A'). You then simply need to shoot it three rails, behind the stick. Since Mike is great with stroke shots, he added that element, making the shot much more difficult.

Setup: The 1-ball is placed on the second diamond line, about a 1/2 diamond from the cushion. The cue ball is positioned only 2mm from the 1-ball (the width of a tip tapper or clay poker chip is about right), and it is aligned at the long rail pocket point as shown. The 8-ball is frozen to the cushion at the third diamond, and the 9-ball is hanging in front of pocket 'B'. The tip end of a jump cue is up against the cushion, and a rack is holding it in place. Angle the cue so that it is one chalk-width from the 8-ball.

Solution: Aim at the first diamond on the short rail using bottom right English (more bottom than right). As you stroke through the cue ball, the angle of aim and the right English should cause the cue stick to deflect off to the right far enough to avoid the double hit on the cue ball. It helps to use a long bridge. The stroke used in this shot requires a little practice to get it just right.

Adjustments: If the 1-ball misses, adjust the alignment of the cue ball as needed. If you double hit the cue ball and it goes forward, try aiming a little more to the left, and lengthen your bridge. If the cue ball is drawing back, but not far enough, use more draw and less right spin.

9.11: Split Sticks

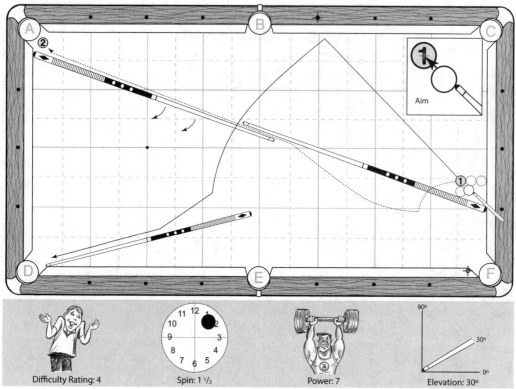

Difficulty Rating: 4   Spin: 1 ½   Power: 7   Elevation: 30°

Split Sticks is another beautiful creation by Sebastian Giumelli. Shoot the 1-ball, causing it to bank, jump over the sticks, hit the third stick, and go into the corner pocket. The cue ball will jump over the stick, curve forward and between the sticks (which were separated by the 1-ball), and eventually pocket the 2-ball. This has become one of my favorite shots and, even though it takes a little while to set up, I try to include *Split Sticks* in all of my shows. When I explain the shot to an audience, it seems impossible because the cue sticks are touching, so how in the world is the cue ball going to squeeze between them? Of course, I leave out the part about the object ball opening up the sticks as it jumps over them.

Setup: The 1-ball is positioned two balls off the cushion and one ball from the stick. The cue ball is about a ½ - ¾ inch from the 1-ball and it is aligned with the third diamond. Hang the 2-ball in front of pocket 'A'. Two adjoining sticks are at a diagonal across the table, one with the butt near the 2-ball, and the other with the end of its butt frozen to the short rail at the first diamond. The tip of a third and shorter cue is wedged into pocket 'D', and it is angled at or near the middle of the opposite short cushion.

Solution: Elevate your cue to about 30 degrees and aim at the center of the 1-ball with high right English. Stroke through the cue ball, and hit it with a little pop (similar to a jump stroke). The 1-ball should bank and, as it jumps over the cues, it will separate them. Make sure that the cue near the 2-ball is far enough away as it has a tendency to hit and make the 2-ball before the cue ball gets there.

Adjustments: Getting the cue ball to jump is the hard part. Pretend you are hitting a standard jump shot. If the cue ball jumps, but doesn't clear the stick, aim thinner on the 1-ball (more to the left). If the cue ball jumps, but doesn't curve back through the opening, aim fuller (more to the right), or add a little more side spin or elevation. Be careful when adding more side spin because this results in less top spin, which can cause the cue ball to run out of steam before it reaches the 2-ball.

9.12: Jump Fouette #1

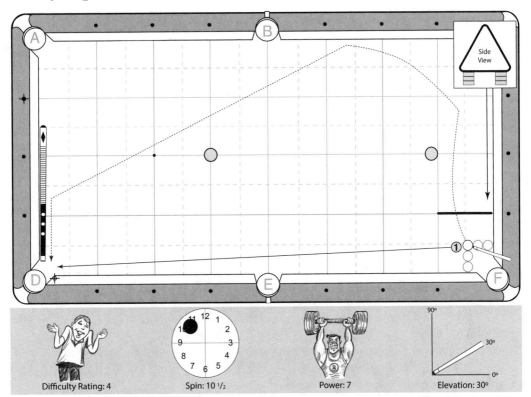

| Difficulty Rating: 4 | Spin: 10 ½ | Power: 7 | Elevation: 30° |

The *Jump Fouette #1* is one of my own creations. Although recent competitions featured numerous shots of this type, this was the one that started them all. The idea is to make the 1-ball in corner pocket 'D'. The cue ball then jumps through the rack, curves around both cups, hits the butt, and goes into the same corner pocket as the 1-ball did. When I introduced this shot in Trick Shot Magic back in the mid-2000s, I was making it about 70-80% of the time during practice. When I got to the competition, I realized that I made a typo in the write-up and said that there were four dominos under the rack when there only should have been three. This extra height was a little too much for me to retain the consistency that I need for television, so I ended up not using a shot that I felt could have earned me some points during that event.

Setup: The cue ball is placed two ball-widths off both the long rail and short rail. The 1-ball is about 1/4 inch from the cue ball, and it is aligned with the long rail pocket point. A rack is positioned along the first diamond, frozen to the rail, and propped up by three dominos. One cup is located along the center line, and its back edge is at the first diamond. The second cup is also on the center line at the third diamond as shown. A butt is up against the short rail.

Solution: Aim at the first diamond on the opposite short rail and elevate to about 30 degrees. Hit this one like a jump shot and pop the cue ball. It should jump through the rack. The top spin will make the cue ball curve around the first cup, and the left spin will kick it off the first cushion, and down the table far enough so that it clears the second cup.

Adjustments: If the cue ball is not jumping, switch to a jump cue. I use a full length jump cue (it's a break/jump cue) with a phenolic tip, which helps with the jump, and yet I am still able to get enough spin on the ball. However, it is very difficult to apply much English on the cue ball with a phenolic tip, so switch to a jump cue at your own risk.

9.13: Jump Fouette #2

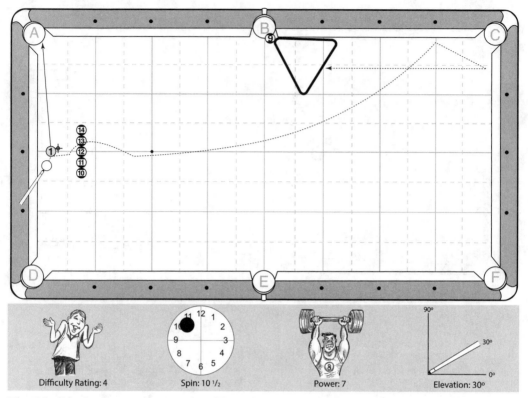

| Difficulty Rating: 4 | Spin: 10 ½ | Power: 7 | Elevation: 30° |

The 1-ball is shot into corner pocket 'A'. In the meantime, the cue ball jumps over the line of blocker balls, then curves around the rack into the long cushion, strikes the short cushion, and spins back into the rack, sinking the 9-ball. The *Jump Fouette #2* was introduced by Gabi Visoiu of Romania in 2010 at the World Cup of Trick Shots. The cue ball and cloth were so new and slippery that neither team could get the amount of left spin required to make the cue ball spin back and hit the rack. This shot is a lot easier on used cloth.

Setup: The cue ball and 1-ball are in hand, but the 1-ball is placed slightly further from the rail. You need about a ½ inch gap between the 1-ball and the cue ball. The line of blocker balls is stationed just before the first diamond line. The 9-ball is hanging in front of pocket 'B', and the rack is frozen to the cushion, and to the 9-ball.

Solution: Aim to cut the 1-ball into the corner pocket, and elevate to about 30 degrees. You must hit this with a jump stroke, so you may want to use a jump cue like I do. The top spin makes the cue ball curve around the rack, and the left spin enables the cue ball to spin back off the short cushion toward the rack.

Adjustments: Assuming the cue ball jumps over the blockers, the problem of the cue ball curving too soon can be solved by aiming more to the right (a thinner hit on the 1-ball), but this may make it necessary for you to change the starting alignment. You can also use more left spin than top. Another mishap is for the cue ball to curve around the rack it, but it fails to spin back enough after hitting the short rail (missing the rack). If this happens, use more left spin.

9.14: Last Man Spinning

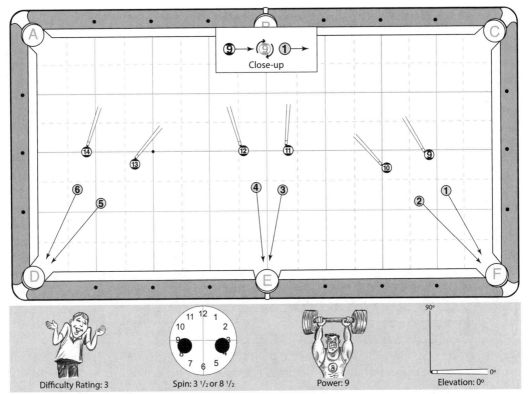

Close-up

Difficulty Rating: 3   **Spin: 3 ½ or 8 ½**   **Power: 9**   **Elevation: 0°**

The *Last Man Spinning* begins by shooting the 9-ball and making the 1-ball in pocket 'F'. Use a lot of side spin so the 9-ball spins in place after contacting the 1-ball. Repeat for the 10-ball, making the 2-ball, and so on down the line. At the conclusion of the shot, all of the stripe balls must be spinning, and no ball may contact any other, or a cushion. *Last Man Spinning* was selected by Mike Dechaine, a top professional 10-ball player, at the 2012 World Cup of Trick Shots. This was Mike's first year on Team USA, and we like to hassle the new guy a little (all in good fun), so, because the balls were all spinning, we told him that the name of this shot was 'The Ballerina'. He reluctantly agreed, but when he selected the shot in competition, he renamed it *Last Man Spinning* without telling any of us in advance. Curses, foiled again!

Setup: You have ball-in-hand for every shot, but the stripe ball must be a minimum of two ball-widths from its corresponding solid ball. Separate the balls far enough apart so that there is no danger of one getting in the way of another.

Solution: Each stripe ball is hit with extreme side spin and a touch of draw. You must use enough spin so that it lasts until you hit the 14-ball and pocket the 6. However, if you are able to put a sufficient amount of spin on each ball, you don't need to move too fast from shot to shot. The less spin and the faster you go, the greater are your chances of missing a ball.

Adjustments: The most common miss is to have one of the stripe balls get away from you by either rolling forward or backward. That can be fixed by applying more or less draw. If a ball rolls to the side and gets in the way of the next set of balls, you didn't have the balls lined up straight, or you cheated the pocket slightly (which is easy to do). Make sure that you take careful aim, and that you hit each solid ball fully in the face.

9.15: Tray Rebound

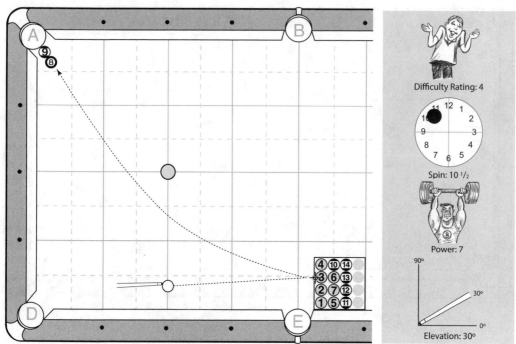

Difficulty Rating: 4

Spin: 10 1/2

Power: 7

Elevation: 30°

When I create new shots for a tournament, I always save a few for a critical moment, which usually happens in the finals (and a lot of times I'm up against Jamey Gray or Nick Nikolaidis). I don't use them in any prior matches for fear of them being seen and practiced during the off-hours by another player. Jamey and I have had candid discussions about how we invent shots specifically to use against each other. In fact, I have a few shots I designed a couple of years ago that no one has ever seen because I have not needed them - yet. The *Tray Rebound* is one of those shots that I came up with back in 2009, and I used it for the first time at the 2013 Masters Trick Shot Tournament. I still have a few tricks up my sleeve, and at some point I'll need to pull them out of the bag. I can only hope I remember how to make them. In this shot, the cue ball is shot straight into the tray, causing it to rebound back, curve around the cup, and pocket the 8-9 combination into pocket 'A'.

Setup: The cue ball is placed on the second diamond line about 1 1/2 inches from the cushion. You can use your first three fingers as a guide for measuring this gap. The 8-9 combo is hanging in front of pocket 'A', and a cup is positioned on the spot. A tray with 12 balls in it (the back row is empty) is aligned with the far side pocket point as shown. You need to use a tray with a flat side (no lip). Caution: You will likely crack some trays, as I have done many times, but this shot is worth it. Make sure to use your own ball tray, or prepare to reach into your wallet. I warned you, so don't send those angry pool room owners my way!

Solution: Aim with top left directly at the third ball from the cushion in the front row of the tray (3-ball). Elevate to about 30 degrees, and make sure to hit the cue ball hard enough so that the spin doesn't run out, or kick in too soon.

Adjustments: The higher you elevate your cue, the more the cue ball will curve. So, if the cue ball is curving into the short rail, or it is not curving enough, elevate more. Alternatively, if the cue ball is curving into the long rail, or it is hitting the cup, decrease the elevation of your cue. You can also adjust your aim point. The closer you aim to the rail, the more kiss back you will get.

10: Massé Shots

Massé shots work for crowds comprised of both amateurs and professionals. The key is in knowing which *massé* shots to perform. When I'm at a trade show or business expo, I perform the easier *massé* shots, guaranteeing that they will go in. For the more advanced crowd, any *massé* will do since that audience will understand the difficulty level of the shot. Either way, *massé* shots are always a crowd pleaser.

BE CAREFUL!!! Playing massé shots can easily rip the cloth or result in damage to your cue stick. Make sure that you use a break cloth under the cue ball at all times, and always start out by hitting the shots softer than is necessary. Get the technique down first before using full power.

One way to avoid ripping the cloth is to shoot the massé shot on the floor (say what?!?). When we were in St. Petersburg, Russia for the 2007 WPA World Artistic Pool Championship (where I won my first World Championship), some of us were hanging around in the hotel lobby one evening when I met Javier Gomez from Mexico, a current trick shot artist/player and the 2013 World Champion in the Bank/Kick Shot category. He told us of a new shot that he was working on, and then proceeded to demonstrate it in the hotel lobby (without a pool table). He placed the cue ball on the marble floor and hit a pretty good massé. The cue ball shot out quite some distance before making a hard right turn, and it almost rolled into one of the shops!

10.1: Tim's Escape

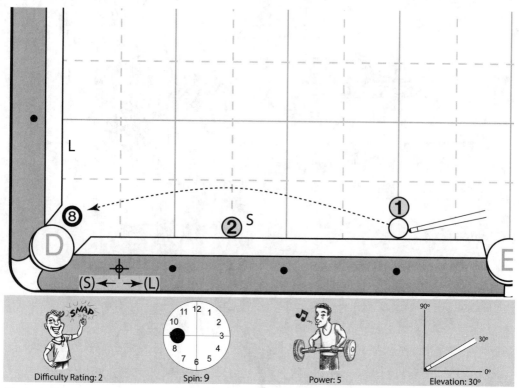

Tim's Escape is an original shot by Tim Chin, the 2010 Ultimate Trick Shot Tour Champion, and a member of Team USA in 2011 at the ESPN World Cup of Trick Shots. When Tim first invented the shot, the intent was to execute a full massé, get the cue ball to come off the rail about a diamond, and then make it curve back to pocket the hanger. As players started practicing this shot, they all found ways to make it easier (as described below). Now the objective is to shoot the cue ball out from under the 1-ball, softly curve it around the 2-ball, and make the 8-ball.

Setup: The cue ball and 1-ball are frozen in line, with the cue ball on the cushion. Both balls are positioned along the third diamond line. The 2-ball is frozen to the cushion at the 1 1/2 diamond mark. Hang the 8-ball in front of pocket 'D'. I prefer to shift the 8-ball slightly toward the short rail jaw (as shown) so the cue ball doesn't need to curve as much.

Solution: Aim 1/2 diamond up the long rail from pocket 'D' and elevate your cue to 30 degrees. If the 1-ball wasn't there, you could aim away from the rail to massé around the 2-ball. Use the same stroke, but aim into the rail. This will compress the cushion and allow the cue ball to escape without hitting the 1-ball.

Adjustments: If the cue ball hits the 2-ball (missing short - 'S'), aim more into the cushion. If the cue ball curves around the 2, but hits the short rail instead of making the 8-ball (missing long - 'L'), aim less into the cushion, or increase the elevation on your cue stick.

10.2: Around the Wall

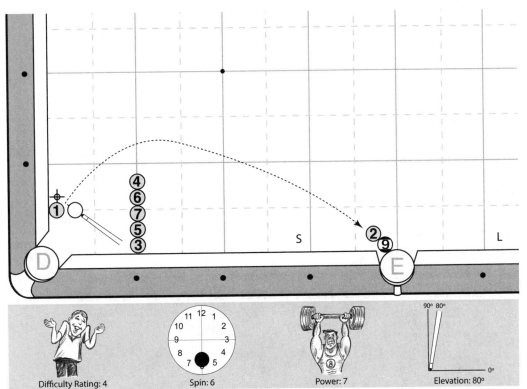

| Difficulty Rating: 4 | Spin: 6 | Power: 7 | Elevation: 80° |

Around the Wall is a pretty shot that I performed for the first time when Jamey Gray used it against me in the finals of the 2010 ESPN Trick Shot Magic competition. Massé the cue ball off of the 1-ball. It will then double kiss back (without hitting the short rail), curve around the wall of blocker balls, and sink the 2-9 combo.

Setup: The 1-ball is frozen to the cushion ¹/₂ diamond from pocket 'D'. The cue ball is placed straight out from the 1-ball, and there is a ¹/₄ - ¹/₂ inch gap between the balls. The 2-9 combo is hanging in the side, and there is a wall of five blocker balls, all frozen in line along the first diamond.

Solution: Visualize a point to the right of the 1-ball, ¹/₂ ball-width from the edge. That is your aim point. Make sure to hit it hard enough for the cue ball to pass the wall before the massé kicks in.

Adjustments: If you miss short, and possibly hit the wall, lower your cue stick elevation. This will add forward momentum to the cue ball, allowing it to travel a little further before curving. If the cue ball circles the wall and you miss short because it is still curving too soon, put a touch (very little) of right English on the ball. If you miss long, increase the elevation, or use less speed.

10.3: The Accidental Massé

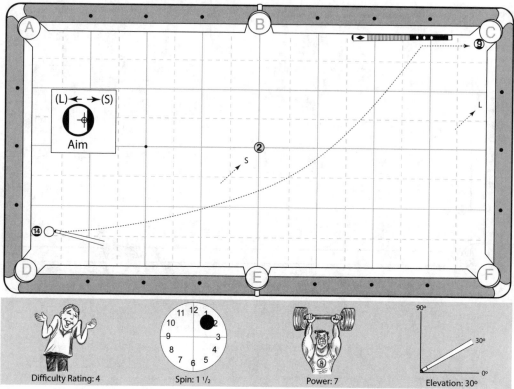

Difficulty Rating: 4   **Spin: 1 ½**   **Power: 7**   **Elevation: 30°**

The Accidental Massé is another one of those shots that I invented - by accident! I was practicing a shot that didn't require the cue ball to curve, but it did have to double kiss off a ball, travel around the table, and pocket another ball. Every once in a while I would miss hit the cue ball, and it would curve. These misses gave me the idea for this shot. The objective is to shoot the cue ball into the 14-ball, causing it to double kiss back, curve around the 2-ball, and make the 9-ball in corner pocket 'C'.

Setup: The 14-ball is frozen to the cushion ½ diamond from pocket 'D'. The cue ball is placed straight out, and there is gap that's the width of the tip of your cue. The 2-ball is located at the center point, and the 9-ball is hanging in front of pocket 'C'. A short jump cue butt is positioned against the long rail.

Solution: I use a stripe ball near the cue ball, and I place the stripe so it is perfectly aligned vertically. The right edge of the colored stripe is my aim point. Elevate to about 30 degrees and use top right English. Make sure that your bridge hand is out of the way when the cue ball shoots back at you.

Adjustments: If the cue ball curves too much and hits the 2-ball (missing short - 'S'), aim for a fuller hit on the 14-ball, which will give you more of a double kiss. If the cue ball doesn't curve enough (missing long - 'L'), aim more to the right and/or increase the elevation.

10.4: The Soft Massé

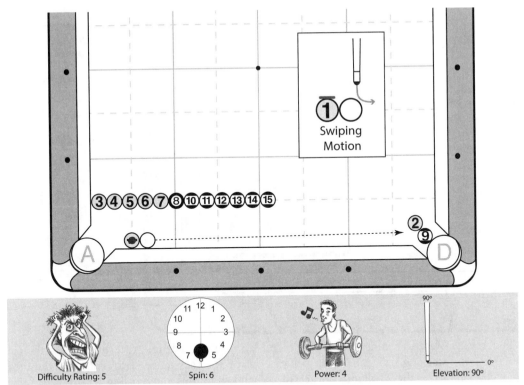

Difficulty Rating: 5   **Spin: 6**   **Power: 4**   **Elevation: 90°**

I always thought that *The Soft Massé* was Bruce Barthelette's shot, but he informed me that Eric Yow originally came up with it, and then showed it to him. Although the shot doesn't look that hard, after you try it a few times, you soon come to realize that it is one tricky little shot. Massé the cue ball into the 1-ball, and make it curve back into the 2-9 combo. The 1-ball must move, but it is not allowed to go into the corner pocket! Most massé shots are hit using a hard stroke, so it is difficult to get a lot of action on the cue ball with a soft massé stroke.

Setup: The 1-ball starts a 1/2 diamond from pocket 'A', and the cue ball is frozen to it. Both balls are frozen to the cushion. The 2-9 combo is hanging in front of pocket 'D'. The row of 12 blocker balls positioned along the 1/2 diamond line forces you to shoot directly into the 1-ball. A coin is balanced on top of the 1-ball to indicate of whether or not it moved. When you play the shot, the coin must fall.

Solution: Do not use a standard massé stroke or else the 1-ball will topple into pocket 'A'. Use a swiping motion with your cue (see close-up). This will create less force into the 1-ball, and yet it will still give you enough momentum to send the cue ball across the table and into the combo.

Adjustments: The most common miss is to make the 1-ball. Try angling your cue stick away from the 1-ball and toward the combination (which is the opposite of a normal massé). This should reduce the force that's going into the 1-ball.

10.5: Stacked Massé

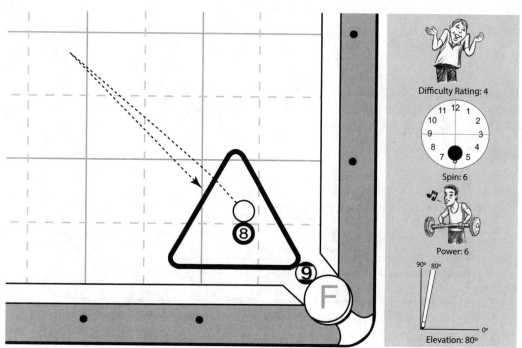

Difficulty Rating: 4

Spin: 6

Power: 6

Elevation: 80°

The *Stacked Massé* was concocted in my secret lab on Long Island. You must massé the cue ball off the stacking ball, causing it to jump out of the rack, curve back and into the rack, which then pushes the 9-ball into pocket 'F'. When I shoot this, the 8-ball rolls slightly forward, however, when I have seen others try it, the 8-ball has slammed into the edge of the rack. The problem when this happens is that the rack will move away from the 9-ball, and the impact of the cue ball when it returns may not be enough to slide the rack back into the 9-ball. Sometimes I'll move the stacking ball forward, to about an inch from the edge of the rack. This makes the jump easier, but if my opponent causes the 8-ball to move too fast, he will likely not make the shot.

Setup: Hang the 9-ball in front of pocket 'F' and place a rack against it. A stacker ball is placed within the rack, and the cue ball is balanced on top of it.

Solution: Aiming is the key. Aim straight out, and use absolutely no side English. Don't follow through too much because hitting the stacking ball with your cue will send it into the top edge of the rack, causing it to move. If this happens, the 9-ball may not fall when the cue ball comes back and hits the rack. You don't need to hit this shot very hard.

Adjustments: If the cue ball curves to the left or right, you accidentally applied some left or right English. If the cue ball fails to clear the rack, lower your stick's elevation, which will increase the cue ball's forward momentum.

10.6: Upside Down Massé

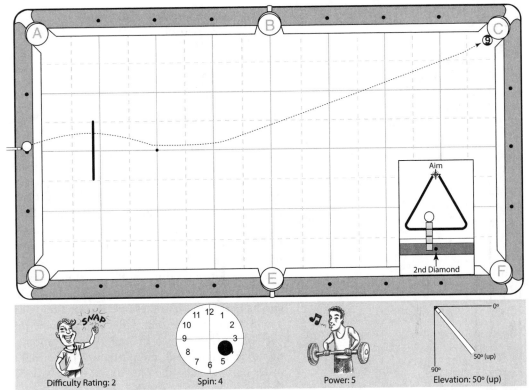

| Difficulty Rating: 2 | Spin: 4 | Power: 5 | Elevation: 50° (up) |

Kneel down and shoot the cue ball up and through the rack. It will then curve to pocket the 9-ball. I invented the *Upside Down Massé* for my first televised trick shot competition, which was in 2003 at the Trick Shot Magic tournament in Baltimore, MD. Bogdan Wolkowski from Poland dropped out due to an injury, and I was called six days before the tournament started. My first match was against Stefano Pelinga, a veteran who played in this competition two or three times before. On both of his attempts, he mistakenly put left English on the cue ball, which made it curve away from the hanger. After I won that match and I was in the semi-finals against Charles Darling, another veteran, he stood behind me as I shot this to see what kind of English I used. He got it right, but fortunately for me, he hit the shot too hard both times, and I was able to pick up a point on him.

Setup: Hang the 9-ball in pocket 'C'. Stand a rack upright, center it at the second diamond, and position it four ball-widths from the cushion. A stack of four pieces of chalk is placed on the rail one inch to the left of the middle diamond. The cue ball sits on top of these chalks.

Solution: If this were a normal massé shot, you would hit it with left English. However, since you are shooting in an upwards direction, you need to use right English. Aim directly at the top point of the rack. It helps to use a shorter cue. I use a massé cue, but you can use a jump cue with a leather tip. A shorter cue enables you to achieve greater elevation because it does not extend far enough to reach the floor.

Adjustments: Speed is the critical element. Get a feel for how hard to hit this shot so you don't hit the rack. If the cue ball is not curving enough, lower your cue so you can hit 'up' on the cue ball even more. Also try using more side English. If the cue ball is curving too much (not a common problem), take some English off the cue ball, or decrease the angle at which you are aiming 'up'.

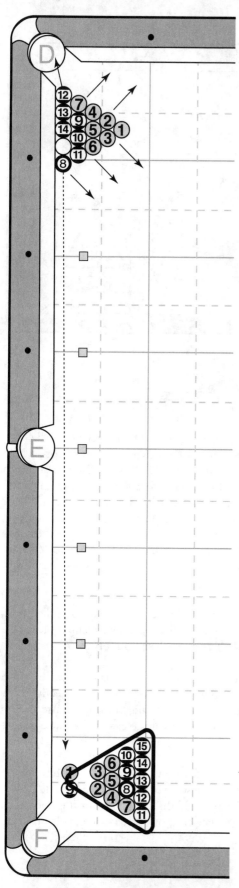

10.7: Bogdan's Massé

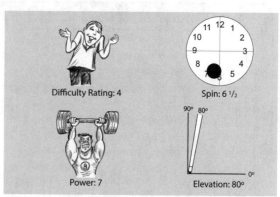

Difficulty Rating: 4

Spin: 6 ½

Power: 7

Elevation: 80°

Bogdan's Massé gets its name from its creator, Bogdan Wolkowski. The version in this book is not his invention, but the concept of doing a massé when the cue ball is stuck in the rack is his idea. Eric Yow introduced me to this version during a Trick Shot Magic competition. If you massé the cue ball correctly, it will escape the rack of balls. The 8-ball will move out of the way, allowing the cue ball to shoot down the rail, hit the combination, pocket the 9-ball, and push the 1-ball into the other balls, causing the rack to fall down around them!

Setup: The 12-ball's edge is positioned even with the pocket point. The cue ball is the second ball in the last row. Another rack of balls sits at the other end of the table, with the lead ball offset so as to prop up the rack. The 9-ball is frozen to this lead ball, making a combination into corner pocket 'F'. Five pieces of chalk are placed 1 ½ ball-widths from the long cushion at each diamond line.

Solution: Aim the massé parallel to the cushion. Use a little bit of side English into the rail so that the cue ball will hug the cushion instead of floating away. The cue stick pushes through the cue ball and it then grazes the 8-ball, causing it to move diagonally away from the cushion (as shown by the arrow), clearing the way for the cue ball.

Tips: The weight of the balls around the cue ball helps with the massé, so don't hit this one too hard. Adjust your aim point on the cue ball until you get that end ball (the 8-ball) to clear away. To play a simpler version, remove the rack of balls at the other end of the table and place a ball hanging in the pocket.

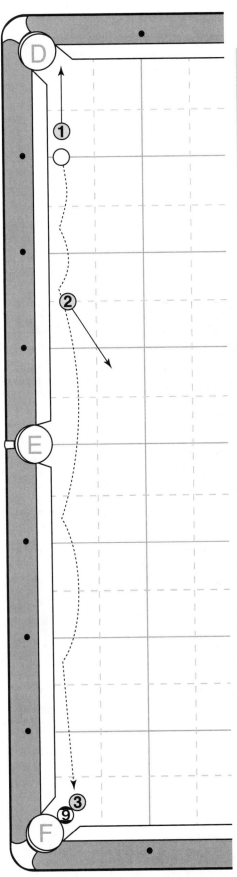

10.8: Silicone Ball

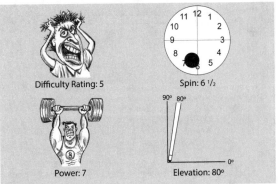

Difficulty Rating: 5   Spin: 6 ½

Power: 7   Elevation: 80°

Massé the cue ball so that you will make the 1-ball in pocket 'D'. The cue ball will reverse its course, come back, and hit the 2-ball, sending it away from the rail. When hit correctly, the cue ball will retain enough spin to cause it to massé again and travel down the table to make the 3-9 combo. While the *Silicone Ball* shot requires that you spray silicone on the cue ball, that step is not necessary if you are playing on brand new equipment, and if you have a very good massé stroke. There are a few players who can make this shot, so when I run up against one of them in a competition, I will execute it without using the silicone, relying more on my massé stroke. One or two of my peers can still make this without the silicone, so I have to be careful not to use it against them.

Setup: The cue ball is placed an inch off the cushion at the first diamond. The 1-ball is located a ½ inch from the cue ball, and the edge of the two balls runs parallel to the cushion. The 2-ball is placed at the 2 ½ diamond marker, and is about ½ ball-width from the rail. The 3-9 combination is hanging in front of pocket 'F'.

Solution: Aim at the center of the 1-ball. You need a lot of elevation, but less than 90 degrees. Use a little side English so that the cue ball will hug the rail, and the English will also pull the cue ball back into the rail after contacting the 2. Spraying silicone on the cue ball is optional, as already explained above.

Adjustments: The most common error comes when elevating the cue. Most players lean over and angle the cue so that it is pointing back into the cushion. This causes the cue ball to hit the rail and then to bounce away from it. The key is to keep your cue parallel to the cushion.

10.9: Speed Massé

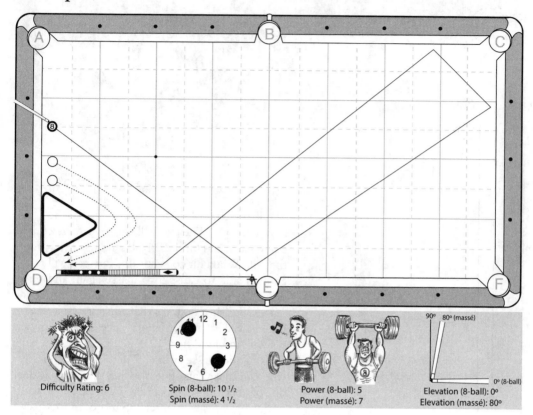

| Difficulty Rating: 6 | Spin (8-ball): 10 ½
Spin (massé): 4 ½ | Power (8-ball): 5
Power (massé): 7 | Elevation (8-ball): 0°
Elevation (massé): 80° |

I created the *Speed Massé* for use in the 2007 ESPN Trick Shot Magic competition. Speed shots are my style, and I find that I can set up and shoot them with a good stroke even when I am rushed and don't have time for practice strokes. On this shot the goal is to shoot the 8-ball three cushions around the table and quickly massé both cue balls, one at a time, of course. The cue balls will go into pocket 'D' first, followed by the 8-ball.

Setup: Place a rack against the cushion and align the edge with the pocket point. A cue stick butt is wedged against the long cushion. The two cue balls are positioned between the rack and the middle diamond, and no more than one ball-width from the cushion. The 8-ball is placed on the 1 ½ diamond line.

Solution: Shoot the 8-ball short, aiming just before side pocket 'E'. Nothing is worse than making both cue balls, only to have the 8-ball come around, hit the top of the rack, and fail to drop. Believe me, I have done it.

Tips: Missing one of the two massé shots is the most common error. You don't need to worry about how much the cue balls will curve. Just put a decent massé stroke on each cue ball, and try to make them hit into the butt.

10.10: The Original Running Massé

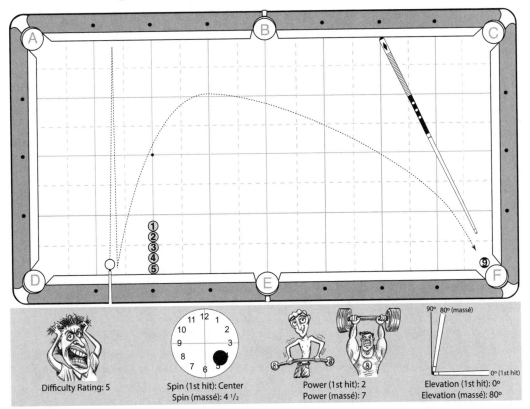

| Difficulty Rating: 5 | Spin (1st hit): Center
Spin (massé): 4 ½ | Power (1st hit): 2
Power (massé): 7 | Elevation (1st hit): 0°
Elevation (massé): 80° |

Recently on television, a few shots have required the player to massé the cue ball while it is rolling. The *Original Running Massé* is the first of this family of shots, and it was invented by Bruce Barthelette for the 2007 World Cup of Trick Shots. Shoot the cue ball back and forth across the table. After the cue ball passes the top of the line of blocker balls (the 1-ball) on its return, massé it before it stops, and before it hits the long cushion so that it circles around the balls and travels down the table to pocket the 9-ball.

Setup: A line of five blocker balls is stationed along the second diamond. Hang the 9-ball in front of pocket 'F' and place a short cue across the table. The cue ball is placed near the long rail on the other side of the blockers.

Solution: Lag the cue ball so that it will barely bank and then return to where it started. Don't worry about how much massé you put on the cue ball because of the helper cue at the other end of the table. You only need a small amount of massé - just enough to pull it back after hitting the cue.

Tips: Regular massé shots are difficult enough, so you need to develop a feel for when to pull the trigger and stroke through on that second hit. Don't hit the second shot (the massé) too hard. The cue ball is coming back toward you, so just a little massé is all that is necessary.

10.11: Running Massé #2

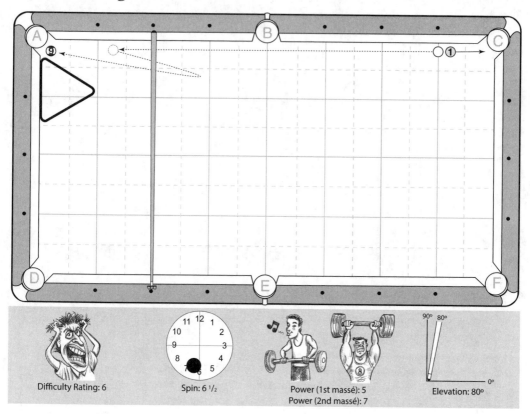

| Difficulty Rating: 6 | Spin: 6 ½ | Power (1st massé): 5
Power (2nd massé): 7 | Elevation: 80° |

The *Running Massé #2* was designed by Florian Kohler and was first seen on television at the 2010 ESPN Trick Shot Magic. This event was Florian's first ESPN competition, and he used this shot against me in the semi-finals after advancing past Stefano Pelinga in his first round match. Here is how it works: Massé the cue ball so that it makes the 1-ball in pocket 'C'. Next, run down the table and wait for the cue ball to pass the bridge. Then re-hit the rolling cue ball with another massé stroke, executing the u-turn shown in the diagram. The cue ball then goes on to pocket the 9-ball.

Setup: The cue ball is on the first diamond line, ½ inch from the cushion. The 1-ball is even with the cue ball, and it is ½ inch from it. Hang the 9-ball in front of pocket 'A', and place a rack against the short rail to enlarge the pocket. A bridge runs across the rail tops at the second diamond.

Solution: When shooting the first massé, a little side English will help the cue ball to hug the rail. Don't hit this one too hard because the faster the cue ball is rolling, the harder it will be to execute the second massé.

Tips: The *Running Massé #2* is a feel shot, so you just need to get used to exactly when to stroke through the cue ball on the second hit. You don't need to hit the second shot too hard because the cue ball has momentum working in the right direction. One trick is to not look at the 1-ball after hitting the first shot. Instead, you want to immediately run down table and prepare for the oncoming cue ball. If you keep your eye on whether or not the 1-ball goes in, you will not have enough time to get down table and prepare for the second massé.

10.12: Jump Massé

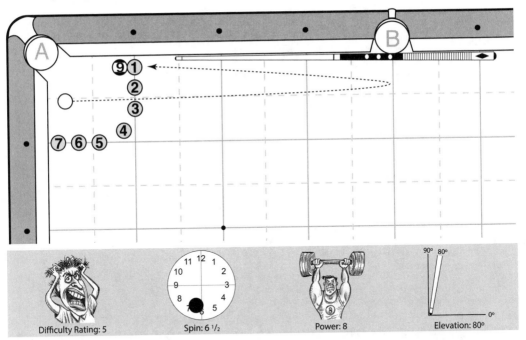

Difficulty Rating: 5   **Spin: 6 ½**   **Power: 8**   **Elevation: 80°**

I first learned the *Jump Massé* from Mike Massey in Kiev, Ukraine, at the 2003 WPA World Artistic Pool Championships. I must have practiced it 200 times while there, missing it almost every time. By the end of the tournament, I had these three things: the proper technique for making this shot, the gold medal for the massé category, and a sore shoulder! Jump the cue ball over the ring of balls. It will travel up table and then massé back along the stick to make the 1-9 combination.

Setup: Make a ring of balls from the first diamond on each rail. The 1-9 combo is slightly off the long rail, and a stick is placed against that rail to help guide the cue ball (which can be placed anywhere inside the ring of balls).

Solution: Hit this shot with a different massé stroke than usual. Use a little more pop, similar to the stroke used when playing a jump shot. Aim slightly into the rail and use a little side English. The English helps to bring the cue ball into the stick.

Adjustments: Elevating less will help you jump the cue ball, but it will remove some of the massé spin off of the shot. Try to find the right balance. If you are having trouble jumping over the ring of balls, position the cue ball so that it will jump over the gap between two of the balls. You can also get rid of the ring of balls and place a rack around the cue ball.

11: Jump Shots

Recently, a ton of different kinds of jump shots have been created for television. The elements used include speed, distance, and height. We have also started using multiple cues, but this will be covered in a later chapter. Specially designed jump cues help with distance or height. While I have never seen these cues used in a standard game of 9-ball, I imagine that they are legal since they meet the required 40 inches in length, and they have a standard phenolic tip.

Be careful when playing jump shots. You can easily rip the cloth with a jump shot, as with a massé. In fact, jump shots tend to rip the cloth more often because the cue is coming in at more of an angle. When your cue is vertical, it is less likely to dig under the cloth. The old signs saying 'No Massé Shots' should really say 'No Massé or Jump Shots'.

The shot titled 'Target Practice' (in chapter 15) is a partner shot, involving two long jumps, which was performed by myself and Bruce Barthelette during one of the ESPN World Cup of Trick Shot competitions. We each had to jump a cue ball the full table length and into a six inch hole cut out in the face of a box (which was also six inches off the table surface). 'Target Practice' was a pretty tough shot already, but we added a little spice by covering the holes with pictures of the television announcers, Mitch Laurance and Allen Hopkins. They had a good time doing commentary on that episode, and Bruce and I are still waiting for them to get us back for our little prank.

11.1: Over, Under, and Over

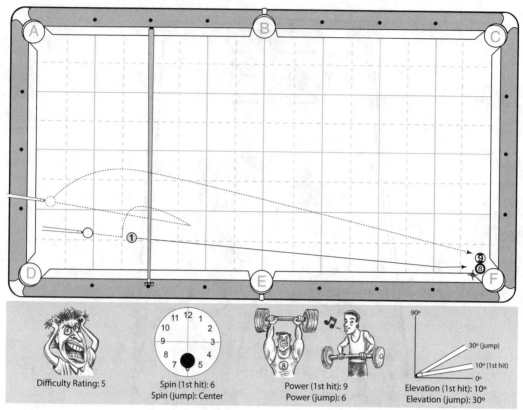

Difficulty Rating: 5	Spin (1st hit): 6 Spin (jump): Center	Power (1st hit): 9 Power (jump): 6	Elevation (1st hit): 10° Elevation (jump): 30°

Bruce Barthelette is great at the long jump (in pool, not track & field, although I have never seen him try it in that setting). The *Over, Under, and Over* is one of his contributions to the ESPN World Cup of Trick Shots. Shoot the 1-ball under the bridge and make the 8-ball in pocket 'F', causing the 9-ball to fall in place. The cue ball will then jump over the bridge and spin back under it. Now it is time to switch cues and jump the cue ball over the bridge (before it hits the short rail), and sink the 9-ball.

Setup: Place the cue ball and 1-ball where you like on the near side of the bridge, and align them for the pocket point on the long rail. The stacker is hanging in front of pocket 'F', but should be a little closer to the long rail. The 9-ball is on top of the stacker, and a bridge is stretched across the rail tops at the second diamond.

Solution: Elevate to about 10 degrees and hit the cue ball with enough power so that it will jump over the bridge. Before switching cues, have the jump cue laying on the table to your left. You can hand the first cue to a friend or drop it on the floor. If you decide to drop your cue, I recommend that you place a pillow on the floor so you don't damage it.

Adjustments: A failure to jump over the bridge results from hitting the shot too softly. Another mistake occurs when the 1-ball pockets the 8-ball, but gets in the way of the falling 9. The solution is to move the stacker closer to the long rail, or adjust your alignment point so the 1-ball hits the 8-ball a little thinner.

11.2: Off the Rail

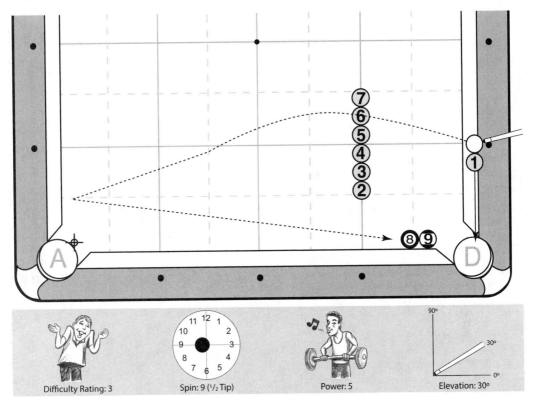

Difficulty Rating: 3	**Spin: 9 (½ Tip)**	**Power: 5**	**Elevation: 30°**

Off the Rail is one of my own inventions. The shot looks simple, but it is actually very tricky. The first step is to jump the cue ball over the line of balls. The 1-ball will roll along the top of the rail and drop into pocket 'D'. The cue ball banks cross corner into the combination, making the 9 in pocket 'D'. Jumping the cue ball off of the rail is tough to judge because you have to hit the cue ball harder than you might think. The aim point and the English is not so easy to figure out, or to execute, especially when you only get three tries, as we do during a match. I got a lot of mileage (and several points!) out of this one before the other players started figuring it out.

Setup: The cue ball is placed on top of the rail at the first diamond, and the 1-ball is frozen next to it. The 8-9 combination is frozen to the short rail with the edge of the 9-ball even with the pocket point. A wall of six balls is stationed along the first diamond line, with the center of that line even with the cue ball.

Solution: Aim at the corner pocket using just a touch of left English (about ⅛ inch off center). Most players initially think that you need to kneel down and shoot up at the cue ball when, in fact, this shot is played like a standard jump shot.

Adjustments: It is easy to hit the cue ball too hard, but this will cause it to fly off the table, or to catch the back rail while in the air and to just stop there. If you miss the combination, keep your line of aim the same, but adjust your English. For example, if you miss by hitting the short rail too soon, hit the cue ball a little closer to the center.

11.3: Rebounding Racks

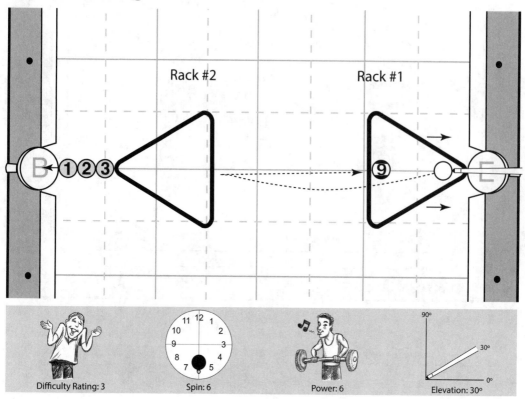

Difficulty Rating: 3   **Spin: 6**   **Power: 6**   **Elevation: 30°**

I can't remember who first came up with the *Rebounding Racks*, but I do remember Matt MacPhail using a similar shot at the 2007 ESPN Trick Shot Magic event. Jump the cue ball out of the rack and hit the other rack. This will send the 1, 2, and 3 balls into side pocket 'B'. The cue ball will then rebound into the first rack, pushing it toward pocket 'E'. The 9-ball will roll into the point of the rack, pushing it over the opening of the pocket, allowing the 9-ball to fall.

Setup: The 1, 2, and 3 balls are frozen in line by side pocket 'B', along the center line. The 9-ball and cue ball are placed inside the other rack on the center line, with the 9-ball frozen to the edge of the rack. The point of the rack is located at a spot even with the pocket cut.

Solution: Jump the cue ball straight over the 9-ball. Speed here is critical; hit the cue ball too hard and it will jump over and into the second rack. If you hit it too softly, you will not clear the 9-ball. The weight of the rack plus three balls should be enough to make the cue ball rebound without the need for a bunch of back spin.

Adjustments: The only adjustment is in the direction that you hit the cue ball. If you hit it at an angle, it could reduce its speed as it comes back, and it might not have enough power to push the rack over the pocket. It helps if rack #2 is heavier than rack #1.

11.4: Sticky Jump

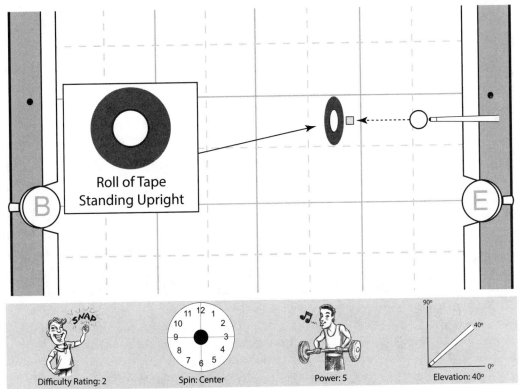

Roll of Tape
Standing Upright

Difficulty Rating: 2 **Spin: Center** **Power: 5** **Elevation: 40°**

Jamey Gray hates the *Sticky Jump*, and it's not because he can't make it... he can. He just thinks that it is the dumbest shot I've ever come up with. He even told me that I am not allowed to shoot this shot in any televised partner match that I play with him. By the way, the first time I ever did use this shot was in the 2008 Trick Shot Magic competition (in the quarter-finals — a non-televised match). My opponent (not Jamey) missed it and I was able to pick up a point at a critical time in the match. You must jump the cue ball into the top of a roll of tape, knock it over, and trap the cue ball inside. So, for all of the above reasons, I hereby dedicate the *Sticky Jump* to Mr. Jamey Gray!

Setup: Stand a roll of tape upright and place the cue ball about two to three inches behind it. I use a standard roll of painter's tape or duct tape. A piece of chalk is placed in front of the tape roll to prevent you from simply shooting the cue ball directly into the bottom of the prop.

Solution: Jump the cue ball lightly into the top edge of the tape. I ensure that the speed is correct by holding the butt end of the jump cue very loosely, forcing a softer hit on the cue ball.

Adjustments: You will need to elevate quite a bit (about 40 degrees) for the cue ball to hit the top of the tape, and to not jump through it. If the cue ball flies out of the tape, you probably hit the shot too hard. If the cue ball jumps right through the tape without touching it, you need more elevation to make the cue ball just catch the top edge. If the tape flips over and lands on its opposite edge, don't adjust – you've just created a new shot!

11.5: Original Double Jump

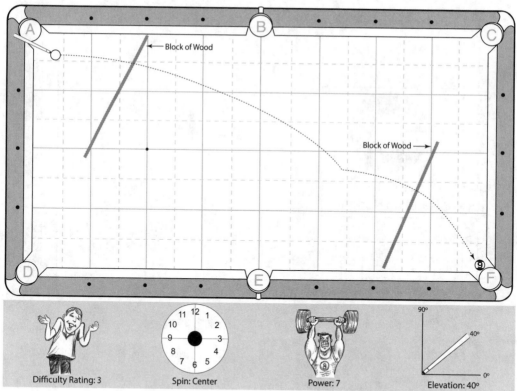

Difficulty Rating: 3   Spin: Center   Power: 7   Elevation: 40°

Lori Jon Jones was a great player on the Women's Professional Billiard Tour, and her former husband, Sammy Jones, also plays very well. (He was once a top player on the Men's Professional Billiard Tour). The three of us used to endorse the same pool table manufacturer, and he showed me the *Original Double Jump* at one of the Billiard Congress of America trade shows in Las Vegas. I first used it in a televised competition at the inaugural ESPN World Cup of Trick Shots back in 2006. The play is to jump the cue ball over the first block of wood. It will then land and bounce over the second block and into the 9-ball, which is waiting in front of pocket 'F'.

Setup: Hang the 9-ball as shown, and place the cue ball somewhere near the short cushion. A block of wood at each end of the table extends from their respective second diamonds to the corner pocket. You can make the shot harder by using a line of balls, which forces you to jump higher.

Solution: Aim directly at the 9-ball and elevate to about 40 degrees. Everyone's stroke is different, so you will need to find the proper position for the second block to match your jump stroke. If you are hitting the wood, move the block closer or further away based on where the cue ball is landing after the first jump.

Adjustments: The most common mistake is to not clear the second block. Even though the cue ball is jumping over a short barrier, it needs to be pretty high in the air for it to bounce high enough to get over the second block of wood. Therefore, pretend that the first jump is 2-3 times its height, and elevate your cue accordingly.

11.6: Double Popper Jump

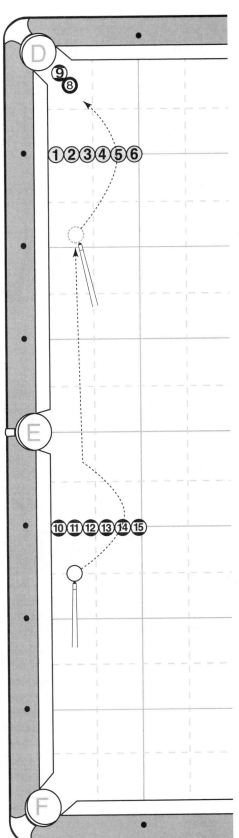

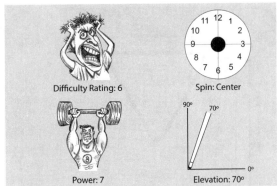

Difficulty Rating: 6

Spin: Center

Power: 7

Elevation: 70°

Florian Kohler originally submitted the *Double Popper Jump* at the 2010 ESPN Trick Shot Magic Competition. Even though I played him in the semi-finals, the shot was first played against me in my quarter-final match against Dave Nangle. The *Double Popper Jump* begins by jumping the cue ball over the first line of balls (the 10-15). As it is rolling, hit it again and jump it over the second line of balls (the 1-6), making the combination on the 9-ball. The cue ball usually flies off the table after the second jump, but in the ESPN competition, that is permitted.

Setup: Six balls are frozen in line along the first diamond, and another six are on the third diamond. The 8-9 combo is hanging in front of pocket 'D', and you have the cue ball in hand.

Solution: This shot can be executed with a standard jump cue, but it is easier with the Popper because it allows you to place the cue ball close (about 2 inches) from the first line of balls. This takes a lot of speed off the cue ball, and it makes the second jump so much easier.

Adjustments: The most common error is to hit the first jump too softly. With the Popper, you can hit the first jump harder and the cue ball will still be rolling slow enough for you to make the second jump. The second jump is all about timing, so you just need to get the feel for it.

11.7: Quick In & Out

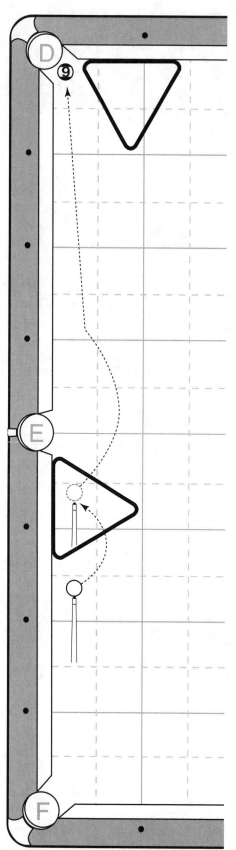

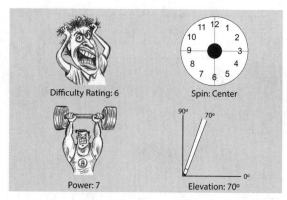

Difficulty Rating: 6

Spin: Center

Power: 7

Elevation: 70°

The *Quick In & Out* was created by Steve Markle, a top trick shot artist from the Philadelphia area. Steve is making a name for himself after a third place finish in 2012 at the Trick Shot US Open in Tunica, and a runner-up finish at the 2013 Masters Trick Shot Championship. You have to jump the cue ball into the first rack without allowing it to hit the rack – then you must hit it again and jump it out of the rack, making the 9-ball in pocket 'D'.

Setup: Hang the 9-ball in front of pocket 'D'. Place a rack against the short cushion, so you have a larger pocket. The other rack is frozen to the long rail (it can be anywhere along that cushion). You have cue ball in hand.

Solution: I have never tried this shot using anything but a Popper jump cue. I don't think you can use a regular cue and still be able to re-hit the cue ball before it contacts the rack. The cue ball is placed close to the rack (1-2 inches). Then use the Popper to jump it almost straight up in the air. If you hit the shot just right, you will have enough time to make the second hit.

Tips When taking your practice strokes, just don't line up on the cue ball. Instead, take two quick practice strokes, one at the cue ball, and the other where the cue ball will be for the second hit. This will help you get the timing down.

11.8: High Bar

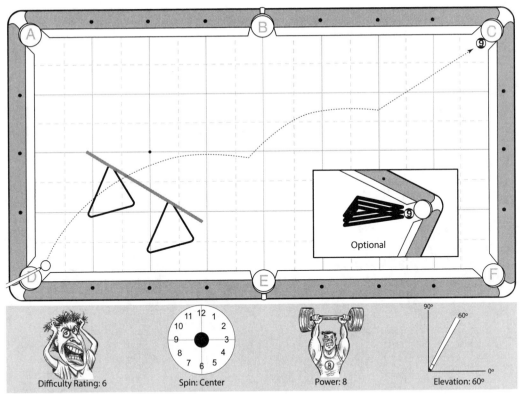

Difficulty Rating: 6	Spin: Center	Power: 8	Elevation: 60°

To make the *High Bar*, you must jump the cue ball over a very high bar (just like in track and field) and make the 9-ball in pocket 'C' (which is omitted from track and field). This is one of Jamey Gray's shots, but we have come up with some interesting variations. The first one that comes to mind calls for jumping the cue ball through a swinging rack, suspended 10 inches above the table. Jamey hits this shot so well that, in some competitions, he adds stuff under the racks to make the bar even higher!

Setup: Two racks are placed in an upright position, and a bar is stretched across the top of them. I use racks that have holes by the points which allow me to slip an old shaft or block of wood through them. You can also stand up a box of balls, or any other tall (unbreakable) object. The cue ball is placed behind this setup, as shown, and the 9-ball is hanging in front of pocket 'C'.

Solution:
Although the *High Bar* can be made with a standard jump cue, it is much easier with the Popper. The cue ball must be hit pretty hard, and you need to almost throw the stick at the cue ball (catching it again as it rebounds). A word of caution: Shoot this at your own risk because it is a cloth-ripper.

Tips:
Don't elevate too much when setting up for this shot (surprisingly). You are looking to make a solid hit on the cue ball so that it flies up and over the barrier. Although televised competitions allow the cue ball to fly off the table, it is illegal in others. To fix this, stack three racks on top of each other against the 9-ball – this will give you a back stop for the cue ball, and a much larger target (see insert).

11.9: Prison Jump

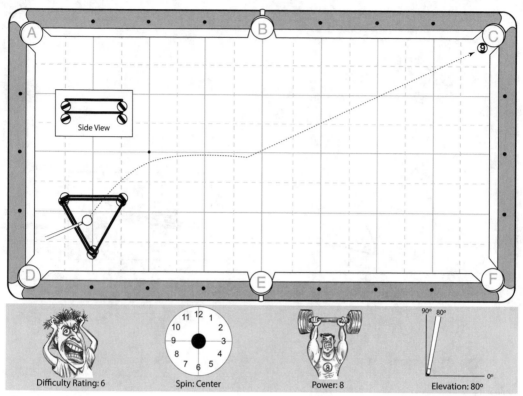

Difficulty Rating: 6	Spin: Center	Power: 8	Elevation: 80°

The only way to escape from jail is to jump out of the prison made up of racks and balls, sending the cue ball down the table to make the 9-ball. *Prison Jump* is another of Jamey Gray's inventions, and it is similar to the previous shot. When I was in Las Vegas for one of the Ultimate Trick Shot Tour Finale events, Jamey, Bruce Barthelette and I were interviewed by National Geographic, and we performed some shots for the show called 'Amazing'. This shot made the cut, but the one shown on the episode was a slightly different version. The setup was located by the side pocket, and Jamey had to jump the cue ball out of the tower and make a ball in the opposite side pocket. The funny thing was he missed it, but the cue ball landed before the hanger, jumped over it, and swished into the side pocket. The director liked that version better, so he ended up using it in the final broadcast.

Setup: Balance a rack on top of three balls. Place three more balls on top of that rack and balance another rack on top of the second group of three balls. The cue ball is then placed inside this contraption. The 9-ball is hanging in pocket 'C' at the other end of the table.

Solution: Use the Popper jump cue and shoot almost straight down on the cue ball. Your stick should be elevated about 80 degrees. You should almost throw your cue at the ball, catching it as it rebounds.

Tips: Try this shot first with only one rack on top of three balls (a minimum security prison), and see if you can jump out of that. Be careful since it is easy to rip the cloth on this shot. Proceed at your own risk.

11.10: Contortion Jump

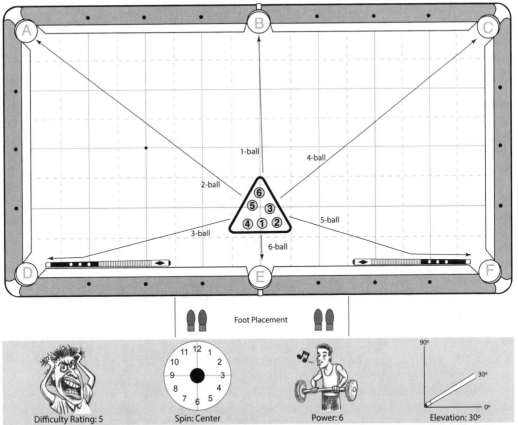

Difficulty Rating: 5 **Spin: Center** **Power: 6** **Elevation: 30°**

I originally came up with the *Contortion Jump* for the 2009 ESPN World Cup of Trick Shots. While standing with your feet no more than 1 1/2 diamonds from the side pocket, jump the 1-6 balls, in order, into the six different pockets. This version is for one player, but the shot was created as a four-man shot, where each player had to perform one or two of the jumps. The 5-ball and 6-ball were reserved for me to shoot, but we never got to them. Bruce Barthelette had to jump the 4-ball behind his back into corner pocket 'C', and it was my responsibility to stand behind that pocket and line him up. After the ball missed, I knew I didn't line him up properly, but it wasn't my fault. The lights were too bright. No... The camera man got in my way. No, wait... I had something in my eye... Yeah, that's it. Something in my eye...

Setup: Center the rack and place it three ball-widths from the cushion. The 1-6 are placed anywhere within the rack and configured as shown to make each jump as simple as possible. Two butts are placed up against the cushions, enlarging corner pockets 'D' and 'F'.

Solution: The 1-ball and 2-ball jumps should not be too difficult. The jump on the 3-ball is tricky because you have to lean over and shoot it backward. The 4-ball would be easy if you could move over, but you have to lean for it. When shooting the 5-ball and 6-ball, remember not to elevate too much. Hold the stick below the joint to allow for minimal elevation.

Tips: I have mastered the backward jump, so I feel like the 4-ball is the hardest of the six shots. You can't quite reach the 4-ball (because of the foot placement rule), and you cannot switch hands (part of the shot rule). I like to place the butt of the cue on the other side of my head (holding it with my right hand, but having the butt on the left side of my head). At other times, I shoot behind the back. Either way, aiming directly into the pocket can prove to be difficult. So, try it both ways and see which one works best for you.

11.11: Nine Ball Contortion

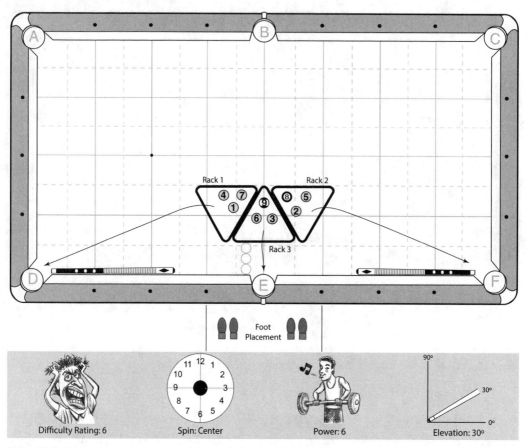

Nine Ball Contortion is a timed version of the previous shot that I devised for the individual competitions. Jump the balls in numerical order, alternating from rack to rack, shooting backward into the three pockets nearest you. Your feet need to remain within one diamond on either side of the pocket, and you have only 18 seconds to finish shooting all nine balls. I can complete this shot faster than that, but the competition guidelines mandate that you may not require less than two seconds per ball hit. You can allow for more time, but you may not force your opponent to shoot faster than the minimum of two seconds per ball hit.

Setup: The middle rack (#3) is centered, and it is placed three ball-widths from the cushion. The other two racks are frozen and aligned. The three balls in each rack are positioned in a triangular formation.

Solution: Keep your feet planted as shifting them for each shot will only cause delays, and you may not meet the 18 second time limit. Remember not to elevate too much – 30 degrees is about right. Start by lining up one of the backward jumps, and make sure your grip is right for the hardest one of all (the 9-ball).

Adjustments: Missing the corner pocket balls can easily happen, so you need to use the butts along the rail. Don't aim for the pocket – aim for the butts. When jumping backward, try to judge how hard you want to hit the ball by jumping it directly into the side pocket. If you hit it too softly, it may bounce first and go over the pocket; too hard and it might directly hit the back edge and bounce back onto the table.

11.12: Back Atcha

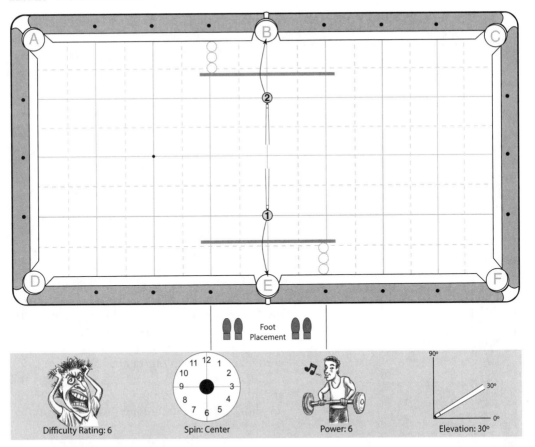

Foot Placement

Difficulty Rating: 6   Spin: Center   Power: 6   Elevation: 30°

It's funny how top players think alike. I was in the process of practicing and inventing shots for an upcoming tournament, and these included the *Back Atcha*. When I got to the event, I saw that another player, Dave Nangle, was shooting a very similar shot, so I guess the credit for this one goes to both of us. Stand with your feet within one diamond of either side of pocket 'E', lean over, and one-hand jump the 1-ball backward into the side pocket. Walk around the table and repeat with the 2-ball.

Setup: A block of wood is placed three ball-widths from the cushion. The 1-ball is placed behind the block. Use the same setup on the other side of the table, only you are, of course, using the 2-ball.

Solution: Lean over and remember not to elevate too much – 30 degrees should work. This shot takes a lot of getting used to. Hold the jump cue at the balance point so controlling it does not become a struggle.

Tips: If I aim at the middle of the 1-ball (as I would for any standard jump shot), I tend to miscue on the left side and under the ball. I compensate for this by aiming my cue high on the ball and to the right of center (from the perspective of the cue stick, it will be left of center). Now, when my stick shifts during my stroke, it will catch the ball dead center. You will, in time, find your own aim point.

11.13: Split Jump

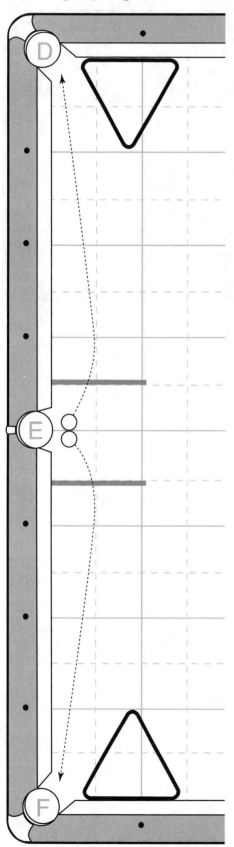

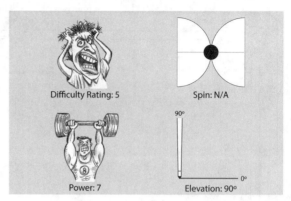

Difficulty Rating: 5

Spin: N/A

Power: 7

Elevation: 90°

Shoot straight down between the two cue balls and they will jump in opposite directions and go into their respective corner pockets. I'm not sure who originally came up with the *Split Jump* – possibly it was Luke Szywala for an older Trick Shot Magic in the mid-2000's. However, I do know that the one-handed version was created by Dave Nangle for the 2010 ESPN Trick Shot Magic, and if my memory serves me well (which is hardly ever the case), he used it against me in our quarter-final match. For the 2013 Masters Trick Shot Championship, I came up with a variation without using the racks. To play my shot, the cue balls are jumped directly into the pockets. This was a much harder version since I also required the balls to be a minimum of one ball-width plus one chalk-width from the cushion.

Setup: Two cue balls are frozen together, and they are centered near side pocket 'E'. Two blocks of wood are placed two ball-widths from the cue balls. Two racks enlarge the pockets at either end of the table.

Solution: Shoot straight down and hit both cue balls at the same time. Make sure to snap your wrist a lot more than normal. It will ensure that the cue stick is perfectly vertical if you let go with your bridge hand and let it hang straight down. Then grab it and shoot.

Adjustments: The most common error is to mis-cue. When this happens, you probably shifted your stick forward or backward – so instead of hitting at the contact point, you are hitting a little closer (or further) from the cushion where there is a small gap between the balls. If one cue ball jumps and the other doesn't, you shifted your cue to the left or right.

11.14: The Original One-Handed Jump

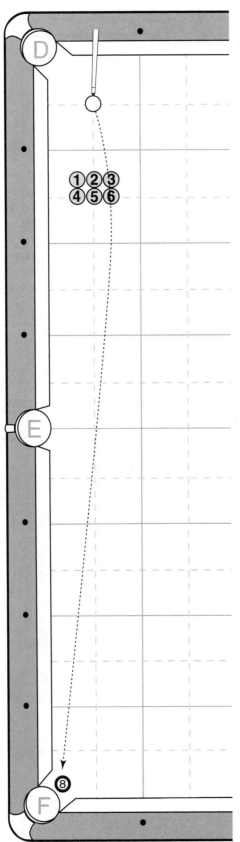

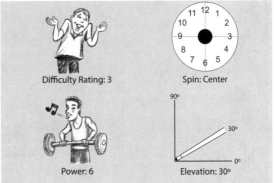

Difficulty Rating: 3

Spin: Center

Power: 6

Elevation: 30°

The Original One-Handed Jump was introduced by Mike Massey at the 2000 Trick Shot Magic competition. Back then it was a brand new shot, so no one had ever tried it. In fact, Mike's opponent didn't even attempt the shot, forfeiting the point! Nowadays, this shot has become so easy that no one even thinks of shooting it in a televised competition. Most players now reserve this shot as a 'hanger' when they need one point to win a match. Several harder variations of this shot have been developed recently, some of which you will see in this book. In this version, perform a one-handed jump over the blocking balls, and make the 8-ball.

Setup: A cluster of six balls is positioned in front of the cue ball. The 8-ball is hanging in front of pocket 'F'.

Solution: I hold the jump cue out in front of me, which enables me to look straight down the shaft. Lean into the shot with your right foot forward (left foot if you are a lefty). Be sure to make a solid hit on the cue ball.

Adjustments: If you are miscuing, see if you are missing the cue ball consistently on one side or the other. Then compensate by aiming to the side of the cue ball.

11.15: Nick's Quick Six Pack

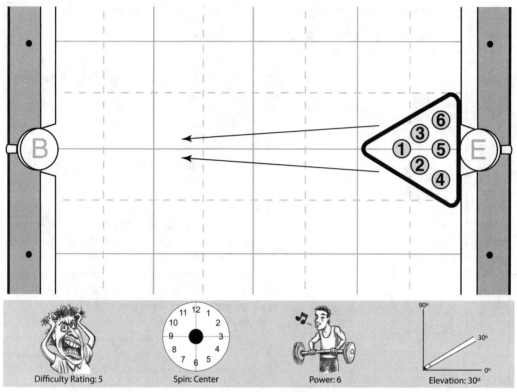

| Difficulty Rating: 5 | Spin: Center | Power: 6 | Elevation: 30° |

Nick's Quick Six Pack is the brainchild of Nick Nikolaidis, who expanded on the one-handed jump concept by making it much harder. Using one hand, jump all six balls out of the rack and into the opposite side pocket. You only have 18 seconds to complete this shot. Nick's stage name is 'Quick Nick' because he is very good at speed shots, especially ones that require one-handed or two-handed jumps. I have seen him perform this shot in well under 18 seconds.

Setup: Freeze a rack to the cushion, centered by side pocket 'E'. The six balls are set up in a triangular formation.

Solution: Keep your grip hand steady and lean into the shot. One-handed jumps take a while to get used to, and this one is harder than most because you have to jump six balls, and you cannot take your sweet time.

Adjustments: The most common mistake is to hit one of the balls off-center, which will make it jump out of the rack and curve away from the side pocket. Make sure your hand is steady and contact each ball right in the middle. When you get into a rhythm, it is easy to concentrate on the jumps and to not look at the side pocket. I can avoid this mistake by glancing up at the pocket between shots.

12: Multi-Cue Jump Shots

With all of the various jump shots that have been invented over the past few years, it was inevitable that the players would start adding extra cue sticks into the mix. Now it isn't enough to simply jump a ball. Today, a lot of the jump shots require the use of two, three, or more cues while jumping multiple balls at the same time. These shots are crowd favorites, especially when they are performed in front of a more experienced audience.

In practice, I have jumped six balls simultaneously over a barrier and into a pocket while holding all six cues. We have Dave Nangle to thank for the Triple Jump, which calls for jumping three balls at the same time, and the Quad Jump (four balls at once). We also have Jamey Gray to thank for the Quint Jump (five balls at once), which he performed successfully in the 2011 ESPN World Cup of Trick Shots. If I ever get the six ball version to the point where I can make it consistently, I'll have so many cues that I may need to start bringing a caddie.

12.1: The First One-Handed Shot That Uses Two Hands

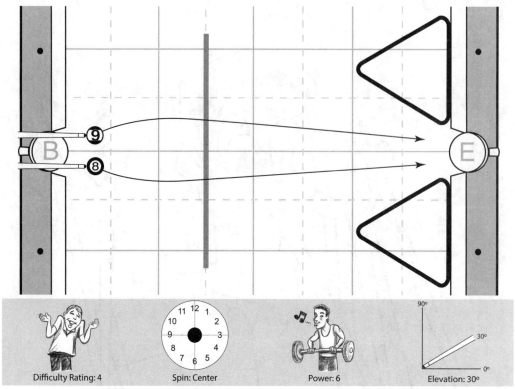

| Difficulty Rating: 4 | Spin: Center | Power: 6 | Elevation: 30° |

Hold one jump cue in each hand and then perform two simultaneous one-handed jump shots, one right-handed and one left-handed. Jump both balls over the barrier and into side pocket 'E'. I use the 8-ball and the 9-ball because I like to have a funny line just in case I miss. For example, if I miss the 8-ball, I will say, "Well, I play 9-ball better anyway"; vice versa if I miss the 9-ball. During a show, when I announce the name of this shot, *The Frst One-Handed Shot That Uses Two Hands*, I get this confused look on my face, which is usually good for a laugh.

Setup: A block of wood (or a butt) is located across the table, and the 8-ball and 9-ball are placed behind it. Two racks enlarge the opening for side pocket 'E'.

Solution: Hold both cues out in front of you, and keep your hands steady. Stroke straight into both balls. Practice shooting each ball one at a time before attempting to make both together.

Adjustments: If you are miscuing, see if this is consistently happening on one side or the other. Then adjust your aim point to compensate for any shifting in your stroke. Once you get the hang of the one-handed jump shots (especially with your opposite hand), you will be able to aim straight at the balls.

12.2: Crisscross

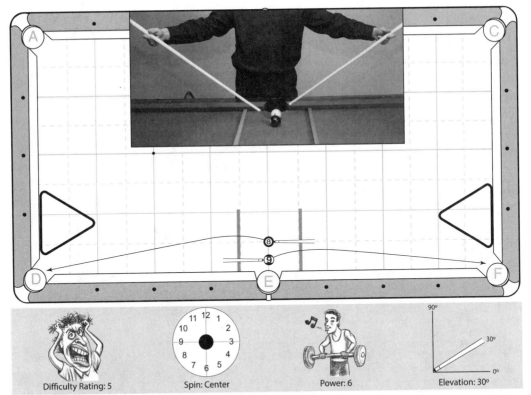

Difficulty Rating: 5	Spin: Center	Power: 6	Elevation: 30°

Jamey Gray selected *Crisscross* when competing against me in the finals of the 2010 Trick Shot Magic competition. He named it 'Crisscross Applesauce', so I almost refused to shoot it because of the name alone. This comes from the same person who was giving me some attitude over the shot where I jump the cue ball into a roll of duct tape!!! (If you are skipping around, see the shot titled *Sticky Jump* in chapter 11). Hold one jump cue in each hand, then perform two one-handed jump shots simultaneously. Use your right hand to jump the 8-ball to the left and into corner pocket 'D'. The 9-ball is jumped with your left hand into the opposite corner pocket. The cues will actually cross each other as you jump the two balls.

Setup: Two blocks are placed about ¹/₂ diamond from side pocket 'E'. Two racks enlarge the corner pockets. The 8-ball and 9-ball are positioned along the center line.

Solution: Hold the cues at the balance point so you don't have to struggle to control them. While you are holding the two cues and are lining up both shots, try only the right-handed jump. Once you have that going pretty well, practice the left-handed jump. Once you are pretty good at both jumps, try them together.

Adjustments: If you are miscuing, see if it is consistently off to one side or the other – then compensate by shifting your starting line of aim.

12.3: Double Back Atcha

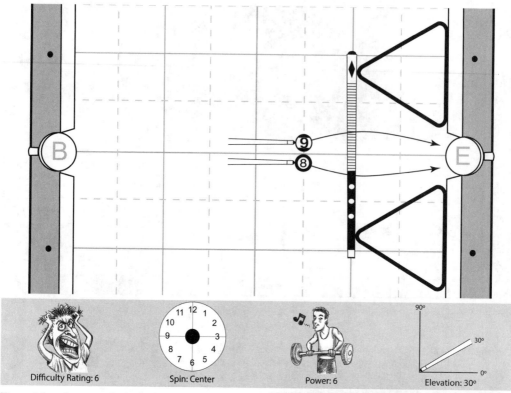

Dave Nangle started shooting the *Double Back Atcha* in one of the Ultimate Trick Shot Tour Finale events. Hold two cues at the same time. Stand behind the long rail, lean over, and backward jump both balls simultaneously into side pocket 'E'. I haven't had much trouble with this version, but I know that Dave is working on a three ball version, and I am working on that one myself as well (shhh... don't tell anyone).

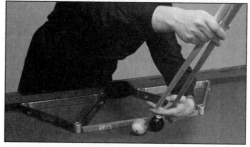

Setup: Two racks enlarge the opening for pocket 'E'. A butt (or a block of wood) is placed on the table flush with the top of both racks. You have ball in hand on the 8 and 9 balls, but they must be behind the butt (or it wouldn't be much of a jump shot).

Solution: Hold the two cues below the joint, and hold your bridge as seen in the close-up. It is a good idea to try this one going forward first. Stand on the other side of the table and move the balls and butt closer to you. Once you master that shot, then try the backward version.

Tips: Remember not to elevate too much, which is a common mistake on all backward jump shots.

12.4: Chopsticks

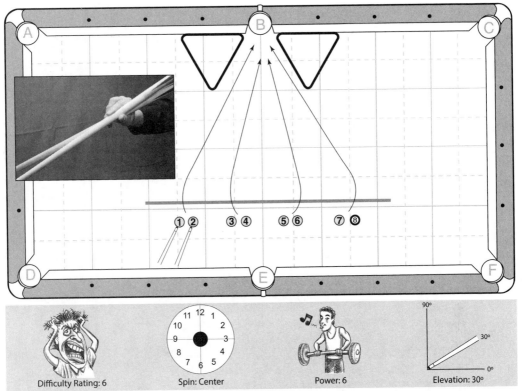

Difficulty Rating: 6	Spin: Center	Power: 6	Elevation: 30°

Chopsticks is one of my own creations, which I performed for the first time at the 2010 ESPN Trick Shot Magic competition against Florian Kohler. To execute this shot, hold two cues in one hand, and then perform four one-handed double jumps. The first two groups are done left-handed, and the last two groups are played with your right hand.

Setup: Two racks are placed along the rail next to pocket 'B' to enlarge the opening. The racks should be weighted down with a reasonably heavy object. A butt or block of wood is stretched across the table, and four sets of two balls each are positioned in a line behind the butt. Each pair should be one inch apart.

Solution: I shoot better with my right hand, so I prefer to jump the left-handed part first so I can get it out of the way. The key is to hold both cues steady, and I do this by pushing my fingers against the cues, and by holding them tight. Once you get the standard one-handed jump down, adding a second cue is all about the grip.

Adjustments: Missing the jump is the most obvious error. The only other thing that can go wrong takes place when the balls get tied up and interfere with each other while they are making their way into the pocket. I always try to have one ball aimed directly into the pocket, and the other is aimed into the rack. This way one will get there sooner than the other, avoiding a collision.

12.5: Viagra Shot

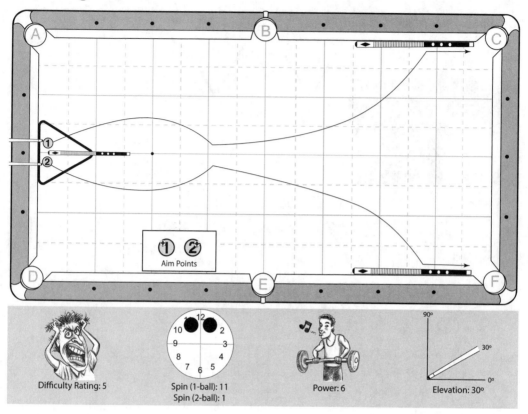

Aim Points

Difficulty Rating: 5

Spin (1-ball): 11
Spin (2-ball): 1

Power: 6

Elevation: 30°

Gordon Hedges is the inventor of the *Viagra Shot*, but it was I who came up with the name. Just look at the initial setup and you will understand why I gave it its name. A long time ago I remember doing an exhibition for Pfizer in Westchester with my friend, Jim Dale. I came up with some other kind of shot called the *Viagra Shot*, but it wasn't nearly as fitting as this one. It's too bad that the show didn't happen after I met Gordon. A quick note to the parents: Sometimes I tell jokes for the adults only – and if the kids get the joke, is that really my fault?

Hold two cues, jump both balls simultaneously out of the rack. They will curve into the butts and go into corner pockets 'C' and 'F'.

Setup: A rack is frozen to the cushion and it is centered on the second diamond. A jump cue butt is placed on the table, and it is propped up on the top point of the rack. This cue is used to separate the 1 and 2 balls, which are placed anywhere within the rack. Two butts are up against the long cushions near pocket 'C' and 'F'.

Solution: Hold both cues as can be seen in the close-up photos of other shots, such as *Triple Jump* (you will be using two cues instead of three cues). The only difference this time is that the two butts are crossed over each other (making an elongated 'X' with the sticks). This will angle the cues properly, and this makes it possible to hit the balls toward each long rail.

Tips: Crossing the cues will still not give you enough of an angle to make the two balls. The answer is to place the balls a little closer together so the cue sticks will hit the outer edges of each ball. After jumping, this will cause the balls to curve a little toward the long rails, just enough to pull them into the two corner pockets or into the butts along the rail.

12.6: Wide Chopsticks

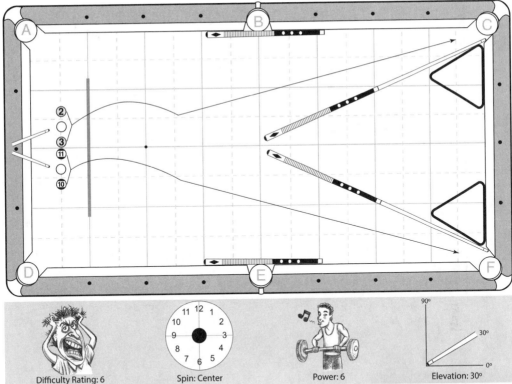

Difficulty Rating: 6	Spin: Center	Power: 6	Elevation: 30°

To perform the *Wide Chopsticks*, hold two cues, jump the two inner balls (3 and 11) simultaneously over the barrier, and into the opposite corner pockets. Next, readjust the cues to make them a little wider, and then jump the two cue balls. Finally, repeat the jumps for the last two balls (2 and 10). When I invented *Chopsticks* (as with others), I tried to focus on one skill – in this case, it is the wide double jump. I am betting that I can perform this skill better than my opponent and, if I perform this part of the shot, I want the rest of this shot to be guaranteed. That is why, on these types of shots, I enlarge the pockets to the point where you cannot miss the shot if you get by the first part. I started getting so good on this shot that I added a fourth set of balls in one competition, and yet I was still able to make it on my first try!

Setup: A barrier (a block of wood or a butt) is placed across the table at the first diamond. The 3 and 11 balls are centered, 1/4 inch apart. The two cue balls are positioned one chalk-width on either side, and the 2 and 10 balls are another chalk-width apart. Two butts are blocking each side pocket. Two cues are stretched diagonally across the table with racks holding them steady.

Solution: The inner set of balls (3 and 11) is a standard double jump shot. If you have practiced it from previous shots, you should be able to execute it on this one. The cues naturally angle outward, so you should have no problem making a ball go into each pocket. Even as you get wider (for the second and third jumps), it is basically the same shot, but holding the cues steadily will become even more difficult.

Adjustments: If you put a finger between the cues, it will help keep them apart, and to keep them steady as well. When aiming the shot, point both tips at the center of each ball.

12.7: Triple Jump

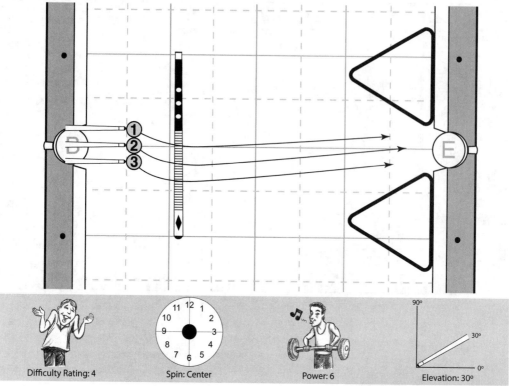

Difficulty Rating: 4	Spin: Center	Power: 6	Elevation: 30°

To play this shot, hold three cues at the same time, and then jump all three balls simultaneously over the butt and into the side pocket. Dave Nangle introduced the *Triple Jump* in Las Vegas back in 2009, and it was just my luck that he first used it against me. After Dave made it, I spent five full minutes fumbling around with the cues, trying to get the grip and bridge right, but with no success. On my third attempt, I finally jumped all three balls, but one of them flew off the table. Nowadays most players are making this shot so easily that only the difficult variations of it are used in competitions.

Setup: Two racks are used to enlarge pocket 'E'. A butt is placed across the table, and three balls are positioned behind it. I prefer to freeze the balls in a straight line, but I have seen players leave a small gap between the balls, or stagger them so the center ball is slightly ahead of the other two balls.

Solution: The three jump cues are jammed in between the four fingers on your right hand (excluding the thumb). The bridge is kind of tricky. One cue is resting between my thumb and first finger (which is bent), another cue is resting against the knuckle of my first finger, and my middle finger, and the third cue is positioned between my third and fourth fingers.

Tips: Play around with your bridge until you get the cues separated to the point where they are hitting the center of each object ball. You can also separate the balls, if necessary, to get the desired alignment.

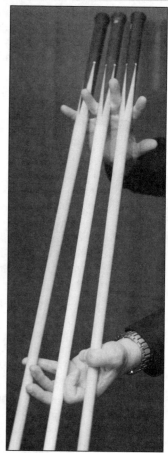

12.8: Four Triples

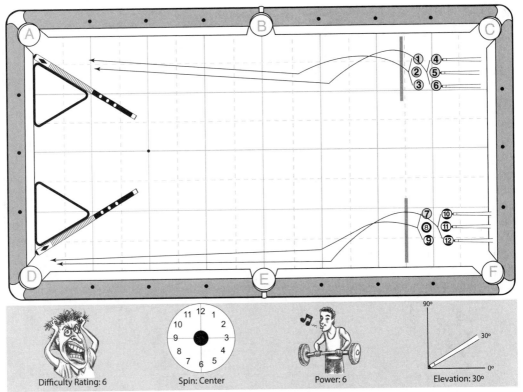

Difficulty Rating: 6   **Spin: Center**   **Power: 6**   **Elevation: 30°**

Four Triples was introduced by Bruce Barthelette during Trick Shot Magic, but there was no speed requirement. All you had to do was jump each set of balls, one at a time, at your leisure. I was the one who added the element of speed to this shot. Hold three cues at the same time, then perform four triple jumps, one after the other. Each set of balls must be jumped before any of the balls from the prior set go into the pocket.

Setup: A rack and a butt are used to enlarge corner pockets 'A' and 'D'. Two blocks of wood are placed on the table, and two sets of three balls are positioned behind each block as shown.

Solution: Make sure to use a solid grip and bridge on the cues (see photo close-up in a prior shot). Because this shot needs to be done quickly, you will not have time to readjust your grip or bridge.

Adjustments: Once you have mastered the triple jump, the most common error is to miss because you are rushing a shot. If you use a little more elevation than normal, the balls will jump higher and roll more slowly, giving you a little more time to move from group to group.

12.9: Progression Speed Jump

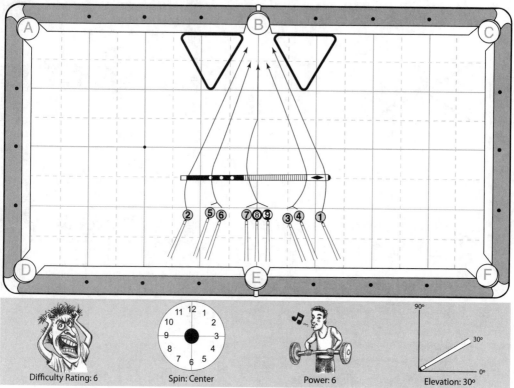

| Difficulty Rating: 6 | Spin: Center | Power: 6 | Elevation: 30° |

To play the *Progression Speed Jump*, you must jump the 1-ball right-handed, switch the cue to your left hand, and jump the 2-ball. Next, pick up a second cue and double jump (righty) the 3 and 4 balls. Switch both cues to your left hand and double jump the 5 and 6 balls (lefty). Finally, pick up a third cue and triple jump (righty) the 7, 8, and 9 balls. Please understand that these are all two-handed jumps. Oh, one more thing: all of this must be completed in only 18 seconds. Nick Nikolaidis came up with this shot for the 2011 World Cup of Trick Shots. Nick is very fast at switching the cues from hand to hand. If I remember correctly, he performed this shot in 13 or 14 seconds (but 18 is now the minimum since there are nine balls being hit, and you need to give your opponent at least two seconds per ball). When it was my turn, I made this shot on my first attempt, but I was 0.3 seconds over the maximum time requirement. Fortunately for me, on my second attempt I completed it with a whopping 0.75 seconds to spare!

Setup: Two racks are used to enlarge side pocket 'B'. A butt is placed across the table, and nine balls are positioned behind the butt, as shown in the diagram.

Solution: You must be pretty quick when switching from hand to hand. It takes me the most time to set up my bridge and grip for the triple jump, so I try to perform the other parts of this shot as quickly as possible.

Tips: This shot is very difficult, so I recommend trying it without worrying about the timer. It is crucial for you to align the tip end of the cues when jumping multiple balls. Stand the cues straight up with the tips down and resting on the table. Don't worry about the chalk being wiped off the tips because, if you hit the center of each ball, you don't even need to chalk up.

12.10: Quad Jump

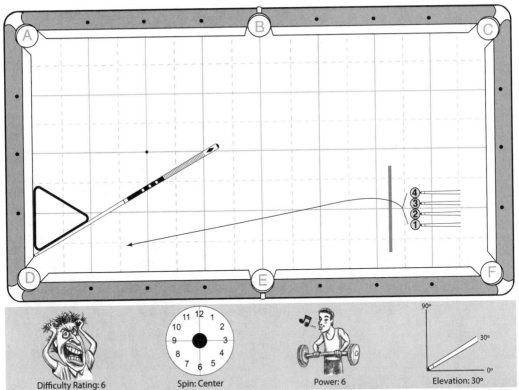

| Difficulty Rating: 6 | Spin: Center | Power: 6 | Elevation: 30° |

Dave Nangle came up with the *Quad Jump*. I always had trouble when practicing it, and I could hardly make it one out of ten times, so I could never select this shot in a competition with that kind of poor make percentage. However, when Dave selected it against me, I would always find a way to make it. Now, I am much better at the *Quad Jump* so I will select it anytime the situation warrants it. Hold four cues and jump all four balls simultaneously over the barrier and into pocket 'D'.

Setup: A rack and stick are used to enlarge the corner pocket. A block of wood or butt is placed on the table, with four balls positioned in a row behind it. Freeze all four balls in line.

Solution: Hold your cues like you would when playing the *Triple Jump*. The fourth cue is held between the thumb and first finger, and the shaft is off to the side of your thumb on your bridge hand. The cue rests on your wrist, and it is pressed up against the outside of your thumb (see close-up).

Adjustments: This fourth cue is the critical one. To keep it steady, I press it tightly against my thumb. There is a tendency for the tip of the fourth cue to rise up slightly as I go forward in my stroke. I compensate by aiming this cue low on the ball while the other cues are aimed directly at the center of their corresponding ball.

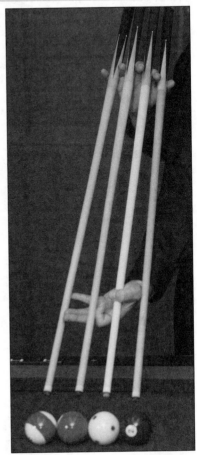

12.11: Triple Chopsticks

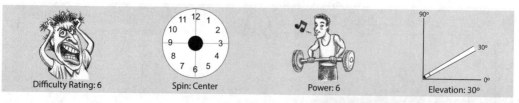

Difficulty Rating: 6   Spin: Center   Power: 6   Elevation: 30°

I invented *Triple Chopsticks* in 2010 for the Southeast Classic held in Atlanta, GA. I was saving the shot for a later match when something unexpected happened – Bruce Barthelette and Jamey Gray were shooting that same shot in their match! As it turned out, they had both worked together and came up with the same exact shot for the same tournament. Well, not exactly the same. Theirs was just a right-handed shot while my version required shooting with both hands. Still, I thought it was interesting that all three of us came up with the exact same new shot for the same tournament. *Triple Chopsticks* requires you to hold three cues in one hand, and to perform a one-handed triple jump making all three balls into the corner pocket. Switch the cues to your opposite hand and repeat with the other set of balls.

Setup: Two sets of three balls are placed behind blocks of wood. Two cues and four racks enlarge the pocket openings at the other end of the table.

Solution: If you have mastered the one-handed jump and the one-handed double jump, then this shot is simply the next step in the progression. Keep a very steady grip on the cues. I push them tightly with my fingers, locking the cues in place.

Tips: Some players like to arrange the balls in a slight 'V' shape because that matches up with how they hold the cues. I leave a small gap (about 1/8 inch) between the balls, but that is something you should adjust based on your grip. Once you get a steady one-handed grip on three cues, see if they are straight across and in line with each other, or if one of them is slightly askew. Then adjust the ball setup accordingly.

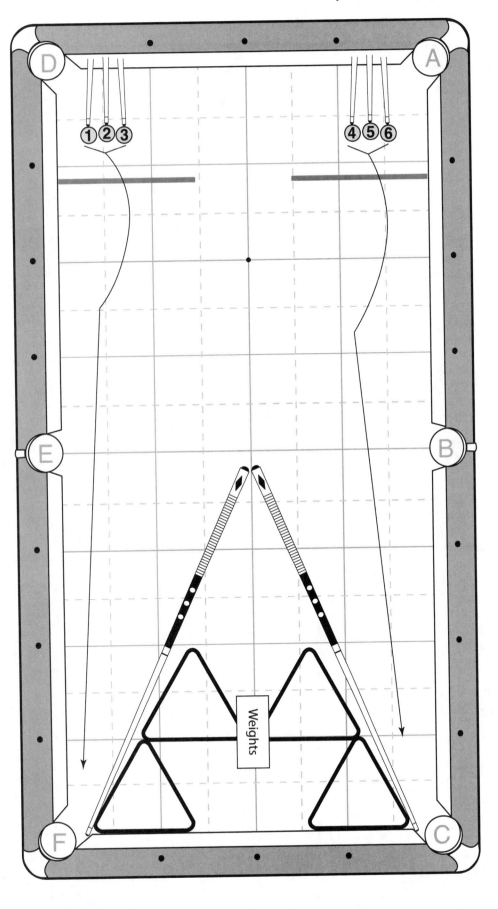

12.12: Triple Chopsticks With Timer

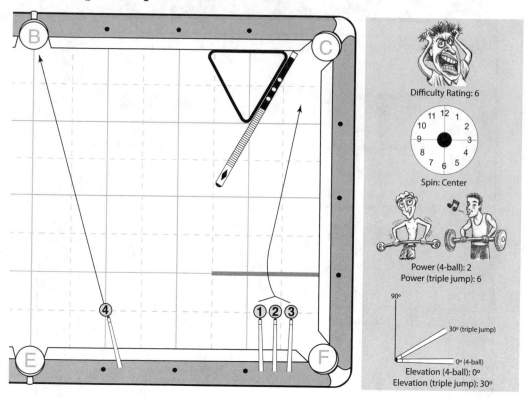

Difficulty Rating: 6

Spin: Center

Power (4-ball): 2
Power (triple jump): 6

Elevation (4-ball): 0°
Elevation (triple jump): 30°

Here is a variation of the *Triple Chopsticks* shot that I created for the 2012 ESPN World Cup of Trick Shots. Hold three cues in your right hand and one in your left, and start by lagging the 4-ball left-handed into side pocket 'B'. Before the ball gets there, triple jump the 1, 2, and 3 balls right-handed into corner pocket 'C'. All of the shots must be performed jacked up, which means that you cannot rest the cues on the rail.

Setup: Our old friends, the rack and the butt, are used to enlarge corner pocket 'C'. A block of wood is placed along the first diamond, and three balls are positioned in a row behind it. The 4-ball is on the third diamond, 1/2 diamond off the long rail.

Solution: Make sure that you have the three cues set up and steady before lagging the 4-ball (see the close-up of how to hold three cues one-handed in the prior shot called *Triple Chopsticks*). You must be able to line up the triple jump and, without moving your body, hit the lag on the 4-ball. If you have to move over and/or adjust your grip on the cues, you may run out of time.

Adjustments: Don't hit the 4-ball too softly, which is a common mistake. You won't need much time for the triple jump if you have the cues steady and prepared to go.

13: Wing Shots

Wing Shots are defined as hitting the cue ball into a moving ball. They have been around for a long time, but I don't know who invented the first one. I am not even sure where the name came from. Maybe the first person to try them said that they were going to roll a ball down the table and 'just *wing* it'. As the trick shot competitions have grown in recent years, *wing shots* have developed with new and interesting variations.

I remember doing an exhibition a long time ago with Earl Strickland in New York City. It was right after the 9-ball U.S. Open in Virginia, and we were performing for a special event at Blatt Billiards. We each did a short set of trick shots – then, during his turn at the table, Earl started doing wing shots. Back then I wasn't even competing in trick shot competitions, so I had never seen those shots before. It was pretty impressive when he made almost all of them. Nowadays, wing shots are played in almost every artistic pool competition.

13.1: The Original Wing Shot

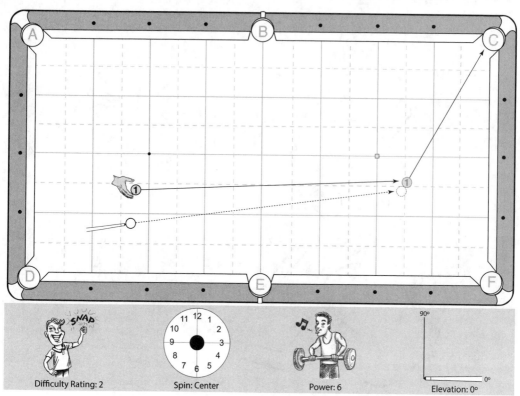

| Difficulty Rating: 2 | Spin: Center | Power: 6 | Elevation: 0° |

There are many variations of the classic 'wing shot', but this is *The Original Wing Shot*, so it's the one that started them all.[13-1] Hold both the cue ball and object ball in your hand, roll the object ball down the table, and place the cue ball behind the second diamond line. Next, hit the cue ball into the moving object ball and make it in corner pocket 'C'. In some competitions, we are given one attempt at seven wing shots. Your score is based on how many shots you make. In other competitions, we are given three attempts, each consisting of three wing shots. Each shot counts for three points, so if you make all three, you score nine points. If you make less, you score fewer points, but then you get two additional attempts to improve your score.

In trick shot competitions, a piece of chalk is placed on the spot. Roll the object ball down the table on the right side of the chalk, and cut it over to the left-hand corner pocket. During my shows, I leave out the chalk (as I would recommend for you), because it makes the shot much harder.

Setup: The cue ball and object ball are both placed in your hand.

Solution: You need to get the timing down for exactly when to hit the cue ball. You want to roll the ball at a consistent speed down the table, and at the same point on the opposite short rail each time.

Adjustments: It is very difficult to get the same roll each time, and you will need to make any adjustments on the fly, with very little time to think about what you are doing. Keep in mind that the faster the object ball is rolling, or the further the travel line is from the corner pocket, the thinner you will need to cut the object ball (and vice versa).

13.2: Reverse Wing

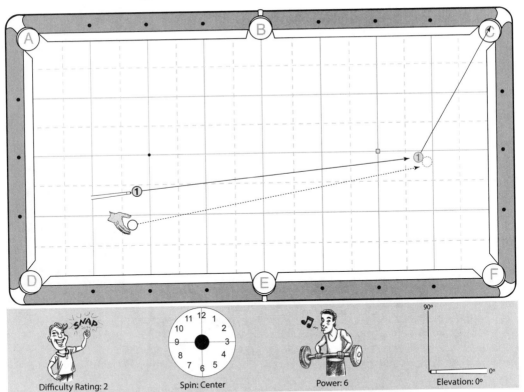

| Difficulty Rating: 2 | Spin: Center | Power: 6 | Elevation: 0° |

To play the *Reverse Wing* shot, hold the cue ball and an object ball in your bridge hand. Roll the cue ball down the table, then place the object ball behind the second diamond line. Shoot the object ball into the cue ball and carom off of it into corner pocket 'C'. As with *The Original Wing Shot*, a piece of chalk on the spot is required for trick shot competitions, but it is optional here.

Setup: You prepare for this shot by placing the cue ball and an object ball in your hand.

Solution: Don't roll the cue ball too close to the pocket or you will not have the proper angle to carom the object ball off of it and into the corner. I find reverse wing shots to be much easier than the standard wing shot – perhaps because I can see the angle much better – and I do have a higher make percentage on this version.

Adjustments: Because the cue ball is moving, the object ball will not travel directly along the contact point's tangent line. Instead, it will roll forward of that line. You must adjust on the fly based on how hard you roll the cue ball, and based on the direction that it takes. The faster it is rolling, the sooner you need to hit the object ball to get it to carom off of the cue ball and to head into the corner pocket; the opposite adjustment is needed with a slow moving cue ball.

13.3: Combo Wing

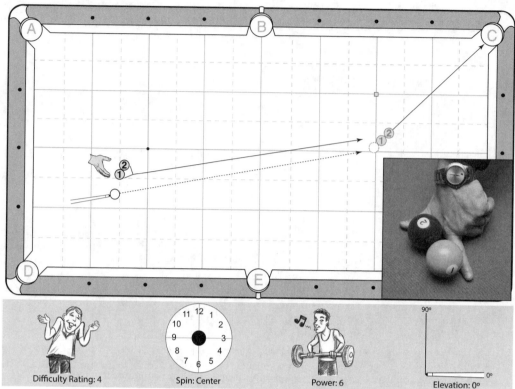

Difficulty Rating: 4   Spin: Center   Power: 6   Elevation: 0°

While holding the cue ball, roll the 1-ball and 2-ball down the table. Place the cue ball behind the second diamond line and shoot it into that moving 1-2 combo, making the 2-ball in corner pocket 'C'. When the *Combo Wing* shot was first used in competition, the players were grabbing the balls and rolling them down table, but this technique sometimes causes the balls separate, which adds to the difficulty of making the moving combination. The person who came up with the idea of placing the balls on the table, and then pushing them between your thumb and first finger was Eric Yow. Ever since then, the *Combo Wing* shot has become easy to make, and it has opened the door to additional variations, which are included in this book.

Setup: Hold the cue ball in your hand and place the 1-2 combo on the table between your thumb and first finger (see the close-up).

Solution: Push the 1-ball and 2-ball down table. Keep the balls at the angle at which you would like them to stay all the way down. If you push them correctly, they will roll together, almost frozen, until the cue ball makes contact with them down table. Of course, all you need to do is time the shot so that you hit the 1-ball when the combo is lined up for the pocket!

Adjustments: If the balls are not staying together, it may be because your hands are sticky. The balls are rubbing against your fingers as you push them, so any moisture will cause them to stick and separate. My recommended solution is to use a glove.

13.4: Triple Combo Wing

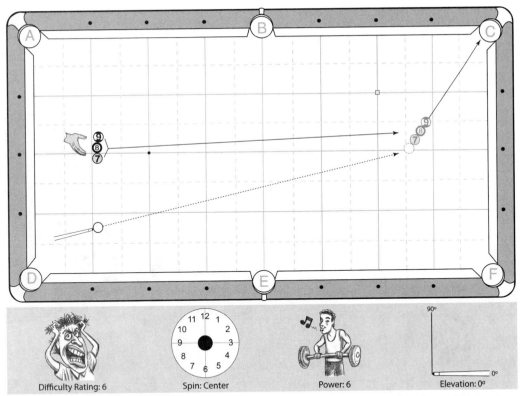

Difficulty Rating: 6   Spin: Center   Power: 6   Elevation: 0°

Bruce Barthelette originally came up with the *Triple Combo Wing*. His hands are bigger than most of the other players, but by crossing my fingers and using my middle finger's extra length, I am able to compensate for having smaller hands than Bruce. Besides, crossing my fingers gives me just enough extra luck to make the shot!

Hold the cue ball in your hand, and roll/push the 7-8-9 combo down the table, all in a row. Place the cue ball behind the second diamond line and hit it into the 7-8-9 combination, making the 9-ball in corner pocket 'C'.

Setup: Hold the cue ball with your last two fingers and press it up against your palm. The 7, 8, and 9 balls are on the table, and they are between your thumb and first finger (see close-up from the previous shot). A piece of chalk at the 2,1 diamond intersection line prevents you from rolling the balls too close to the corner pocket.

Solution: Push the three balls down the table. It may be a little difficult to keep the balls together, but even if they separate, hopefully the 8-9 will stay together. If this happens, you need to be a bit more accurate when shooting the 7-ball into the 8-ball.

Adjustments: The three balls don't quite fit along my index finger, so I cross my index and middle finger, which gives me a little more room to work with. Try this maneuver if you are having problems keeping the 9-ball in place as you push the balls.

13.5: Combo Wing + 1

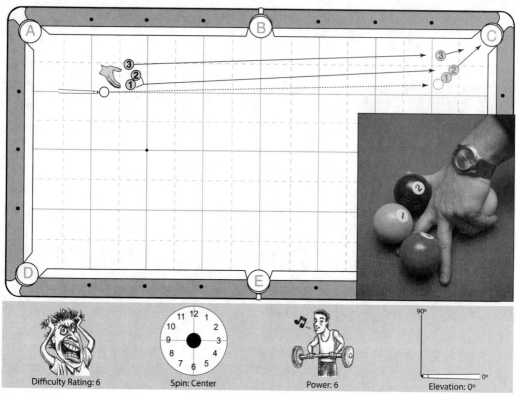

Difficulty Rating: 6   **Spin: Center**   **Power: 6**   **Elevation: 0°**

Some tournaments have a fixed shot program while others use a more free-style approach that allows the players to shoot anything they want. The contestants are even permitted to modify a shot from match to match! At a tournament in Las Vegas, while Jamey Gray and I were experimenting on the practice table, we both worked together to come up with the infamous *Combo Wing + 1* shot. We used it in most of our matches for the remainder of the competition until, of course, we played each other. Hold the cue ball in your hand and roll all three balls down the table. Place the cue ball behind the second diamond line and shoot it into the 1-2 combo. The 3-ball is rolled straight at corner pocket 'C', and the 2-ball must go in before the 3-ball does.

Setup: Hold the cue ball with the last two fingers while pressing it against your palm. The 1, 2 and 3 balls are placed on the table between your fingers (see close-up).

Solution: It helps to use a glove for this shot because any moisture on your hand will cause the balls to separate or to roll at varying speeds. If you push the balls properly, the 1-2 combo will roll slightly ahead of the 3-ball. Concentrate on the 3-ball since you must roll this one straight into the pocket.

Adjustments: When shooting the cue ball, you could carom off the 1-ball and knock the 3-ball off course, so aim to hit the 1-ball as fully as possible. The angle of the combination will cause the 1-ball to go to the right (away from the 3-ball), and the cue ball should not travel to the left because you are hitting directly into the 1-ball.

13.6: What Goes Up Must Come Down

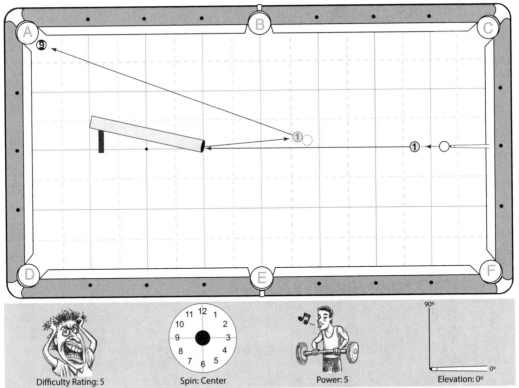

Difficulty Rating: 5	Spin: Center	Power: 5	Elevation: 0°

What Goes Up Must Come Down was created by Bruce Barthelette for a Trick Shot Magic competition in the mid-2000's. Shoot the 1-ball into an elevated tube. The 1 will roll up the inside of the tube, come back down, and roll toward you. When it returns, shoot the cue ball into the oncoming 1-ball, causing it to make the 9-ball in corner pocket 'A'. It would seem that the hard part is hitting the moving ball when, in fact the most difficult part is to get the 1-ball into and rolling up the tube, as there is very little room for error. It is almost like shooting into half of a pocket.

Setup: A standard shipping tube with a four inch opening is elevated on the table, with the opening at the third diamond. The cue ball and 1-ball are lined straight up the table for the opening of the tube. The 9-ball is hanging in front of pocket 'A'.

Solution: You must be very precise when shooting the 1-ball. If you don't hit the opening directly in the middle, it will not enter the tube. Instead, the 1-ball will hit the edge and bounce back. According to the rules, the 1-ball must disappear from view (from the player's perspective) for the shot to be considered good.

Adjustments: This shot has a different feel to it because you must hit a moving ball that is coming right at you. With a standard wing shot, you need to over-cut the ball slightly because the forward momentum alters the angle at which it is hit. Since this ball is moving toward you, it is necessary to *under-cut* the ball. So, attempt to miss the 9-ball by aiming about an inch or two to the left of pocket 'A'. If executed properly, the backward momentum will cause the 1-ball to shift its travel path, and head directly for the 9-ball.

13.7: Push Wing

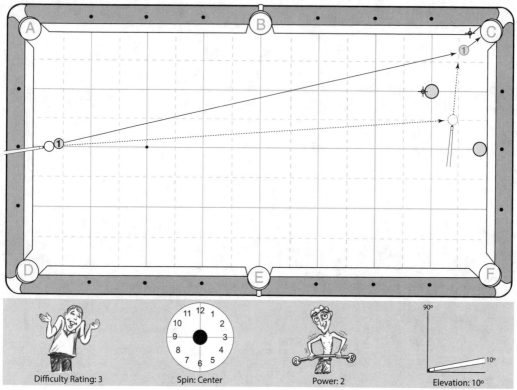

| Difficulty Rating: 3 | Spin: Center | Power: 2 | Elevation: 10° |

Push Wing is another of Jamey Gray's inventions, and he used it to surprise me in the 2010 Ultimate Trick Shot Tour Finale. Shoot the cue ball into the 1-ball so that both balls will roll down the table. Run down to the other end of the table and re-hit the moving cue ball between the cups to make the 1-ball in corner pocket 'C'. Both balls must be moving when the re-hit takes place. The tricky part is hitting the cue ball so that both balls roll down table at the correct speed. Hitting it a hair too high or low makes the cue ball arrive too early, or too late.

Setup: The cue ball is placed one ball-width from the cushion on the middle diamond. The 1-ball is frozen to it, and both balls are lined up for the long rail corner pocket point. A plastic cup is positioned on the 1,1 diamond intersection line, and another cup is frozen to the short cushion at the second diamond.

Solution: Aim at the cup on the 1x1 diamond intersection line. The two balls will split apart; the 1-ball going left, and the cue ball going right. If your speed is right, you will be re-hitting the cue ball into the 1-ball which, by now, is almost hanging in the pocket. If the speed is not right, re-hit the cue ball with less speed – hoping this will slow it down just enough so that it can still clip the oncoming 1-ball into the pocket.

Adjustments: If the cue ball is arriving down table ahead of the 1-ball, hit it slightly below center on your next attempt. If the cue ball is too slow in getting down table, hit it slightly above center. These adjustments are only 1/8 inch up, or 1/8 down.

13.8: Quadruple Combo Wing

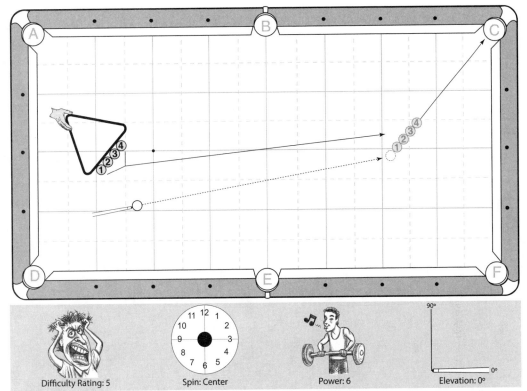

| Difficulty Rating: 5 | Spin: Center | Power: 6 | Elevation: 0° |

It is a little risky putting this shot out there for my peers to see as I have never used it in competition, although I have made it many times in practice. When I first came up with the *Quadruple Combo Wing*, I tried to roll the balls along my arm. Once I tried it using the rack, I found that it was much easier. Use the rack to push all four balls down table. Next, move the rack out of the way and place the cue ball behind the second diamond line. Shoot the cue ball into the four ball combination, making the end ball (the 4-ball) in corner pocket 'C'.

Setup: The cue ball starts in your hand. Four balls are against the forward edge of the rack and your fingers act as bookends.

Solution: Push the rack forward so that all four balls roll down the table together. After placing the cue ball as shown, try to judge when the four balls will be lined up for the pocket as this will tell you when to pull the trigger on the cue ball.

Tips: If the balls separate, chances are that only the 1-ball leaves the group. The others should stay close to each other. If this happens, try to cut the first ball into the lead ball of what is now a three ball combination. Of course if all of the balls separate, all I can say is, "Good Luck!"

14: Miscellaneous Shots

The shots in this chapter don't fall into any of the other categories. You probably can find something that would place them in one or the other but, generally speaking, they are a collection of nice shots that don't fit into any other chapter. However, I wanted to include them in this book. Some require an uncommon skill or a crazy prop.

One shot requires that the cue ball starts within an inflated balloon. In another, you toss the cue ball up in the air before shooting it. I really think that you will get a kick out of *Finish Your Drink*, where you massé a pint glass around a line of balls – and make the 9-ball for the win!

Try them out. I think you will enjoy them.

14.1: Karate Chop

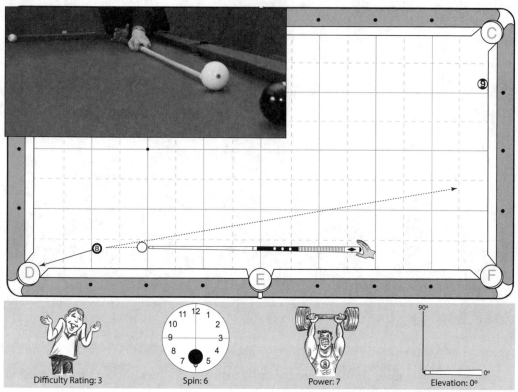

Difficulty Rating: 3	Spin: 6	Power: 7	Elevation: 0°

To execute the *Karate Chop* shot, stand behind the short rail, place your cue stick on the table, and hit the butt end with your hand. The cue ball will make the 8-ball in corner pocket 'F', and then draw back for position on the 9-ball that's waiting near pocket 'C'. In an ESPN style competition, 'getting position for the 9-ball' is too subjective. As a result, the selecting player usually picks a diamond line which the cue ball must cross. Typically, the cue ball must at least hit the short rail, but this has become routine for most players, so now players usually have to rebound off that cushion and pass the second diamond line – and sometimes even further. In an Artistic Pool competition, players are awarded three points if the cue ball crosses the second diamond line (before hitting the short cushion), six points if the cue ball contacts the short rail, and nine points if the cue ball bounces off the short rail and goes beyond the second diamond line.

Setup: In most competitions, the player has both cue ball and object ball in hand beyond the second diamond line. However, I prefer to place them in the second 1x1 diamond zone from the corner. The back edge of the cue ball is on the second diamond line, and the 8-ball's forward edge is on the first diamond line.

Solution: Position the tip about an inch or two behind the cue ball. Stretch out and, using the thumb and first two fingers of your bridge hand, raise the shaft of the cue so the tip is very low on the cue ball. When you hit the butt with your back hand, use a well cushioned spot on your palm so you don't hurt yourself. Be careful!!!

Adjustments: If the cue ball is not drawing back far enough, lower the starting position of your tip. Your stick gets wider as you get closer to the joint, so the tip will naturally raise up if your bridge is solid. Be sure to aim low enough, even though it will seem like you are going to miscue.

14.2: Lift

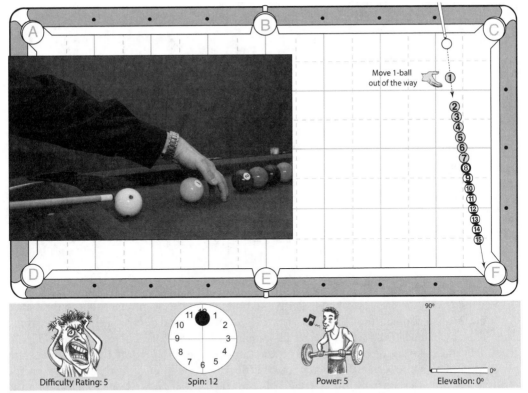

| Difficulty Rating: 5 | Spin: 12 | Power: 5 | Elevation: 0° |

Lift was created by Sebastian Giumelli, but I first used it against Mike Massey in a Trick Shot Magic competition. I don't think Mike had ever seen the shot before, but being the great player that he is, one attempt was all that he needed to figure it out. You must shoot the cue ball into the 1-ball (one-handed). Grab the 1-ball with your other hand and lift it up and out of the way. The cue ball will follow into the 2-ball, making the long combination and sending the 15-ball into corner pocket 'F'.

Setup: Line up 14 balls straight into the corner pocket as shown. The cue ball and 1-ball are in the same line, but they are back a little with some space between them.

Solution: When shooting one-handed, rest your cue on the rail and push it down so that it's very steady. Aim with top spin, but don't follow through too much or you could double hit the cue ball. Your other hand is positioned in front of the 1-ball, and it is ready to grab it.

Adjustments: The key is to make a full hit on the 1-ball. If the cue ball drifts to one side or the other, adjust your aim on the next attempt. If the cue ball is rolling too slowly, use more top spin. You will need to hit this one with a little speed so that the cue ball will transfer enough force to make the 14 ball combination.

14.3: Chain Lift

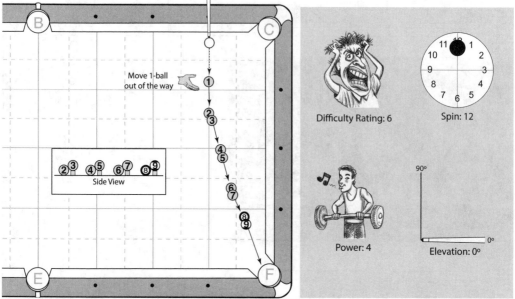

To play the *Chain Lift*, use a two-handed grip and bridge, and shoot the cue ball into the 1-ball. After the cue ball contacts the 1-ball, grab it with your bridge hand before the ball hits anything else. The cue ball will follow into the 2-ball, knocking the 3-ball off a piece of chalk. The 3-ball will hit the 4, knocking the 5-ball off of another chalk, and so on until the 9-ball goes into pocket 'F'. The name 'Chain Lift' came from lifting the 1-ball out of the way and from the chain reaction that's set off by hitting the 2-ball, causing the ball on the chalk to fall and hit the next ball, and so on.

The original 'Lift' shot was supposed to be done this way as well, using a two-handed bridge instead of the method used in the previous shot (titled *Lift*). The shot was submitted by Sebastian Giumelli (Argentina), who doesn't speak English very well – so when we wrote the instructions for this shot for Trick Shot Magic, he wasn't very clear about the requirements, and he never corrected anyone during the tournament. A few years later Sebastian submitted another shot similar to the *Chain Lift* (it also used the concept of starting with a two-handed grip). It was only then that he mentioned (through an interpreter) that the original shot from a few years prior was intended to be this way. The version shown here is my variation on his invention.

Setup: The 1-ball is placed five ball-widths off the cushion, and along the first diamond line. The 2-ball is two ball-widths from the 1-ball, and is also positioned along the first diamond line. The 3-ball sits on top of a piece of chalk, and it is frozen to the 2-ball. The 4-ball and 5-ball are set up in a similar manner (both balls frozen with the 5-ball on a chalk); again, the same setup is used for the 6-7 and the 8-9 pairings. The cue ball may be placed anywhere along the first diamond line, but should be close to the rail.

Solution: *Chain Lift* is a tricky shot because you need to hit it with a lot of top spin, but softly at the same time. If you hit it too hard, you will not have time to grab the 1-ball before it hits the 2-ball. Remember, you must use a two-handed grip, so your bridge hand can't be placed in front of the 1-ball like it was in the previous shot.

Tips: The most obvious miss comes from not grabbing the 1-ball in time. You will have to play around with the amount of power that you use. I also advise that you start your grabbing motion before the cue ball hits the 1-ball. You can't touch it until they hit each other, but at least you can start to move your hand forward immediately after hitting the cue ball.

14.4: Pop It Back

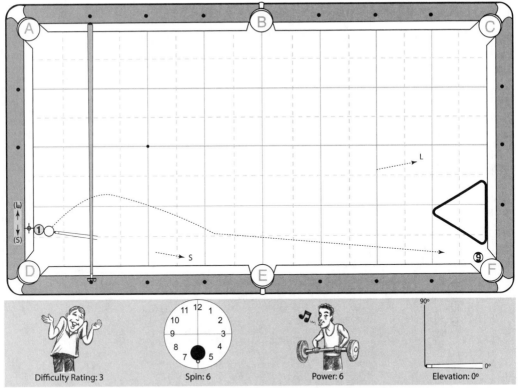

| Difficulty Rating: 3 | Spin: 6 | Power: 6 | Elevation: 0° |

Pop It Back was created by Luke Szywala of Poland. He originally placed a rack around the cue ball, balanced with one end on the rail top, and the other end on some balls a few inches from the cue ball. A cover sat on top of the rack, and it had a small square hole in it. You had to shoot a blind shot under the rack, hit the cue ball, make it bounce up through the hole, roll down table, and pocket a hanger. The same basic thing happens in this variation, but you are shooting under a bridge, and you can see the cue ball.

Setup: The 1-ball is frozen to the cushion near pocket 'D'. The cue ball is frozen to the 1-ball, and it is aligned directly at the 9-ball, which is hanging in front of pocket 'F'. A rack is placed near the 9-ball to enlarge the pocket.

Solution: Shoot the cue ball straight into the 1-ball with draw. The cue ball should fly back up, and pretty high (so watch yourself – proceed at your own risk). The back spin on the cue ball turns into follow as the cue ball travels down table. Don't stroke through this one. Instead, be sure to poke at the cue ball with little follow through.

Adjustments: If the cue ball misses by hitting the long rail, or it flies off the table, shift the butt end of your cue toward the long rail so you are aiming more to the right. Make the opposite adjustment if the cue ball is staying on the table, but it is missing on the other side of the rack.

The lower you aim on the cue ball, the less chance there is that the tip will get in the way and push the cue ball left or right.

14.5: Rainbow Shot

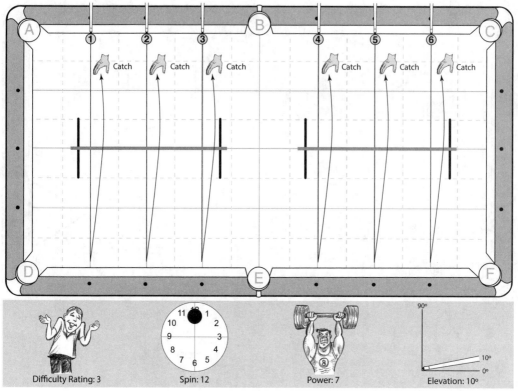

Difficulty Rating: 3	Spin: 12	Power: 7	Elevation: 10°

The *Rainbow Shot* is one of Jamey Gray's favorites. He makes it almost every time, and it is very pretty to watch him play it. The shot got its name because of the arc that the balls take when they jump off the cushion – which is in the same shape as a rainbow. Shoot the 1-ball across the table. When it hits the opposite long cushion, it will fly up in the air back toward you (and over the bar). Catch the 1-ball and place it into a pocket. Repeat this process for the 2 through 6 balls, alternating hands by shooting the odd numbered balls righty, and the even numbered balls lefty.

Setup: Place the 1-6 balls frozen to the cushion at their respective diamond markers. Two pairs of two racks each are placed upright, and a shaft or block of wood rests on top of them. I use racks with holes at the top which hold the shafts in place.

Solution: I use a full length break/jump cue. The balls must be slightly airborne when they hit the opposite cushion. BE CAREFUL ON THIS SHOT. It is very easy for a ball to fly back at you at high speed, or to fly forward at an even faster rate. Do not attempt this shot if anyone is standing in front of or behind you – and remember to keep your eye on the ball because it can hit you as well. In addition, do not attempt this shot if there are table lights. We reserve this shot for television or tournaments where the lights are embedded way up in the ceiling.

Tips: The most common mistake appears on the lefty portion of this shot. I find that it helps to elevate the cue a little more, and to hit the balls a little harder. My advice is to try it without the racks and shafts, and to start by using only your right hand.

14.6: Pop It Up

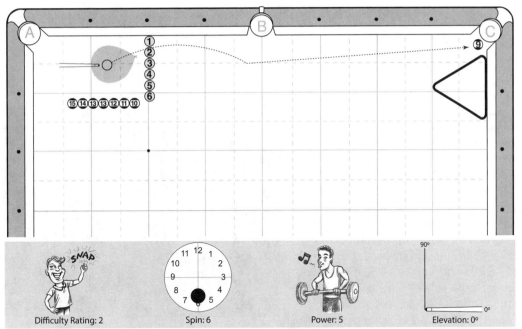

| Difficulty Rating: 2 | Spin: 6 | Power: 5 | Elevation: 0° |

Even though *Pop It Up* is one of my inventions, the concept of putting a cue ball or object ball inside a balloon was introduced by Rick Hawkinson. He used to come up with acts for the circus, so what better way was there to spend his spare time than to come up with crazy trick shots with things commonly found at a circus (like balloons – good thing he didn't try to use elephants, although I shouldn't give him any ideas). To *Pop It Up*, jump the cue ball out of the balloon (which then pops), then over the line of balls, and down the table to make the 9-ball in corner pocket 'C'. Since this shot is made by scooping under the cue ball, it is an illegal jump. Of course, this doesn't matter because the cue ball would never be inside a balloon in the first place! I have made this without scooping the cue ball, but it is much harder. When using the 'scoop' method, the balloon might not pop if you don't inflate it enough. This happened to me once in a competition. The cue ball AND the balloon rolled down table. Luckily, right before they reached the far end of the table, the balloon popped (a blessing from the pool gods) and everything else worked out as planned. Whew!!!

Setup: The 9-ball is hanging in front of pocket 'C', and a rack enlarges the pocket. The cue ball is placed inside a balloon, which you will then need to inflate. The balloon with the cue ball inside is placed on the table where shown, and a wall of balls is stationed around the balloon.

Solution: Aim right at the 9-ball and shoot very low – you want to hit the balloon and the table at the same time. Push your stick all the way through to the cue ball. The balloon should pop and the stick should miscue under the cue ball, causing it to jump over the wall of balls. Once you practice this shot enough times, you can probably remove the rack.

Adjustments: If you are not jumping the cue ball straight ahead, adjust your aim. Make sure you are stroking straight through. Don't look at the balloon – just concentrate on the cue ball.

14.7: A Game of Jacks

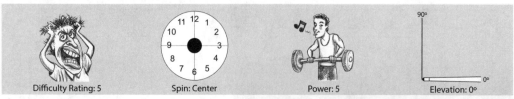

Difficulty Rating: 5   Spin: Center   Power: 5   Elevation: 0°

I came up with this variation for *A Game of Jacks*, but the original idea was invented by Matt MacPhail for the 2007 ESPN Trick Shot Magic competition. Hold a cone and a rubber ball, bounce the ball out of the cone one time, and then hit the 1-ball down table toward the middle diamond on the short rail. Then catch the ball in the cone. The 1-ball must be hit after the bounce, but before the catch. As the 1-ball comes back toward you, bounce the rubber ball again, this time hitting the 1-ball into corner pocket 'C'. The 1-ball must pass the bridge and again be hit between the bounce and the catch. Repeat this process with the 2-ball, bouncing the ball twice each time, and then hitting the ball after the second bounce, and before the catch. Repeat with the 3-ball, bouncing three times. I usually require that all hits be made with the cue jacked up, so you can't rest it on the rail.

Setup: The 1, 2 and 3 balls are in hand behind the bridge. I keep them closer to pocket 'D' so that they are out of the way. A bridge is stretched across the second diamond – and you may need to prop it up with a piece of chalk so the balls can fit underneath it. A rack is placed at the other end of the table to enlarge the corner pocket.

Solution: You need to acquire one of those plastic cones that you can squeeze easily because it will keep you from dropping the ball too soon. Turn the cone upside down and squeeze, holding the ball in place. Once you are lined up on the 1-ball, drop the rubber ball. As the ball returns, turn the cone upside down (the opening is up). Concentrate on the 1-ball and stroke it after you *hear* (not see) the ball bounce. It gets harder to stay focused when the balls are returning for the second hit, especially when you are on the 3-ball (three bounces). If you don't have a cone, use just the rubber ball, but you can't throw it up into the air because that would be cheating. Turn your hand over and just let it drop.

Tips: The easiest way to miss is by dropping the ball, so make sure that the cone is perfectly vertical. If it is angled a little, the ball will bounce and move sideways, making it harder to catch, and also adding the possibility that it could get in the way of the oncoming ball. Keep your eye on the object ball while keeping the bouncing ball in your peripheral vision. Only when you have hit the object ball should you look at the rubber ball and then catch it.

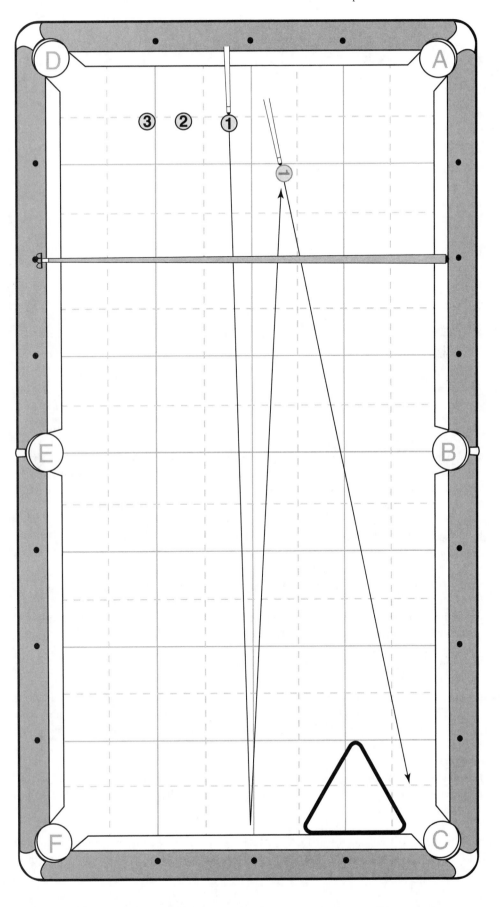

14.8: An Aerobic Game of Jacks

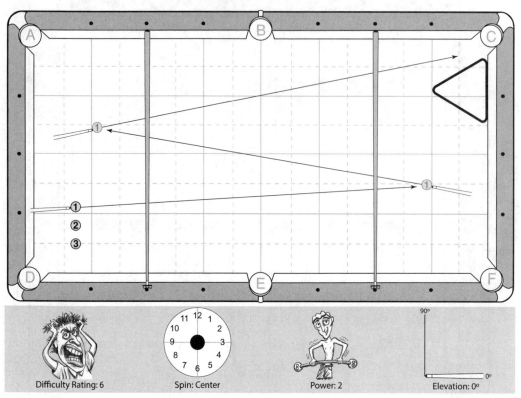

Difficulty Rating: 6	Spin: Center	Power: 2	Elevation: 0°

The World Cup of Trick Shots is a team event at which we try to come up with shots that use multiple players. An *Aerobic Game of Jacks* is a one-player variation of a multi-player shot. Use a cone and rubber ball, bounce it once, and hit the 1-ball across the table (one-handed and jacked up). Run to the other side and bounce the rubber ball and hit the 1-ball back. Run back to the starting point and repeat, this time making the 1-ball in corner pocket 'C'. Repeat this routine with the 2-ball and 3-ball, using two and three bounces respectively (as described in the previous shot, *A Game of Jacks*). You must hit the balls after they pass the bridge, but before they hit the short rail.

I first performed this for the team event with Bruce Barthelette and Jamey Gray. Bruce began by bouncing the rubber ball and making the initial hit on each balls. Next, Jamey bounced a rubber ball and hit the balls back up table where I waited to perform the same task, only I would shoot them into the corner pocket. I devised this single player variation while on my way to Montreal for a one-on-one, five day challenge match against Nick Nikolaidis. Not only is this a great shot to play in a competition, but practicing it for 30 minutes is a better workout than walking on a treadmill.

Setup: Two bridges are spread across the table at the second diamond lines. You may need to prop them up with a piece of chalk so that the balls can fit underneath. A rack enlarges corner pocket 'C', and the 1, 2 and 3 balls are positioned behind the first bridge. Hold a cone and rubber ball in your left hand.

Solution: As with the previous shot, you must keep your eye on the object ball to be hit and try to time the bounces correctly. Only after you have hit the object ball should you look at the bouncing ball to catch it.

Tips: The first hit is angled toward the center of the table, so you have room to bounce the ball. Don't hit the second shot too far over for the same reason. Instead, hit it straight down the center of the table.

14.9: Toss

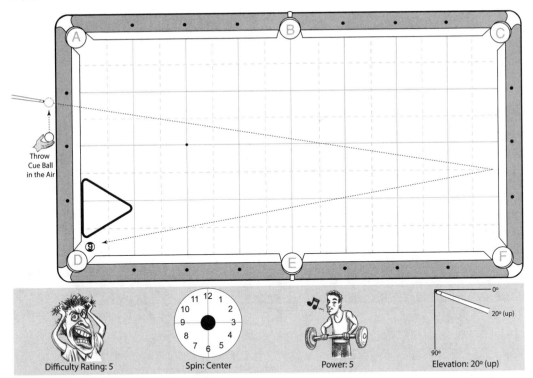

Difficulty Rating: 5	Spin: Center	Power: 5	Elevation: 20° (up)

Throw the cue ball up in the air. Then, using a two-handed closed bridge grip, hit the cue ball onto the table, causing it to bank one rail, and to pocket the 9-ball. I invented *Toss* back in 2004 for the Trick Shot Magic competition. I originally performed it by throwing the cue ball up and hitting it with a cue that was being held in my other hand (one-handed). This is a much easier version because the cue stick is ready to go, and you don't need to throw it up too high. My opponent in '04 hit the ball right out of his hand. Unfortunately (for me), the referee gave him the point because, in his opinion, the cue ball was thrown up a fraction of a millimeter. I am not one to argue, and I didn't see much chance of reversing his decision, so I kept quiet. I always knew whenever this episode had been aired because I would get an email from some random person asking me why I didn't say anything. Eventually the shot was modified to its current version, and it was introduced by Mike Dechaine, one of the best 9-ball players in the world and a member of Team USA, at the 2012 World Cup of Trick Shots. I liked the idea of forcing a two-handed closed bridge grip, so I have been performing it that way ever since.

Setup: The 9-ball is hanging in front of pocket 'D', and a rack is used to enlarge the pocket. You begin with the cue ball in your hand. By the way, this is what you get when you give a trick shot artist *ball in hand!*

Solution: Throw the cue ball up. It should be high enough so that you have time to re-grip your cue with a standard closed handed bridge. If you shoot too hard, the cue ball will bounce, and it may be airborne when it hits the back rail. This will cause it to die right there, or to fly off the table.

Tips: You can make this shot with a level cue, hitting it straight onto the table, but that is the hard way. A much easier approach is to aim and hit the cue ball at an upward angle. Essentially, the cue ball is falling onto the tip of your cue, and you will find that this method gives you a better chance of making solid contact with the cue ball.

14.10: Finish Your Drink

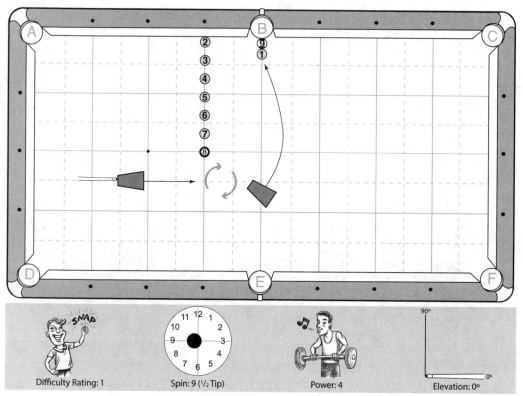

Difficulty Rating: 1   Spin: 9 (½ Tip)   Power: 4   Elevation: 0°

This shot was invented by Luke Szywala. The name that I gave it, *Finish Your Drink*, comes from my style of presentation. I start with the cue ball on the table and a glass hidden on the floor. I then ask the audience how they would make the 1-9 combo, and I get the usual answers (jump, curve, bank, etc). I always follow-up their answers with, "Sorry, I forgot to mention that you can't jump (or bank, etc)". Eventually I tell them that they need to remember three things when faced with a shot like this. First, replace the cue ball with a pint glass; second, hit it with ½ tip of left side beer glass English; third, make sure you finish your drink or else it will spill all over the table. Shoot the pint glass forward. After it passes the line of balls, the shape of the glass will cause it to curve around to the left and into the 1-9 combo.

Setup: The 1-9 combination is hanging in front of side pocket 'B', aligned straight out (perpendicular to the long rail). The 2-8 balls are positioned along the third diamond line, with gaps between them so that the line will stretch out to the middle of the table. A pint glass is placed on the 1 ½ diamond line, directly behind the second diamond.

Solution: Shoot the glass forward with a touch of left 'English'. This small offset (from the center) will make the glass twist. Once the forward movement stops, the momentum will cause it to roll, and since the opening (of the glass) is wider than the base, it will roll along a curved path. If you get the speed just right (and you have a large margin for error), it will contact the 1-ball and sink the 9-ball.

Adjustments: If the glass twists too much, you used too much left 'English'. Shift your cue so you are hitting the glass only ⅛ inch from the center. The most common error comes from using the incorrect speed on the glass, and it could take a little practice to get it just right, so be patient.

14.11: Corner to Corner Spin

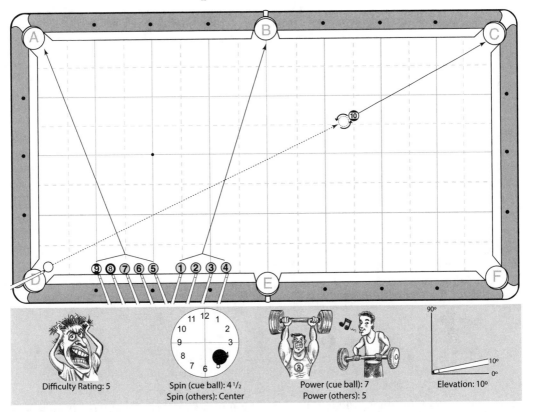

| Difficulty Rating: 5 | Spin (cue ball): 4 1/2
Spin (others): Center | Power (cue ball): 7
Power (others): 5 | Elevation: 10° |

The *Corner to Corner Spin* is actually a little easier for the top 9-ball players than it is for professional trick shot artists because their shot making is far more accurate. Even though Mike Dechaine created this shot, you may want to ask him about the lunch he had to buy me because of this shot. We were practicing for the 2012 World Cup of Trick Shots and after he missed a few attempts, I came up and knocked it in on my first try! Of course, I didn't give him a chance to continue the bet because I knew that if we kept going, I would end up buying his meals for a long time. Shoot the cue ball into the 10-ball, sending it into corner pocket 'C'. Use extreme side English so that the cue ball spins in place. Before it stops spinning, pocket the 1-4 balls in side pocket 'B', and the 5-9 balls in corner pocket 'A'.

Setup: The 1-9 balls are frozen to the cushion in line. Make sure there is enough space between the balls so they have a clear path into their respective pockets. The cue ball is placed between the pocket jaws. The 10-ball is placed on the 2 1/2 diamond line, and it is adjusted slightly so you have a straight-in shot across the diagonal of the table.

Solution: Use extreme 4 1/2 English. The draw is necessary because the cue ball is not allowed to hit a rail. If (and this is a big IF) you make the 10-ball, you should have plenty of time to pocket the remaining nine balls.

Tips: When beginning this shot, don't think about shooting the 1-9 balls. Put all of your focus on making the 10-ball. This shot is plenty hard without using any English, and when you add extreme right spin, it becomes very difficult, even for a top player. Try to keep a consistent speed and grip tightness on the cue's butt, as this will give you the same amount of deflection on each attempt.

14.12: Rebound

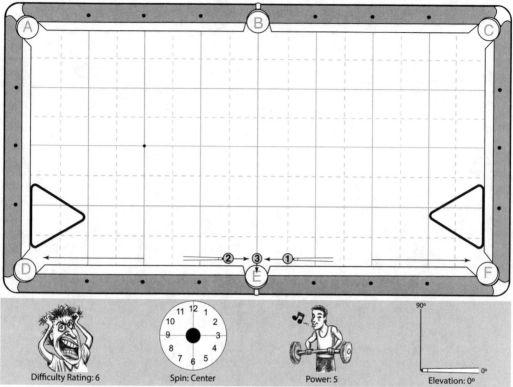

Difficulty Rating: 6   **Spin: Center**   **Power: 5**   **Elevation: 0°**

Rebound is my own invention, and it is also a variation of a classic shot that most people have seen or heard of at one time or another. In the classic version, two balls are placed at the opposite corner pockets on the line running diagonally across the table. Two players simultaneously hit the balls toward each other. The balls collide near the middle of the table and rebound, each going into the corner pocket where they started. I decided to come up with a single player version, and *Rebound* was the result. Hold two cues, one in each hand, and simultaneously shoot the 1-ball and 2-ball toward the 3-ball. They will hit the 3-ball and rebound into their corresponding corner pockets. The 3-ball goes into side pocket 'E'.

Setup: The 3-ball is placed close to the side pocket, right in the middle. The 1-ball and 2-ball are positioned on either side, about two ball-widths from the 3-ball. Two racks are placed at either end of the table as shown to enlarge the pockets.

Solution: Stand right in the center as this helps you to get a simultaneous hit on both balls. This is critical because, if one ball gets there before the other, nothing will work. I use two jump cues, and I hold them in a fist about 3-4 inches from the tip.

Adjustments: If you are okay with making the 1 and 2 balls, but are having difficulty making the 3-ball, place the 1-ball and 2-ball a little further from the rail. Aim both balls back toward the cushion to contact the 3. If the shot is hit correctly, the balls will still rebound as planned, and the backward angle will squeeze the 3-ball into the side. Try it a few times without the 3-ball, then add it once you can consistently make the 1 and 2 balls.

15: Partner Shots

When the World Cup of Trick Shots was created back in 2006, the original plan was to use the same format as Trick Shot Magic, which is an individual competition. One of the players on the USA Team would select a shot and shoot it, and then a player from Team Europe would answer, and so on. I asked the producer if we could include shots that incorporated multiple players. His simple 'yes' led to a whole array of new shots.

At that first event, Bruce Barthelette and I led off, and we selected the first televised partner shot in competition, *Bruce's Weave*, which is included here. Later in the four-man match, Team USA led off with a partner version of Steve Mizerak's *Just Showin' Off Shot*, the one that was diagrammed in the introduction and that was used in the famous Miller Lite commercial.

A number of the partner shots from television are really individual shots, only repeated twice so each player has to make it. I will not include these shots in this chapter, but I will show you a group of unique shots that we have come up with over the years.

15.1: Bruce's Weave

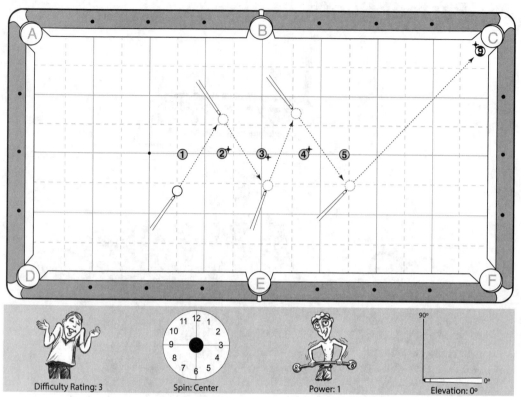

| Difficulty Rating: 3 | Spin: Center | Power: 1 | Elevation: 0° |

No, this shot wasn't named after Bruce's hair. Instead, *Bruce's Weave* comes from the way the cue ball weaves through the line of balls. The first player shoots the cue ball through the first gap. The second player shoots the cue ball through the second gap, and so on until the first player shoots the cue ball directly into the 9-ball, making it in corner pocket 'C'. Bruce Barthelette and I came up with this shot for the first ESPN World Cup of Trick Shots back in 2006. I shot the cue ball first, and finished the shot by making the hanger. When I am playing, I usually don't notice anything other than the shot on which I am concentrating. Later, when I was watching the show on ESPN, something happened that I didn't notice when I was performing the shot. I realized that after Bruce made his second (and last) hit on the cue ball, he yelled 'YES' as if we had already completed the shot. Of course, this was before I had even shot the cue ball into the hanger! It's a good thing that I didn't let him down.

Setup: Hang the 9-ball in front of pocket 'C'. The 3-ball is centered in the middle of the table, and the other balls are along the center line with gaps that are three ball-widths wide. Though you have cue ball in hand, it should be placed about five or six inches from the 1-ball where shown.

Solution: Control your speed, and be sure not to baby these shots. The other player should be able to return the ball even if you hit it a little faster. However, try not to hit it too fast. It is easy to increase the speed for each hit on the cue ball, and eventually it could be too fast to handle.

Adjustments: The most common mistake is to run into one of the blocker balls. The trick is to use the cue ball's momentum and to aim accordingly. After the cue ball goes through the first gap, the second player needs to hit it between the 2-ball and 3-ball. That player should aim at the edge of the 2-ball because the momentum of the cue ball should alter the path from the aim line, thereby causing it to go right through the center. You need to use some judgment because a slower moving cue ball will not have as much momentum.

15.2: Pitcher & Batter

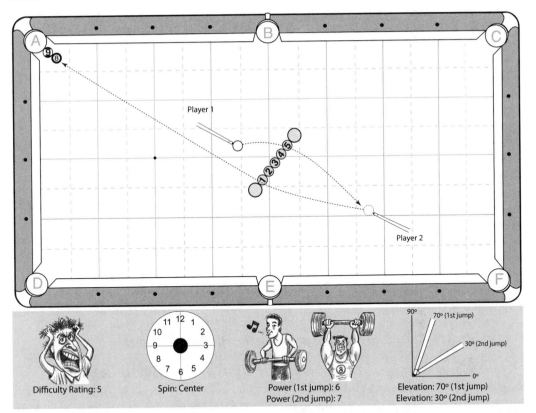

Difficulty Rating: 5	Spin: Center	Power (1st jump): 6 Power (2nd jump): 7	Elevation: 70° (1st jump) Elevation: 30° (2nd jump)

Pitcher & Batter is another original from Bruce Barthelette and myself. The first player jumps the cue ball over the line of balls toward the second player, who, in turn, jumps it back over the line, making the 8-9 combo into pocket 'A'. We made this shot at the 2006 ESPN World Cup of Trick Shots, and while the two players from Team Europe (Nick Nikolaidis and Bogdan Wolkowski) had never practiced it before, they were able to come as close as possible without making it. Nick served up the first jump shot perfectly, and Bogdan hit the return jump very well, but ever so slightly to the right. The cue ball landed and bounced over the edge of the combination without hitting it.

Setup: Five blocker balls are frozen in line near the center of the table. Two plastic cups are placed at each end of the line. The 8-9 combination is hanging in the corner pocket 'A', and you start with the cue ball in hand.

Solution: The first player should jump the cue ball as high as he possibly can, as this will slow it down and make it easier for the second player to jump the ball. During the televised competitions, the cue ball is allowed to fly off the table, so the second player doesn't have to worry about hitting the shot too hard. Still, you must be careful because, while it may be legal for a ball to fly off the table in a tournament, it can still break something, or hurt someone.

Tips: Both parts of the shot can be played using a normal jump cue, but we use the Popper for the first shot, and a standard jump cue for the second shot. When this shot was first used in competition, I was the one performing the first jump, and the Popper enabled me to put the cue ball very close to the line of blockers. It worked because the cue ball was barely moving when my partner jumped it back.

15.3: Cue Ball Toast

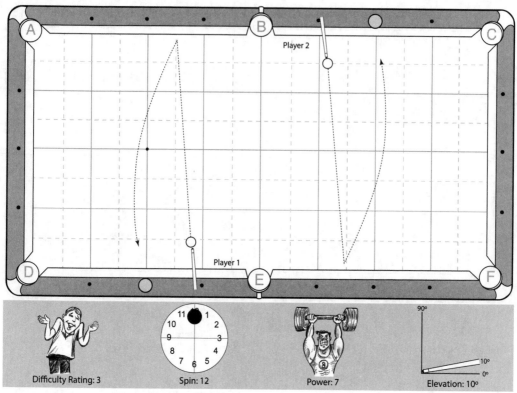

Difficulty Rating: 3   Spin: 12   Power: 7   Elevation: 10°

Cue Ball Toast was first performed during the 2006 ESPN World Cup of Trick Shots by Mike Massey and Tom Rossman. Two players shoot cue balls across the table at the same time. Both balls hit the opposite rail and fly back at the shooter, who picks up a plastic cup and catches the cue ball. The two players then make a toast to a successful shot (without actually drinking the cue ball).

Setup: Each player places a cue ball near the long rail, and a plastic cup on the rail top where shown.

Solution: When you are shooting the ball across the table, elevate slightly (not too much). The cue ball must be about 1/4 inch in the air when it hits the opposite cushion. If the cue ball is travelling too low, it will simply roll back toward you. If it is too high, it will jump forward and away from you. The cup is placed near your bridge hand so that you can pick it up with ease.

Tips: I use a full length jump/break cue, and I like to place the cue ball against the rail. I suggest that you find the right starting position for your stroke as everyone has their own preference. If you pretend that you are jumping over a shaft, this should give you the right elevation and power to complete the shot.

15.4: Newton's Line

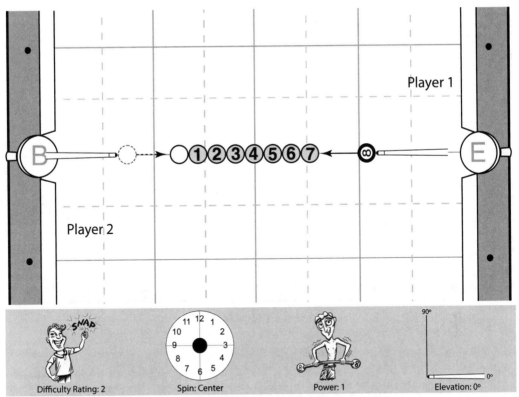

Difficulty Rating: 2   Spin: Center   Power: 1   Elevation: 0°

Tom Rossman and I came up with this shot while practicing at Willow Billiards in Hoboken, NJ. Tom came in for a show and we spent the day working on new partner shots for the upcoming Team USA match against Team Europe. We called it *Newton's Line* because it resembled 'Newton's Balls', which is a novelty item that you may find in a shop which sells office desk accessories. I started out by shooting the 8-ball into the line of balls, causing the cue ball to separate and travel toward side pocket 'B' while the 8-ball stayed right there and joined the line of balls. Tom then shot the cue ball back into the line, causing the 8-ball to roll away. We repeated this process one more time, hitting the 8-ball, then the cue ball, and on that final hit, Tom made the 8-ball in side pocket 'E'.

Setup: Balls 1-7 are frozen in line along the center of the table, the 4-ball goes on the exact center spot, and the cue ball is frozen to the 1-ball. The first shooter may place the 8-ball anywhere along the center line.

Solution: Hit the 8-ball and cue ball slowly, using just enough speed to make the opposite ball in the closer side pocket. The speed must be slow enough to allow your partner to hit his ball back with accuracy. You also need to make sure that you aim for, and hit, the center of the end ball in the line. Anything off center will cause the line to twist, and the balls to roll sideways.

Adjustments: It seems natural to use a stop shot stroke, but that will not work because the weight of eight balls in the line would cause the cue ball (or 8-ball) to draw back a little. Any separation between the balls makes the shot exponentially more difficult. Use center ball, or even $1/2$ tip of top spin.

15.5: Lightening & Thunder

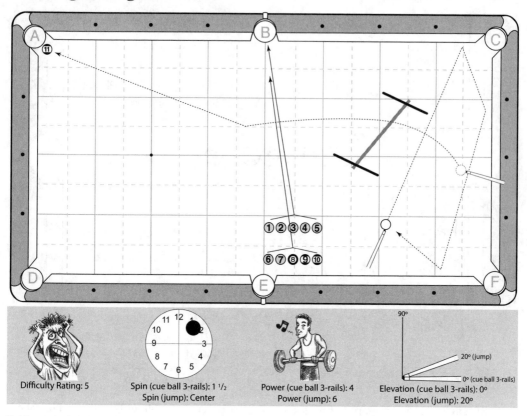

| Difficulty Rating: 5 | Spin (cue ball 3-rails): 1 ½ Spin (jump): Center | Power (cue ball 3-rails): 4 Power (jump): 6 | Elevation (cue ball 3-rails): 0° Elevation (jump): 20° |

Lightening & Thunder is another shot Bruce Barthelette and I came up with for the World Cup of Trick Shots. The first player shoots the cue ball three cushions and, while it is rolling, quickly pockets the 1-5 balls into side pocket 'B'. The same player re-hits the cue ball three cushions, and then pockets the 6-10 balls in the same side pocket. The same player again re-hits the cue ball for the third time, but this time only two cushions. The second player jumps the moving cue ball between the racks and over the prop, making the 11-ball in corner pocket 'A'. I have since turned this shot into a one-player version, where I do all the work.

Setup: The 6-10 balls are between the side pocket and third diamond, and they are one ball-width from the cushion. The 1-5 balls are aligned with the other balls, two ball-widths from the first row. You have cue ball in hand, and the 11-ball is hanging in front of pocket 'A'. A block of wood is flanked by two upright racks.

Solution: Don't hit the cue ball too softly. If you don't use enough speed on the cue ball, it may be difficult to get a solid second hit. You should have plenty of time to make the five balls in the side pocket.

Tips: You need to change your aim angle when hitting the cue ball for the third time. Aim a little closer to corner pocket 'C' so that the cue ball is far enough away from the rail. This ensures that your partner has enough room to form a solid bridge for the jump portion of the shot.

15.6: Target Practice

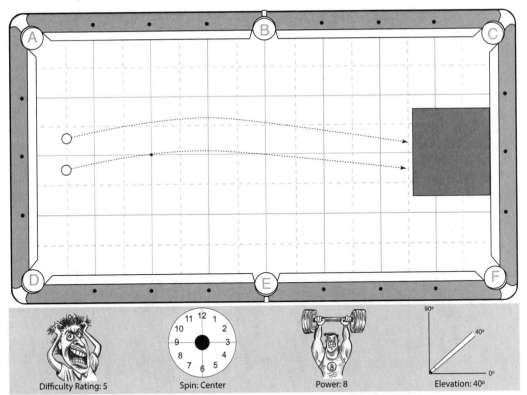

| Difficulty Rating: 5 | Spin: Center | Power: 8 | Elevation: 40° |

Bruce Barthelette and I got into a little bit of trouble at an ESPN event when we first invented *Target Practice*. The idea is that we each take turns jumping the cue ball through one of two holes cut out of the box at the other end of the table. The announcers were Mitch Laurence and Allen Hopkins, so we decided to print out photos of Mitch and Allen, overlay them with a sniper's target image, and tape them to the box so they covered the holes. Bruce jumped through Mitch's picture, and I jumped through Allen's. Needless to say, they had fun during the commentary. When it was Team Europe's turn to answer, we gave them pictures of Bruce and me to give them an added incentive to make the shot.

Setup: A large box made of hard plastic is frozen to the end cushion. Two holes are cut into the front that are six inches in diameter, and that are six inches from the bottom. Two paper targets are taped over the holes (optional). The two shooters have cue ball in hand, but they may be no more than two ball-widths from the short rail. The illustration leading off chapter 11 will give you an idea of how this shot is set up.

Solution: There is no real trick to this shot. Just jump the cue ball as far as you can. Make sure you get a solid hit on the cue ball because if you contact it even a fraction of an inch off center, that will take away some distance. CAUTION: It is very easy to jump the balls off the table or rip the cloth on this shot, so please proceed with caution, and at your own risk.

Tips: Try one of these methods if you are having trouble jumping as far as *Target Practice* requires. Bruce Barthelette uses an open hand bridge on the rail. I put my leg up on the rail and use a closed bridge, braced on my leg. Jamey Gray does the same thing, but he uses a dart style grip (pinky forward, thumb back). This just goes to show you that each player has his own technique for long distance jumps. So, give these a try, or find your own method.

15.7: Motion Resistance Draw

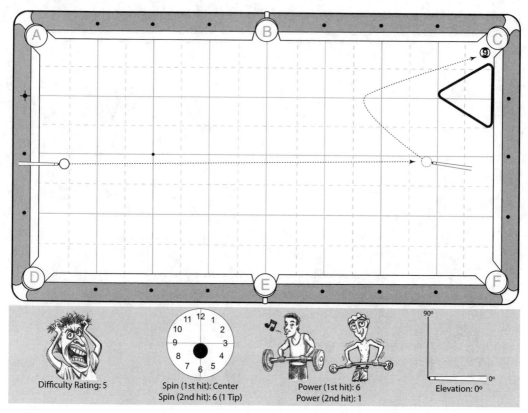

Difficulty Rating: 5	Spin (1st hit): Center Spin (2nd hit): 6 (1 Tip)	Power (1st hit): 6 Power (2nd hit): 1	Elevation: 0°

The concept for the *Motion Resistance Draw* has been around for a while, but this two-player variation was invented by Jamey Gray and Bruce Barthelette. The first player shoots the cue ball toward the second player, who hits it forward with a little draw, causing it to bend around the rack and to make the 9-ball in pocket 'C'.

Setup: The 9-ball is hanging in front of pocket 'C' and a rack enlarges the pocket. You have cue ball in hand at the far end of the table.

Solution: The second player is down in his stance and ready with his cue angled slightly to his right so that he is aiming at the first diamond on the far short cushion. Aiming on this shot is all on the first player, who must hit the cue ball directly into the second player's cue.

Tips: The first player must hit this firmly enough. Pretend that you want to lag the cue ball down table, back toward yourself and then back to the other end again. The second player should just poke at the cue ball with a touch of draw (not too low). The cue ball's momentum will cause it to curve around the rack. The cue ball should almost bounce off the second player's tip.

15.8: Double Wing Shot

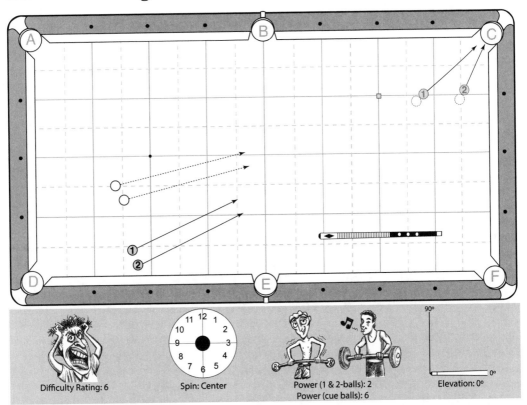

Difficulty Rating: 6   **Spin:** Center   **Power (1 & 2-balls):** 2
Power (cue balls): 6   **Elevation:** 0°

Tom Rossman and I came up with the *Double Wing* shot for the 2010 ESPN World Cup of Trick Shots. The following year, Tim Chin and Bruce Barthelette gave this one another try. The first player shoots the 1-ball and then the 2-ball down table. The second player shoots the first cue ball, making the 1-ball (wing shot), and then shoots the second cue ball to make the 2-ball (another wing shot). The 1-ball and 2-ball must both be rolling before the second player is allowed to shoot at them. Since wing shots are Tom's specialty, I shot the object balls, and Tom shot the cue balls.

Setup: The two cue balls are placed between one and two diamonds off the long rail, while the 1-ball and 2-ball are closer to the rail as shown. A cube of chalk is positioned on the 1,2 diamond intersection line to prevent the first player from shooting the balls too close to the corner pocket (which would make the shot too easy). A butt is placed on the table to catch the first cue ball, and to stop it from interfering with the rest of the shot.

Solution: Even though the second player has to make the wing shots, the first player's task is just as tough because he must control the speed of the two object balls, which must be hit with the exact same power. Don't hit them too softly, and be sure to wait until the 1-ball is past the halfway point on the table before shooting the 2-ball. This should separate the balls enough so that the second player doesn't have to be in a rush to hit both cue balls.

Tips: If both players are shooting right-handed, as was the case with Bruce Barthelette and Tim Chin (when we used this for the World Cup of Trick Shots in 2011), the players can get in each other's way. To solve this problem, have the first player shoot the object balls lefty (which is exactly what Tim Chin did!). Yes, it makes it a little more difficult to get the speed and control, but it does allow the second player to be in position, and ready to shoot.

Part III

The Lighter Side

16: Funny Stories

16.1: Andy Segal

When I first started doing trick shots and playing professional 9-ball, I did a lot of shows for Blatt Billiards in NYC. Most of the shows were for free (or a small fee), and I did them mainly to get my name out there. A few higher priced shows came out of it, so I will always be grateful for my time working with Blatt Billiards and Barry Dubow, who is their marketing manager.

One of the events was booked at an exclusive clothing store just off Madison Avenue, around 65th street – right in the middle of where everything costs a fortune. The event was a photo shoot for a European designer, so a custom made shirt and tie were given to me to wear at this event. All I had to bring was black slacks, dress shoes, and my pool cues. Jennifer Barretta was also performing, and I believe she had an outfit custom made for her as well (though the name of the designer escapes me). I had my slacks cleaned earlier in the week along with some other clothes, and I took the slacks to work with me that day, still wrapped in plastic.

After arriving at the venue, I went into the back room to change, and came out looking white as a ghost. Barry Dubow was there, and he asked me what was wrong. I informed him in as steady a voice as I could manage that I had accidentally brought a pair of my wife's black pants instead of my dress slacks. I was in the middle of my fifth apology when he asked me if I was insane. I stopped just long enough to hear him tell me that I was performing in a clothing store, and that I should go select one of a hundred pair of black pants hanging on the racks.

If I had made that mistake anywhere else, I would have been sunk. What can I say? Maybe I am the luckiest guy in the world.

16.2: Sal Conti

Sal Conti started playing on the trick shot tour back in 2004. His first event was the North-eastern Artistic Pool Championship at Shooter's Billiards in Southington, CT (his home room, which he owns). Sal quickly moved up in the rankings and eventually he was invited to the 2007 ESPN Trick Shot Magic competition, held at the ESPN Zone in the New York New York Casino in Las Vegas, NV.

Bruce Barthelette was on Team USA for the World Cup of Trick Shots at the time and, being good friends with Sal, he came along for moral support, and to help him prepare for the event. A few weeks before the tournament, Sal had an allergic reaction at one of his son's sporting events and was taken to the hospital, in need of a shot of steroids to help him get through this episode.

Everything turned out well and Sal was looking forward to the upcoming ESPN event. That was when I received a call from Bruce, who told me this story and was wondering what kind of practical joke we could play on Sal. We put our heads together (which is very dangerous) and came up with a plan. We would write a letter and put it on fake ESPN letterhead. The letter would go on about how there are new sporting regulations which require all competitors to take a urine test for drugs, steroids and HGH. Bruce and I printed up three copies and had the producer put them in Sal's, Matt MacPhail's and my player envelopes, which get handed out during the players meeting. Matt and I sat on either side of Sal during this meeting, and we pulled out our copies so that Sal would see them and then assume that we all got one. The idea was to get Sal to stand up and complain about this 'new policy' during the meeting, and we would all have a good laugh. But as it turned out, he didn't say a word!

Afterwards, each player had 15-20 minutes of private practice time, so Bruce went into the room with Sal to help him. When they were done, Bruce informed me that Sal was very upset, that he was throwing the balls around the table and was complaining about how he dedicated six months of hard work practicing for this event. Now it would be all over because of some stupid allergic reaction, and that there was no way he was going to pass this urine test. It was then that Bruce told him it was all a joke, adding of course that it was all my fault.

Now for the kicker. Sal and I ended up playing each other in the first round of the tournament, and I am sorry to say that he got his revenge. Of course, if you ask Bruce, he will tell you a slightly modified version of the story. He says that it was all a ploy to motivate Sal into winning our match since he was acting as his coach and was simply doing a coach's job. The only good thing that came out of this (from my point of view) was that Sal ended up setting a record in the semi-finals by making 10 out of his 10 selected shots, something no one else has ever been able to do.

Anyway, here is a copy of the letter:

The National Sporting Agency and ESPN now have stricter
guidelines regarding the use of performance enhancing drugs for
any televised sporting event. Because of this, all players in this
year's Trick Shot Magic will be required to undergo tests for the
following:

1. Drugs
2. Steroids
3. Human Growth Hormones (HGH)

Positive tests will result in disqualification from this and future
events.

Doctors will be available from 9:30pm - 10:00pm in room AA224,
which is on the second floor (follow the signs off the elevators).
Players are asked to go down for testing immediately following
the players meeting. It should take no more than 5-10 minutes
per player.

Thank you for your cooperation.

16.3: Matt MacPhail

I get calls from agents all of the time asking me to do shows around the country. Whenever I am unavailable, I refer them to friends in the business. A number of years ago I was asked to do a show in Arizona for a private corporate event. The dates they needed me for were already booked, so I referred the show to a friend of mine, Matt MacPhail. At the time, Matt was an up and coming trick shot artist who was doing exceptionally well in most events, and who was invited to the 2007 ESPN Trick Shot Magic tournament in Las Vegas.

I put Matt in touch with the agent, and they worked out a price. A few weeks later he was off to Arizona. When he returned, I called to see how the event went and he told me it was the easiest work that he ever did. I'm now thinking that since he is a trick shot artist, performing IS more fun than standard work. Makes sense, right? Wrong. This is what actually happened; Matt arrived at the hotel, found the agent, and asked where the pool table was. The agent told him that they didn't like the way the pool table looked in the room, so they removed it. "Oh, and by the way, here is your check and you are welcome to hang out and enjoy the party."

I wish I could get jobs like that. It figures – I refer this job to a friend and...

16.4: Tony Robles

Tony Robles is one of the best professional 9-ball players in the world, and he is a 7-times Tri-State Player of the Year. Tony is currently running the amateur/pro Predator 9-ball Tour in and around the New York City area, and he is the founder and CEO of the National Amateur Pool League.

Back when I was playing, we traveled together to some events. I never had a billiards instructor, but Tony is probably the closest person to a mentor that I had when I first started out on the 9-ball tour.

Tony and I would sometimes refer each other to shows that the other one of us couldn't make. On one occasion I remember referring Tony to a spot on a soap opera as a body double, and as a technical advisor for a pool scene. I have always been confused about that since we were going to act as a body double, shooting the shots on camera, and Tony's skin complexion is far darker than mine. I have the 'pool room tan' which means I am white as a ghost, so I never understood how they could consider both of us as an on camera double for the same actor!

Some time later Tony referred me to a job at Pressure, a beautiful club in New York City. Pressure has a different activity on each floor (pool, bowling, etc), and it is the same place where I filmed a 12-week teaser series for Spike TV called Bikini Pool Shark. I believe some of the videos are still up on Spike's website. The show Tony gave to me was for the re-launch of Teen Magazine. I had no idea what Teen was all about until I found myself in a room with over 200 girls, all between the ages of 21 and 30. There were at most four or five men present that weren't on the staff – and I was one of them and, of course, the main attraction for the evening. It is safe to say that I enjoyed working that event, and when I told Tony all about the gig the next day, I could feel his pain.

16.5: Adam Ferrara

In my freshman year of college in the late 1980's I met Jim Dale, who became one of my best friends. We were attending Carnegie Mellon University in Pittsburgh. While there, we played pool more often than our parents would have liked. Summer breaks were no exception, especially since we lived close to one another – I in Queens, New York, and Jim in Long Island. I would usually take the train out for the weekend, and we would spend most of our time at the Huntington Village Billiard Club (which has since closed down). One of the regular players there was named Adam Ferrara. Adam was a comedian whose career was taking off. He was performing stand-up at Governor's Comedy Club in Levittown, New York., but soon thereafter he appeared on The Tonight Show, Late Night With David Letterman, and Comedy Central.

One afternoon we were shooting around at the pool room, but we had plans to go see Adam perform later that evening. Jim and I started doing a few trick shots, and I got Adam involved in one of them. The shot is more of a gag. You tell the mark that you can place two quarters on the table with a third on top. If you hit into the upper quarter, the other two will pop up and fly through the air. The mark should stand behind the table and catch them, but since that would be too easy, they have to start with both hands in their pockets, and have to wait until the cue ball is hit before they can remove them. Obviously, all of that is a lie because the real goal of the shot is to have the cue ball go up the ramp created by the center quarter and hit the mark where it counts.

Adam had never seen this shot before, so he fell right into the trap. After the business with the cue ball was done, he fell on the floor but was not in pain. Adam was laughing so hard that he couldn't remain upright. Jim and I didn't realize until we were driving to the comedy club that we had a huge problem. We were going to be both sitting in the front row during the show to watch a comedian who earlier that day had been the victim of a successful practical joke. Expecting more pain than we inflicted, we sat nervously waiting for the torture to start. Fortunately Adam's memory was short-lived, so we were spared.

16.6: Team USA

The World Cup of Trick Shots competition is between two teams, one from the USA, and one from Europe. There are four players on each team. The first two matches are called the semi-finals even though they are not standard semi-finals with the winner advancing. The winning team in each semi-final gets one point to carry over into the final match, which pits all four players on each team against each other. We always tried to come up with partner shots because these were unique, and were very rarely seen on television. Team USA originally consisted of myself, Bruce Barthelette, Mike Massey, and Tom Rossman. Since Bruce and I lived the closest to one another, we would get together a few times to develop some partner shots. Sometimes we worked on four-player shots, each of us performing two parts. When Mike and Tom arrived about a week before the tournament, we practiced them to see which ones worked, and which ones didn't. Here is the original diagram of one such four-player shot that Bruce and I submitted into the World Cup of Trick Shots program.

Tom Rossman and I were the fastest on the team, Mike had the best draw stroke, and Bruce could long jump better than anyone, so we tried to incorporate all four of those skills into one shot as follows:

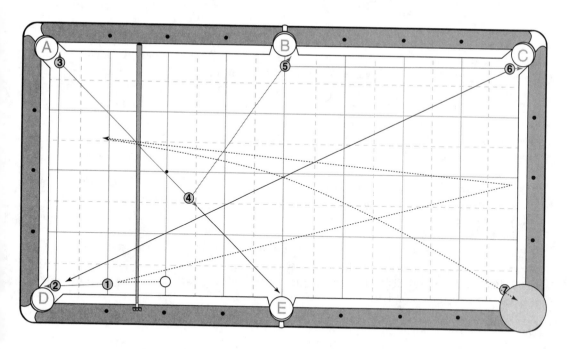

Setup: The 2, 3, 4, 5, and 6 balls are all balanced on top of coin wrappers. A bridge is spread across the table, and a large 8-ball pillow is wedged into the corner pocket, keeping the 7-ball from falling.

Part 1: Mike Massey shoots the cue ball into the 1-ball, making it in corner pocket 'D', travelling under the 2-ball, and causing it to fall in place. The cue ball will draw up table and back down again. The rest of the shot happens after Mike hits the cue ball, and while it is still rolling.

Part 2: I shoot the 2-ball into corner pocket 'A', under the 3-ball, causing it to fall.

Part 3: Tom Rossman shoots the 3-ball into side pocket 'E', under the 4-ball, causing it to fall.

Part 4: Mike gets out of the way, and I then shoot the 4-ball into side pocket 'B', causing the 5-ball to fall.

Part 5: Tom shoots the 5-ball down the long rail and into corner pocket 'C', causing the 6-ball to fall.

Part 6: I run around and shoot the 6-ball straight into corner pocket 'D', where I started (where the 1-ball was made).

Part 7: Bruce has been waiting patiently while all of this has been going on. Assuming Mike hit the cue ball with enough draw (which he *always* did), it should be just rolling under the bridge by this time. Once clear, Bruce jumps the cue ball over the bridge and into the pillow at the other end of the table. The 7-ball was wedged under the pillow, hanging over the pocket opening. Once the cue ball hits the pillow off the table, the 7-ball will fall into the pocket, completing the shot.

All of this sounded great on paper, but we never had the opportunity to choreograph the shot with all four of us present until about three days before the competition. On our first attempt, Mike put a massive stroke on the cue ball and stood up, keeping his cue pointed in front of him. I shot the 2-ball as planned, and started to run around Mike. Unfortunately, I ran eye first into the tip of his cue stick. My feet kept going forward while my head shot straight back. It seemed as if I hovered in the air for a second before I fell flat on my back, like in a cartoon. While I am grabbing my eye and everyone else is hovering over me to see if I'm okay, all I can think about is how we are going to find my replacement three days before the tournament. Lucky for me I had just started wearing contact lenses, one of which now had a perfect blue circle on it from Mike's tip. I'm sure you have seen scenes in movies where someone gets stabbed and the victim has a book or wallet in his pocket, which prevents the knife from hurting him? "Eye" am living proof that it works.

We renamed that shot 'The Eyeball Shot', and then quickly pulled it from the tournament.

16.7: Three Amigos

I used to work on Wall Street for Standard & Poor's, which is down on 55 Water Street, only a five-minute walk from the World Trade Center, which was attacked on 9/11. Most of you from the northeast probably know about the Super Billiards Expo, which is held every year in Valley Forge, PA (it has since moved to New Jersey). Allen Hopkins does a great job, and the Expo is one of the large events that everyone looks forward to every Spring. Mike Massey came into town to stay with Bruce Barthelette for a few days before the tournament, and on the Wednesday right before the event, Bruce, Mike, and Sal Conti all drove down to meet me at my office. We were planning to have lunch in the city and then drive down to Valley Forge together. Downtown New York was the perfect place for them to take a break from their six hour trip.

Right before a major tournament, my head is completely focused on playing pool, not on work. So even though we were scheduled to leave around 2 P.M., my mind had left work as soon as I woke up that morning at 5:30 A.M. My wife Kim showed up a little earlier than the boys, so we decided to take a walk around South Street Seaport. Bruce called about 10 minutes before they arrived, I told them where the office garage was located, and Kim and I started walking back to meet them. The parking garage is on Old Slip, right between Water Street and the FDR Drive. As Kim and I got to the corner of Water Street and Old Slip, we saw something strange - Mike Massey was on his knees behind a parked car, reaching underneath for something, Sal was walking around looking for something else, and Bruce was running down the street.

After the attacks on 9/11, security at office buildings was heightened, and searches were done on all cars coming into the garage. Bruce was stopped as he pulled in, and a guard did a camera sweep under his car for explosives. The guard then asked Bruce to unlock the back of his SUV, which he did. As soon as he opened the back, three boxes of pool balls, which had been packed standing upright, fell out and the balls started bouncing and rolling all over the place. There were balls rolling down the sidewalk, under cars, into the garage, and everywhere else you can possibly imagine. These were the balls that were going to be used for the tournament, so it would be a pretty big problem if they were lost. Fortunately all but one was recovered, the only casualty being a spotted Aramith cue ball.

Since this was a big expo, we were able to get one of the vendors to give us a replacement cue ball for our tournament. I think the funniest part was thinking about the people I worked with, and imagining what they would think when they left work and found a cue ball rolling around the street, knowing that I had left earlier that day for a pool tournament.

16.8: Jerry Orbach

I was performing one of my earlier shows for Blatt Billiards at the New York Athletic Club for the annual cue maker's show. Hundreds of people were there including news crews, photographers, actors, etc. It was a very big night for me, to say the least. Paul Sorvino and Jerry Orbach, two famous actors, local to New York City, were among those present. Both were very big pool fans who I would run into on weeknights from time to time, playing at one of the Amsterdam Billiard Clubs on the Upper East Side or on the Upper West Side. Mainly it was Paul as Jerry didn't come around that much unless there was a big event going on. Just so you know, Paul Sorvino is a pretty decent pool player. When he was in town, we would regularly play in a Chicago ring game with George San Souci ('Ginky') and a rotating fourth based on attendance that night. Paul could run 30 when playing straight pool if he was in stroke, which isn't bad for someone who doesn't play all that much.

Back to that night. A pool table was in the center of the room, and about a hundred people were surrounding it with a 6-foot gap between them and the table. A few photographers were taking stills, and there was one person filming the show. About halfway through my 15 minute set, I was doing a shot where the 5-ball was down at the other end of the table. I was going to shoot around it a bunch of times before eventually making another ball.

I was in the middle of my pre-shot patter when Jerry Orbach walked out from the crowd, picked up the 5-ball, and started explaining something to a friend of his. He was pointing at the table, talking about some shot that probably came up a while ago, completely oblivious to the show, the cameras, and the hundred or so people around him. Without skipping a beat, I worked Jerry into the show. I asked for a volunteer to hold the 5-ball, looked at him and said, "Oh, thank you sir" (he was still not paying attention, but I had the crowd laughing and they were on my side now). Every time he pointed around the table, I would say, "I will hit the cue ball there, no, over there, actually it will be right there…", and so on, following his finger each time. Eventually Jerry's friend stopped listening to his story and saw what was going on, and he motioned for Jerry to look at me. He did, then looked surprisingly around at the crowd and apologized. You can't write this kind of stuff, and if we had planned this in advance, it wouldn't have been nearly as funny.

The first time I met Jerry Orbach was at the Amsterdam Billiard Club on the Upper East Side of NYC. I was playing on the front table and had my break cue sitting against a stool. Jerry grabbed the cue and started swinging it around like he was Tom Cruise in The Color of Money. Needless to say, I ran right up with my hand outstretched, trying to get my cue back. Jerry held out his hand and shook it, saying "Nice to meet you." Being a celebrity, I guess he is used to things like that happening. I responded with, "Nice to meet you too. Now can I please have my cue stick back?"

When my mother lived in New York, she was a big fan of *The Fantasticks*, an off-Broadway show and the longest running musical play in history. Jerry Orbach was one of the original members of the cast. When he passed away in 2004, the world lost a great actor - and he will be missed.

16.9: Mitch & Ewa Laurance

The 2005 Trick Shot Magic was not a fun competition. Actually, I shouldn't say that. It was a good event, but I got knocked out in the first round. That year, the producers decided to have two events, one for the men, and one for the women. One of the competitors was Ewa Laurance, one of the all-time great players and a member of the Hall of Fame. Ewa has always done trick shot shows, but the shots she does in her shows differ greatly from shots that are done in a competition. Bruce Barthelette, Mike Massey, and I were practicing together for the men's event even though we were competitors, and Ewa came over for some coaching. We all took turns helping her out with new shots that she could use to fool her opponents. When all was said and done, Ewa won her event, and the three of us all got knocked out right from the gate!

The top prize was a check for $25,000, which Ewa received immediately following the tournament. What happened next is told by Mitch Laurance:

At the end of an intense, terrific final matchup against Allison Fisher for the title of International Trick Shot Champion at the New York New York Hotel in Las Vegas in 2005, my wife Ewa finally made the final shot to secure her victory. After an emotional reunion with me when the match ended (I was in the production truck during the recording of the telecast) and the usual post-final events, Ewa and I were thrilled to be able to share the thrill of victory with the many good friends who rooted her home.

Ewa and I are often fortunate enough to be together when one of us receives a check for our work, so it is our custom that one of us will entrust their check to the other for safekeeping, usually depending on who is less, shall we say, "energetic" at the moment (Note from Andy: Bruce adds that Ewa wanted to hold onto the check, but Mitch insisted that he hold it for safe keeping). *Ewa proceeded to give me her huge check that represented the Champion's well-earned reward. After a fabulous and memorable dinner at the hotel, Ewa and I went out to look for a few gifts for our family. When I went to pay for the gifts, the sickening feeling came over me that the check Ewa had 'entrusted' to me a few hours before was not there. Panic. Despair. Quadruple check of my wallet. My pockets. Her purse. Nothing.*

We hurried back to the hotel, went to the restaurant, and asked if it had been found. Zip. I went hurriedly over to the Lost and Found. Still Lost, Not Found. Ran (for real) over to the hotel police and asked for help. They said that all they could do was to file a report and hope that it turned up. More walking, retracing every possible step from the time Ewa gave me the check yielded only more heartburn.

The only saving grace was that I knew, and kept assuring Ewa, that in the worst case we could have Matt & Bettiane Braun, the wonderful producers of The Trick Shot Championship, void the check and write another, which they gracefully and kindly did.

Needless to say, I gave the new check to Ewa. It has, however, given us lots of laughs since then. Hindsight is a beautiful thing.

Now for the kicker. A men's 9-ball event was also going on the day before. During one of the matches, a couple of beautiful girls from a morally questionable Vegas 'hospitality' service were watching in the audience. The camera men were constantly turning in their direction, so it was a wonder that they got any match footage at all.

Anyway, when Bruce and Sal Conti got word that Mitch had lost Ewa's check, he put on his practical joker's hat and went to work. He purchased a shirt from the establishment where those two beauties were from, poured perfume all over it, stuffed it in an envelope along with a note, and off it went. A few days later, Mitch and Ewa received the package and proceeded to read the note, thanking 'Mitchie' for a great time in Las Vegas, and especially for the $25,000 check he gave them for their 'college' education. The note also said to say hi to all the boys in the truck, and how they were looking forward to seeing him (Mitch) again.

Bruce says, "To this day, I still don't know how the girls got Mitchie's address."

16.10: Andy Segal Reprise

In 2004, a major trick shot tournament called the Las Vegas Artistic Pool Open, was held in conjunction with the APA National Team Championship at the Riviera Hotel and Casino in Las Vegas. Thousands of amateur players were competing, and they loved watching the tournament and seeing the trick shot guys that they had come to know from watching us perform on television. We were constantly being asked for autographs, and to pose for photos.

Picture of Andy Segal with his wife Kimberly right after the awards ceremony at the 2004 Las Vegas Artistic Pool Open.

I had just won the tournament and had spent about 45 minutes taking pictures with various people. We were all set to go out for dinner with a group when I took a long walk to use the restroom. On my way out, I passed a bar where there was a group of about five or six people sitting there drinking. They stopped me and asked if I would take a picture. I smiled and said sure, putting my arm around the guy and posing like I had just done for my fans numerous times during the past hour. They all looked at me like I was crazy, and one of them then said, "No, we want you to take a picture of us." Oops.

17: Photo Gallery

The first World Cup of Trick Shots (2006)
Mohegan Sun Casino
Uncasville, CT
Andy Segal with Bruce Barthelette, right before their semi-final match.

2006 World Cup of Trick Shots
Good friends from Long Island,
coming up to root for Team USA
and getting into the spirit.

2006 World Cup of Trick Shots
Kim Segal with Bogdan Wolkowski
from team Europe, fraternizing
with the opponents.

2010 Southeast Classic
Atlanta, GA
Andy Segal and Nick Nikolaidis,
borrowing the table number
lights during the tear-down.
Can you guess who finished 1st and 2nd?

2012 World Championship
Oak, PA
L to R: Jamey Gray, Andy Segal,
Nick Nikolaidis

2012 US Open
L to R: Steve Markle, Andy Segal,
Abram Diaz

Action shot during practice time
at the 2012 US Open
Tunica, MS

2006 World Cup of Trick Shots
Jessica Segal wishing that her dad will win the event.
Better to throw the coin in the fountain rather than waste it in a slot machine.

2006 World Cup of Trick Shots
Team USA after receiving
our gold medals.
L to R: Mike Massey, Tom Rossman,
Mark Dimick, Andy Segal,
Bruce Barthelette

Andy's daughter Jessica drew a
good luck picture of Team USA
before the 2006 event.
Looks like it worked.

2011 World Championships
King of Prussia, PA
Top 2 finishers from both
the trick shot and the 10-ball event.
L to R: Frank Del Pizzo,
Ralph Souquet, Rob Saez,
Andy Segal, Jamey Gray

2011 World Championships
Andy Segal with the Comcast team,
who filmed the very first
billiard competition in 3D.

2011 World Championships
After beating Jamey Gray in the finals,
we took a candid shot
in front of the trophies.

This is what Jamey was
REALLY thinking.
This shot was taken at
Madame Tussaud's Wax Museum
in New York City.

The 2010 World Cup of Trick Shots
team did a recreation of the
famous Rat Pack photo.

2011 Duel of Champions
Montreal, Canada
Andy Segal with Nick Nikolaidis
during the awards ceremony
announcements.

2006 World Cup of Trick Shots
Andy Segal with Team USA,
receiving their gold medals.

2009 Trick Shot Magic
New York New York Hotel & Casino
Las Vegas, NV
Andy Segal with runner up
Sebastian Giumelli

2009 Trick Shot Magic
Andy Segal with producer
and founder of the event, Matt Braun

2009 Trick Shot Magic
The after-party at the bar,
celebrating the win.
L to R: Dan Flynn, Jason Kane, Jason
Lynch, Andy Segal, Jamey Gray
(behind-turning away), Kim Segal,
Bev Gray (back), Bruce Barthelette

The welcome home party from the
2009 Trick Shot Magic competition.

2004 Las Vegas Open
Andy Segal with his wife
Kimberly Segal immediately after
his second major championship win.

2004 Las Vegas Open
During the APA National
Team Championship at
The Riviera Hotel & Casino.
Top 3 finishers.
L to R: Tom Rossman, Andy Segal,
Mike Massey

Before the 2004 Las Vegas Open,
some of the players went down to a local
pool room and held a mini-tournament
as practice for the main championship.
L to R: Gerry Woodlief,
Charles Darling, Luke Szywala,
Andy Segal, Nick Nikolaidis (leaning),
Paul Danno, Mike Massey

2013 – Walt Disney World
Magic Kingdom
Andy Segal with his daughter Jessica,
and two guests of honor in the
background.

2013 – Walt Disney World – Epcot
I'm Andy Segal and I approved this
photo – NOT!

2012 US Open Tennis
with his daughter Jessica
Arthur Ashe Stadium
Queens, NY

Andy Segal with his daughter
Jessica during a trip to
Colonial Williamsburg in 2010

2012 Mohegan Sun at the World Cup of Trick Shots,
with two good friends from our college days at
Carnegie Mellon University.
L to R: Steve Carpenter, Andy Segal, Jim Dale

2013 – Just returned from a round
of golf at Bruce Barthelette's club in
South Hadley, MA.
Now it is time to start practicing for
the 2013 WPA World Artistic Pool
Championship (4 days before the event).
L to R: Jim Glanville, Mike Massey,
Andy Segal

2009 – Andy Segal with
his mixed martial arts instructor
Sensei Jean.

2009 World Cup of Trick Shots
After the tournament,
the entire Team USA went
up to northern Massachusetts
to perform for the APA.
L to R: Mike Massey, Andy Segal,
Bob Grudzinski, Tom Rossman,
Bruce Barthelette

After the show, Bruce Barthelette
and Andy Segal signing photos
and a special Team USA shirt that
Bob Grudzinski had custom made
for his APA players.

2006 World Cup of Trick Shots
After the tournament,
hanging out with some friends.
L to R (front): Mark Dimick,
Tom Rossman, Andy Segal
L to R (back): Bogdan Wolkowski,
Mike Massey, Stefano Pelinga,
Dawn Hopkins, Nick Nikolaidis,
Bruce Barthelette, Luke Szywala

An old picture from the mid 1990's,
taken at Romine's High Pockets
in Milwalkee, WI during a
professional 9-ball tournament.
L to R: (unknown), JR Calvert,
Jason Kane, Tommy Kennedy (front),
(unknown), Andy Segal, Tony Robles

2007 World Championships
Andy Segal with Eric Yow

2007 World Championships
Top 3 finishers.
L to R: Sebastian Giumelli,
Andy Segal, Mike Massey

2007 World Championships
The Lider Club, St. Petersburg, Russia
Andy Segal after making the winning
shot.

2011 – On the set of
Person of Interest, cast as a detective.

2012 – On the set of
Boardwalk Empire, cast as a
WWI veteran, set in the 1920's.

2011 – On the set of The Dictator,
starring Sacha Baron Cohen and
Ben Kingsley, cast as a boom operator
as part of a three-man news crew
covering The Dictator and
his general's arrival into
New York City.

An old shot from 1998.
Andy Segal with Sean Penn and
Uma Thurman (in the background),
on the set of Sweet and Lowdown,
a Woody Allen film

Andy Segal with former presidential candidate Rick Santorum, while performing at
The Benefits & Selling Expo in 2013. Lincoln Financial Group brought
Andy Segal in to perform at their expo booth and they also brought
in Rick Santorum to make the keynote speech.

While performing in Hong Kong
(2010), there was a little time to spare
to do some sightseeing around the city.

Overlooking Hong Kong
on a very foggy day.

2012 Meucci Factory
Byhalia, MS
Bob Meucci holding up the first
Andy Segal signature series cue
(work in progress)

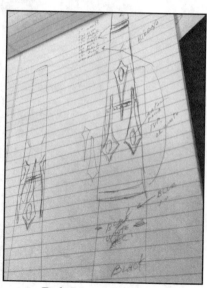

Bob Meucci's sketch
of the AS-4 model.

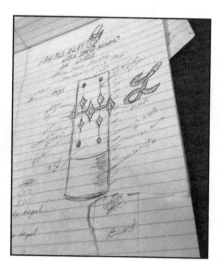

Another sketch of the AS-4
model.

Andy Segal with Buddy Hall
at the Meucci factory.

2010 Trick Shot Magic
Green Valley Ranch Casino
Henderson, NV

2010 Trick Shot Magic
Andy Segal with Florian
Kohler having a discussion
during a break in the
semi-final match.

2010 Trick Shot Magic
Andy Segal with Jamey Gray,
toasting another successful
1st and 2nd place finish.

2010 Trick Shot Magic
The after-party down at the bar.
L to R: Florian Kohler,
Andy Segal, Jamey Gray,
Dave Nangle, Gabi Visoiu (front).

2009 World Cup of Trick Shots
Mohegan Sun Casino, Uncasville, CT
Andy Segal hanging out with some friends from his
mixed martial arts class who came up to see the event.

18: About the Author

Andy Segal started playing pool in High School at JC's in Rego Park, NY. In a group of friends, one will excel at one activity, and another will excel at something else, and so on. Well, pool was Andy's gift. Every weekend he found himself walking the 30 minute trek to the pool room, often playing with friends, but sometimes alone. After Andy entered college, things were no different. He spent hours at night playing on various tables around campus with his best friends, Jim Dale and Alan Gilds. Once they ran out of competitors at Carnegie Mellon, they migrated to the Student Union at the University of Pittsburgh, a much larger school with a Billiard Club. The competition was much stronger at Pitt, so it took a little while to get used to it, but they soon found themselves playing up to the level of the best players in the club.

At the time, JR Calvert (founder of Inside Pool Magazine) was attending the University of Pittsburgh, and he and Andy had many tough matches. JR introduced Andy to the professional side of pool, taking him to his first major competition, The Akron Open, held each year at Starcher's Billiards in Akron, OH. Andy's first match was against Jose Parica, a billiard superstar from the Philippines. After a rough 11-0 loss, Andy then lost his next match 11-2, but he kept going back every year because he knew that this was the next step to improving his game, and he eventually started winning a few matches.

It was at the Akron Open that Andy first met Mike Massey, a future member of the BCA Hall of Fame. While meeting Mike, a funny situation developed. Andy had always done magic growing up, and when he approached Mike and asked him to do a trick shot, Mike said, "Later, but here is a magic trick I can show you." Mike then pulled out a trick deck of cards but, as it turned out, Andy had the very same deck in his pocket! So he pulled his out and said, "Do you mean this trick?", and they have been good friends ever since.

A number of years later, Mike got Andy involved in professional trick shots, and he first competed in the 2002 North American Artistic Pool Championship, at Hippos Billiards in Utica, NY. He received the shot program from Tom Rossman, and then practiced diligently every day for a few months. Andy came in fourth and, after that high finish, he never played professional 9-ball again. He was so consumed by trick shots that he didn't want to do anything else. Later, when he was invited to be one of four representatives from America to play in the 2003 WPA World Artistic Pool Championships in Kiev, Ukraine, Andy jumped at the chance. He finished fifth out of 11 players, but won the Gold Medal in the Bank/Kick discipline, and he shared the Gold Medal in the Jump Discipline with Massey.

When Bogdan Wolkowski had to pull out of the 2003 ESPN Trick Shot Magic event, Andy was recommended by a few players. He got the call and, with only six days of notice, he started practicing and inventing new shots in an effort to try to fool the veterans. His very first match was against Stefano Pelinga from Italy. After beating Stefano, Andy advanced into the semi-finals the next day against Charles Darling, the 2001 World Champion from Missouri. A few hours later, Andy got a call from his wife Kim. She was on a train and was scheduled to arrive in Baltimore in just under an hour. That was a nice surprise, and her presence helped to calm Andy's nerves. He made it past Darling by way of a tie-breaker shot, but he ended up losing in the finals to Mike Massey, who won his third Trick Shot Magic title in four years.

Ever since that tournament, the table was set for his career in trick shots, and Andy moved up quickly through the ranks. The following year he won the 2004 Northeastern Open and the 2004 Las Vegas Open. Later that year, Andy lost again to Mike in the semi-finals of Trick Shot Magic, but he got a rematch in the finals of the 2005 Masters Championship, and he was able to defeat Mike for the first time.

Andy won his first World Championship in 2007 at the Lider Club in St. Petersburg, Russia. The tournament came down to the final shot, where Andy had to make the most difficult massé shot on his first attempt to tie Sebastian Giumelli, a superstar from Argentina. After his successful first attempt, the players squared off in a sudden death tie-breaker for the title, which Andy won. Ever since that event, Andy has occupied the top spot in the WPA world rankings in Artistic Pool.

Below is a complete list of Andy Segal's titles and achievements as of the writing of this book. For more information, visit his website at www.andysegal.com.

World Championships

2013 WPA World Artistic Pool Champion
2012 WPA World Artistic Pool Champion
2011 WPA World Artistic Pool Champion
2007 WPA World Artistic Pool Champion

ESPN Championships

2010 Trick Shot Magic Champion
2009 World Cup of Trick Shots Champion (with teammates Bruce Barthelette, Mike Massey and Tom Rossman)
2009 Trick Shot Magic Champion
2008 World Cup of Trick Shots Champion (with teammates Bruce Barthelette, Mike Massey and Tom Rossman)
2006 World Cup of Trick Shots Champion (with teammates Bruce Barthelette, Mike Massey and Tom Rossman)

Masters Championships

2013 Masters Champion
2013 Masters Doubles Champion (with partner Dave Nangle)
2009 Masters Champion
2007 Masters Champion
2005 Masters Champion

US Open Championships

2012 US Open Champion

UTS Tour Championships

2012 VIP Billiards Champion
2011 Las Vegas Open Champion
2011 Hi-Tech Billiards Champion
2011 Shooter's Billiards Champion
2011 Southeast Classic Champion
2010 Willow Billiards Champion
2010 Shooter's Billiards Champion
2010 Big Shots Billiards Champion
2009 Las Vegas Open Champion
2009 Herbert's Billiards Champion

Other Championships

2011 Duel of Champions Winner
2008 Comet Classic Champion
2007 Artistic Cup (I) Champion
2005 Comet Classic Champion
2004 Las Vegas Open Champion
2004 Northeastern Open Champion

Discipline Medals

2013 Masters - Best Make %
2013 Masters - Most Creative Shot (by player vote)
2012 US Open - Stroke Champion
2012 US Open - Massé Champion
2012 World Championship - Massé Champion
2011 Artistic Cup (V) - Trick & Fancy Champion
2011 Artistic Cup (V) - Follow Champion
2011 Artistic Cup (V) - Jump Champion
2011 World Championship - Special Arts Champion
2011 World Championship - Draw Champion
2011 World Championship - Massé Champion
2010 Masters - Trick & Fancy Champion
2010 Masters - Special Arts Champion
2010 Masters - Follow Champion
2009 Masters - Trick & Fancy Champion
2008 Masters - Jump Champion
2007 World Championship - Draw Champion
2007 World Championship - Follow Champion
2007 World Championship - Jump Champion
2007 US Open - Special Arts Champion
2007 US Open - Follow Champion
2007 Masters - Massé Champion
2005 Comet Classic - Special Arts Champion
2005 Masters - Trick & Fancy Champion
2005 Masters - Jump Champion
2004 Las Vegas Open - Special Arts Champion
2004 Las Vegas Open - Draw Champion
2004 Las Vegas Open - Massé Champion
2004 Northeastern Open - Trick & Fancy Champion
2004 Northeastern Open - Special Arts Champion
2004 Northeastern Open - Draw Champion
2004 Northeastern Open - Jump Champion
2004 Northeastern Open - Massé Champion
2003 World Championship - Bank & Kick Champion
2003 World Championship - Jump Champion
2003 North American Championship - Draw Champion
2003 North American Championship - Massé Champion

Other Achievements

Technical Advisor for the Woody Allen film 'Sweet and Lowdown'.
Urban Tarzan on Spike
     Played the role of "Mike" (property owner).
Scorned, Love Kills (Episode: Rules of Engagement) on Discovery ID
     Played the role of "Detective"
Featured player in 'Spin Doctors' (Comcast 3D).
Featured player in 'The Wondrous World of Artistic Pool' (Comcast 3D).
Appearance on Good Morning America (ABC).
Appearance on Amazing (National Geographic).
Performance of trick shots on commercials for All Detergent and AT&T.

Appendix

Footnotes

1-1: If you place a ball on the table and tap it with another ball a couple of times, it will create a small indentation in the felt. Once that ball is removed, it becomes simple to reposition it in the exact same spot. Move the ball close to where it originally was and it should fall right into the mark on the table. Only a light tapping is necessary, as you can then brush the table and everything will be back to normal. Don't tap too hard or the indentation in the felt will remain for some time and the owner of the pool room will not be too happy.

1-2: Matt & Bettiane Braun are the creators and producers of the ESPN trick shot events, starting them in 2000 and still going today. Matt Braun is also an accomplished writer, with 56 published novels and 40,000,000 copies in print worldwide. He is published in fourteen foreign countries, winner of the Owen Wister Award For Lifetime Achievement, winner of Western Writers of America Golden Spur Award, winner of the Festival of the West Cowboy Spirit Award and has a lifetime appointment as Oklahoma Territorial Marshal. CBS created a six-hour miniseries adapted from his novel Black Fox and TNT made a movie adapted from his novel One Last Town.

2-1: There are actually four ways since the cue ball can come from the other side of the ball, hitting the other rail first or nicking the ball on the other side. In order to simplify this explanation, only one side is discussed.

2-2: The term headstring refers to the second diamond line from where a shooter would break. The term footstring refers to the second diamond line on the other side of the table from where a player would rack. Since trick shots don't require a typical break shot, we usually say 'second diamond' instead.

2-3: Bob Meucci, the owner and founder of Meucci Cues, has a warehouse and pool room in Byhalia, MS.

2-4: The World Cup of Trick Shots is produced by Billiards International (Matt and Bettiane Braun). The event was started in 2006 and matches up the best from the United States and the best from Europe. Each year it has been filmed in October at the Mohegan Sun Casino in Uncasville, CT.

3-1: The point aiming system is used only when I play in trick shot competitions. When playing 9-ball, I don't use this system nor do I use the one where you think about half ball hits and so forth. Instead, I try to visualize the shot I am about to take. When my body gets down to shoot, my brain has already made the shot and my body simply obeys the order. That's the best explanation I can give, and it may not be right for everyone but it works for me.

3-2: The Popper jump cue was invented by Mark Dimick, a professional trick shot artist from Oklahoma.

3-3: Most snooker cues also have this type of taper.

3-4: Massé shots, requiring a vertical cue stick, will rarely rip the felt since the tip is going straight down into the table (perpendicular). Rips are usually caused by massé shots where the cue stick is not straight up and down. When elevated about 60-75 degrees, the tip goes into the felt and slides, possibly under it through the hole it just made. Of course it is possible to rip the felt with a vertical massé, especially if you are new to massé shots.

5-1: Hitting the lower ball too full will cause the cue ball to get in the way when the upper ball falls. This results in the upper ball hitting the cue ball on the way down and rolling slightly. Hitting the lower ball too softly will result in the same thing, but this time it will be caused by the lower ball still being in the way.

5-2: Back in 2005, Mike Massey was playing Luke Szywala in the semi-finals of Trick Shot Magic. Luke pulled out a shot that had two balls balanced on shot glasses (real glass) and required you to shoot one into the other, while landing the cue ball on a third shot glass. As Mike Massey was unfamiliar with this shot, he hit it a little too hard and shattered one of the shot glasses. The following year there was a different shot, also using shot glasses, and they were broken as well. After that, glass props were removed from competition.

7-1: The term 'pocket speed' refers to hitting a ball just hard enough to reach the pocket.

7-2: When playing on TV, we never know what kind of table we will have. Sometimes the table's pockets will hold seven balls, and sometimes it will hold fifteen. Since we need to submit our shots in advance, I always try to come up with shots where no more than six balls will be made in any one pocket. That way, no matter what kind of table or pockets we're presented with, my shot will work. In the 2012 ESPN World Cup of Trick Shots, Team Europe submitted one shot where eleven balls needed to go into one pocket, but after we all arrived, we found out that only ten would fit. Fortunately we're all friends so we agreed to let them remove one ball from the shot. If the reader has the opportunity to watch a recording or re-run of that event, the shot is called 'Speed Demon', presented by Nick Nikolaidis in the finals (four vs. four) match.

7-3: The first person I saw do this was Dave Nangle.

13-1: One of the foremost authorities on the wing shot is Tom Rossman. While writing this book, I asked Tom for information on the origin of wing shots. He mentioned that he has seen many old-time players performing them here and there, but Tom was responsible for creating the current wing shot format (original and reverse) that you not only see in this book, but that is also included in the current Artistic Pool shot programs of today. According to Tom, he was introduced to the two-ball combination wing shot in 1980 by Steve Geller. I would like to thank Tom for this valuable information he has provided, and add that Tom Rossman is almost single-handedly responsible for showcasing the wing shot, and it multiple variations, around the world.

Getting Involved in Professional Trick Shots

Artistic Pool

The Artistic Pool professional tour has been around for a while. I started playing in it back in 2002 at the North American Championships. The structure and format has changed over the years, but it is still based on a book outlining a shot program that is divided into eight categories, or 'disciplines'. Players are not allowed to improvise and introduce new shots, as they are required to select shots out of this book. The eight disciplines are Trick & Fancy (setup shots), Special Arts (miscellaneous shots), Draw, Follow, Bank/Kick, Stroke, Jump, and Massé. The original program had 40 shots, five in each discipline, and in a competition, players were required to shoot all 40 shots. Each shot was given a point value, and players were given three tries and were awarded points based on whether they made the shot on their first, second, or third attempt (a nine-point shot was valued at eight points if made on the second attempt, and seven points for the third). At the time, Artistic Pool competitions were more like a golf tournament where everyone went through the entire course of shots and the best score at the end would win instead of being matched up head-to-head.

Over the years, the shot program evolved to incorporate more shots. Each discipline contained 15 shots, and these were grouped by the degree of difficulty. There are three six-pointers, three seven-pointers, and so on up to shots worth ten-points. Players still need to shoot 40 shots, but now they have a choice as to which shots they may select. However, they must pick one shot of each point value in each discipline. For example, I would start out by selecting a six-pointer in the Trick & Fancy discipline, shoot it, and hopefully make it on the first attempt to get the full six points. The other players in my group (and in the entire field) would also select a six-pointer, but it didn't necessarily have to be the same shot that I chose, as there were two other shots to pick from. An event would proceed like this until all players shot 40 shots. The maximum score is 320 (6+7+8+9+10 times eight disciplines). The top 12 players would then advance into a single elimination phase, with the top four players getting byes. These head-to-head matches were structured exactly like the ESPN competitions, but players had to select shots from the program, and they had to select at least one shot from each discipline. The winner of each match would advance until there would be only one player left, who was crowned champion. This type of tournament was fun to watch, very strategic, and it gave everyone a chance to win. In fact, we have had players come out of the preliminary rounds in 11th place who then went on to win the competition.

In 2012 there was some push-back from some of the old school players, who wanted to revert back to the original format where there were no playoffs. The winner was simply the player who had the highest score. I personally enjoy both formats, but I feel that the playoffs are good for the crowd, and they are definitely good for television. The only two events that we had filmed (other than the ESPN tournaments) were the 2005 and 2011 WPA World Artistic Pool Championship, and both shows were structured in a similar manner to the ESPN events (two semi-finals and one final). Fortunately, for the players who are looking for more head-to-head competition, there are alternatives.

For more information about trick shot competitions, you can visit www.artisticpoolplayers.com. This website lists all of the major tournaments and some of the smaller events as well. It incorporates not only the Artistic Pool events, but those from ESPN and other tours.

Ultimate Trick Shot Tour

Bruce Barthelette, Sal Conti and I started what is known today as the Ultimate Trick Shot Tour back in 2008. These events are structured so that the players can utilize their full creativity on the fly, and come up with new and exciting shots. All matches are head-to-head, and they are run in a round-robin format, allowing new players the opportunity to participate in many more matches and to avoid being knocked out in one or two rounds.

The first event was at the 2008 APA National Team Championship at the Riviera Hotel & Casino in Las Vegas. We had an elite field of 10 players (by invitation only), most of whom were known from prior appearances on ESPN. The rules were simple: players were allowed to come up with any shot and challenge their opponent. Each shot was worth one point, and you had three tries. We decided that one point was a better choice for scoring a match than to subjectively assign a degree of difficulty to each shot, since a hard shot for one person may be an easy shot for another. Eight shots were chosen by each player during a match, and we were on our honor to mix up the shots. A player is not allowed to exploit a weakness in another player's skill by selecting, for example, eight massé shots or eight jump shots in the same match. We also put in place rules regarding props. On ESPN, the producer encouraged new and sometimes crazy props since that is what the TV audience wanted. In these events, however, we wanted to avoid one player having an advantage over another simply because he was used to using a non-standard prop. We eventually came up with a list of approved props (racks, bridges, sticks, etc.) that were common to every pool room, whether commercial or home-based).

Before this big event, we would usually get six to eight players together to practice at Shooter's Billiards, Sal Conti's room in Southington, CT. One day we decided to play head-to-head matches instead of just randomly practicing, and that was the moment when the Ultimate

Trick Shot Tour was born. We started booking four or five smaller events around the New England area, all leading up to the year-end finale in Vegas.

For more information about the Ultimate Trick Shot Tour, you can visit www.ultimatetrickshottour.com and register to receive email alerts for upcoming tournaments. In addition, all of the larger events will be included on www.artisticpoolplayers.com.

ESPN Events

Trick Shot Magic

Matt Braun, a very accomplished western novelist, created Trick Shot Magic back in 2000. The event featured an eight player field of the top trick shot artists in the world, each competing for the title. A single elimination format was used, and players would challenge their opponent with whatever trick shot they could think of. There were no specific rules about shot selection or props, and players were encouraged to come up with the most entertaining shots they could possibly imagine. Two attempts were given per shot, and ten shots were selected by each player per match, with one point awarded for a successful make. Mike Massey, to no one's surprise, won the first two years hands down.

As the shots grew more and more complicated, a few issues became apparent. First, the players were forced to spend more time explaining the shot to the referee than performing it, eating up valuable camera time. Second, the referee was put under enormous pressure to remember all of the requirements. Third, players tended to make their own shots, and to miss their opponent's, something that is not good for television. Starting in 2005, the producer required that all shots must be written down and submitted in advance, with each player given an allotment of 25 shots. In each subsequent year, the prior year's shot list was carried forward, and each player was allowed to add a few additional shots.

The tournaments were all held in an ESPN Zone, first starting out in Chicago, then moving to Baltimore (where I first played), and finally out west to Las Vegas. During the last few years the competition was held at the ESPN Zone at the New York New York Casino, but the very last year it was moved off the strip to the Green Valley Ranch Casino in Henderson, NV.

Getting invited to this premier event is the ultimate goal of all trick shot artists. Each year, Matt Braun selects eight players based on their performance in competitions throughout the past year. He mixes it up by selecting about half the field from Europe, and the other half from America. The only way to get invited is to win a major trick shot competition, or to finish very high behind other players who were already invited to Trick Shot Magic.

All prior events are currently listed on www.artisticpoolplayers.com.

World Cup of Trick Shots

Players from Trick Shot Magic were always throwing ideas at Matt Braun for other possible events. Eventually one stuck, and in 2006, Matt launched the first annual World Cup of Trick Shots. This was held in conjunction with the International Challenge of Champions, which features a 9-ball event for the men and one for the women, with only four invited players in each field. These events were held at Mohegan Sun Casino in Uncasville, CT in the Wolf's Den, a 200+ seat arena. The first team representing America consisted of Mike Massey (captain), Tom Rossman, Bruce Barthelette, and myself. Europe was represented by Stefano Pelinga (captain), Luke Szywala, Nick Nikolaidis, and Bogdan Wolkowski.

Team USA, winners of the
2006 World Cup of Trick Shots
L to R: Mike Massey, Andy Segal,
Bruce Barthelette and Tom Rossman.

In 2007, Matt Braun decided to include one woman

on each team. Unfortunately, I was the one replaced with Jeanette Lee, and Bogdan Wolkowski was replaced by Ewa Laurance. In 2008, I returned as captain, and I have been captain ever since. Mike Massey retired from official competition in 2010 and Jamey Gray was added to the team to take his place. In 2011, Tom Rossman was replaced by Tim Chin, who won his way onto the team by his victory at the 2010 Ultimate Trick Shot Tour Finale in Las Vegas. In 2012, Tim was replaced by Mike Dechaine, a top 9-ball professional who has a very good feel for trick shots.

As with most other events, results and upcoming information can be found at www.artisticpoolplayers.com, but there is also a dedicated website: www.trickshotworldcup.com.

Difficulty Rating Index

Every reader has their own skill level and finding appropriate shots to practice should be made easier by this index, which organizes shots based on their difficulty rating. The overall average rating is slightly under 4.3, but some chapters have a higher or lower average based on the category. For example, shots involving multiple cues and one-handed jumps will tend to have higher difficulty ratings than bank shots. The averages by chapter are given below, followed by the difficulty rating index for the entire collection of trick shots.

6: Bank/Kick Shots (2.5)
7: Speed Shots (4.8)
8: Juggling Shots (4.1)
9: Stroke Shots (4.2)
10: Massé Shots (4.3)
11: Jump Shots (4.7)
12: Multi-Cue Jump Shots (5.5)
13: Wing Shots (4.1)
14: Miscellaneous Shots (4.2)
15: Partner Shots (4.3)

Inventors Index

Some of the shots in this book come from concepts that have been around for a while, but most are new, having been invented while trick shots were becoming more popular on television. If a shot is not included below, this means that the original inventor is not known to me. Some shots are listed multiple times. While a shot may have been created by only one player, I feel that credit should also be given to the person who came up with the original concept. Also, with the ESPN World Cup of Trick Shots team event, some shots were created by a collaboration of multiple players. In all of these cases, I will list the co-inventor's initials after the shot name. For example, shot "15.7: Motion Resistance Draw" was the product of Bruce Barthelette's and Jamey Gray's creative minds. This shot is included under Bruce's group, with "(JG)" appended to the shot name, indicating that Jamey Gray also gets credit. Similarly, this shot is also listed under Jamey's group, with "(BB)" appended to the shot name, giving Bruce credit.

I would like to thank all of the players below (listed alphabetically) for their beautiful creations which I am honored to have as a part of Andy Segal's Cue Magic.

Tim Chin (TC)

Sal Conti (SC)

Mike Dechaine (MD)

Ralph Eckert (RE)

Sebastian Giumelli (SG)

Jamey Gray (JG)

Rick Hawkinson (RH)

Gordon Hedges (GH)

Florian Kohler (FK)

Finally, here is the list of shots which I invented. I hope you enjoy them: I know I have!

Andy Segal (AS) continued

Hiring Andy

Shows and Exhibitions

Andy Segal is available for shows and exhibitions all over the United States and around the world. Some of the countries he has performed in include: China, Canada, Russia, and Ukraine. Andy has been to almost every state, giving performances at pool rooms, trade shows, hotels, private clubs, and even some outdoor events. His corporate clients include: Raymond James & Associates, Lincoln Financial Group, Citigroup, Harley Davidson, and Morgan Stanley. Andy has also performed at numerous private events and he is a crowd favorite at birthday parties, graduation events, VA hospitals, and senior centers. Andy also makes appearances at religious organizations and events, president and executive council events for top performing sales people, and university billiard clubs/freshman orientation events. Why, Andy even did a show in Washington, DC (with Bruce Barthelette) where people from the United States Senate were in audience.

Clinics

Andy started out as an accomplished 9-ball player, so he has given many clinics and lessons throughout his career on all facets of the game including basic skills such as holding a cue, proper stance, aiming techniques, and intermediate and advanced skills such as run out patterns, game strategy, and the proper use of English.

While in Pittsburgh, Andy was the instructor at the University of Pittsburgh's Panther Pocket Billiard Club. He also gave regular lessons at his own school, Carnegie Mellon University. After moving back to New York, he was the lead pool instructor for New York City's *The Learning Annex*. He taught some celebrities, including Sean Penn, for either movies or commercials.

Tournaments

Andy has over eight years of experience at promoting trick shot tournaments, so he can help organize and run trick shot events in a casino, hotel, shopping mall, or at your local pool room.

Cue & Book Sales

For bulk or individual ordering information of this book (including special autographed copies), or for Andy's custom signature cue line, please visit the websites below or contact him via email.

Film & Television

Andy Segal is currently a member of SAG-AFTRA, and is available for film/television work. In addition to numerous background roles, he has been cast in two principle roles, one for Discovery ID called "Scorned, Love Kills", episode "Rules of Engagement" (cast as a detective), and one for Spike called "Urban Tarzan" (cast as "Mike", a property owner).

Contact Information

Andy Segal can be reached at andy@andysegal.com, or visit his website: www.andysegal.com. Even if you don't need anything listed above, drop him a line if you have comments about this book, or if you are having trouble with a shot and need a push in the right direction. You may also contact Billiards Press at www.billiardspress.com.

Billiardspress.com

Listed below are other pool instructional books from Billiards Press.
For further information on these books, please visit billiardspress.com.
Dealer inquiries can be directed to Phil Capelle at capellepublishing@gmail.com

Play Your Best Pool
Your Complete Textbook on Pool
ISBN: 978-0964920484
464 pages -
400+ Illustrations
$29.95 U.S.

Capelle's Practicing Pool
Your complete guide to practicing pool.
ISBN: 978-0-9649204-9-1
292 Pages -
Spiral bound
$29.95 U.S.

Play Your Best Eight Ball
Your Complete Guide to Eight Ball
ISBN: 978-0964920491
456 Pages - 535 Illustrations
$29.95 U.S.

A Mind For Pool
How To Master the Mental Game
ISBN: 978-0964920415
120 lessons on the mental game
320 pages - $19.95 U.S.

Play Your Best Straight Pool
A Complete Course on 14.1
Features a New Player's Guide
ISBN: 978-0964920422
416 pages - 355 Illustrations
$29.95 U.S.

Capelle on 9-Ball - Archer vs. Reyes
Book and companion guide to the video of a pro match.
ISBN: 978-0964920453
200 pages / 2 Hours 15 Minutes
Book/DVD $49.95 U.S.

Mike Massey's World of Trick Shots
ISBN: 978-0964920460
300 pages - 180 Illustrations
$19.95 U.S.

Break Shot Patterns
How to Close 14.1 Racks Like a Pro
110 four ball patterns by the champions
ISBN: 978-0-9649204-4-6
Spiral bound book - 240 Pages
2 Hour DVD - $49.95 U.S.

Andy Segal's Cue Magic
Inside the World of Modern Trick Shots
A world champion's 121 favorite shots
Detailed diagrams and instructions
Packed with funny stories
ISBN: 978-0-9898917-0-7
236 pages - $19.95 US